INDIA'S UNDECLARED EMERGENCY

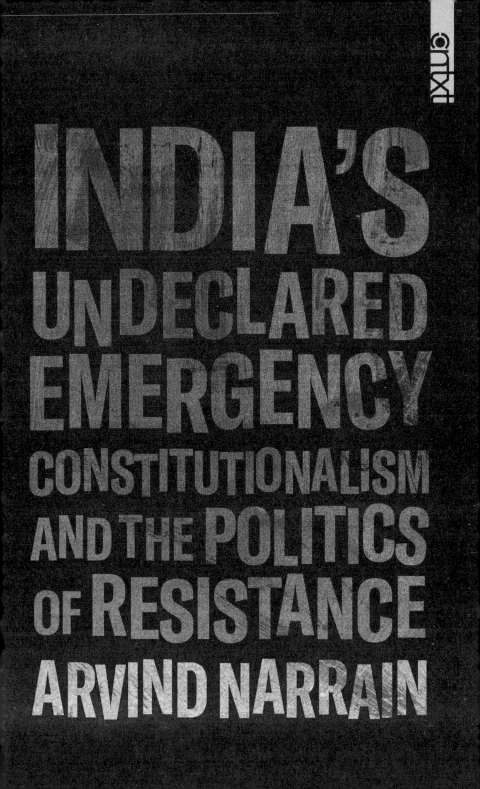

INDIA'S
UNDECLARED
EMERGENCY
CONSTITUTIONALISM
AND THE POLITICS
OF RESISTANCE

ARVIND NARRAIN

cntxt

cntxt

First published by Context, an imprint of Westland Publications Private Limited, in 2021

1st Floor, A Block, East Wing, Plot No. 40, SP Infocity, Dr MGR Salai, Perungudi, Kandanchavadi, Chennai 600096

Westland, the Westland logo, Context and the Context logo are trademarks of Westland Publications Private Limited, or its affiliates.

Copyright © Arvind Narrain, 2022

ISBN: 9789390679119

10 9 8 7 6 5 4 3 2 1

Typeset by R. Ajith Kumar

Printed at Thomson Press (India) Ltd.

MIX
Paper
FSC FSC® C010615

This book is dedicated to the BK-16 who, at the time of the publishing of this book, are still unjustly incarcerated.

This book is also in remembrance of Father Stan Swamy (1937–21), whose inspirational life embodied the struggle to fulfil the promise of the Constitution.

Contents

Introduction

THE NATIONAL DEMOCRATIC ALLIANCE (NDA) GOVERNMENT LED BY Narendra Modi's Bharatiya Janata Party (BJP), first elected in 2014 and brought back to power with a resounding mandate in 2019, poses the most serious challenge to the Indian Constitutional order after the Emergency of 1975–77.

A fundamental precept of democracy is the freedom to question or challenge the government, a legacy of the Independence movement. With the ascendance of this new regime, this freedom is under increasing threat as the government has overtly instrumentalised criminal law to deal with dissent. This campaign of the government against dissent has become symbolised by what is referred to in the media as the arrest of the 'Bhima Koregoan 16', or the 'BK-16', under the draconian Unlawful Activities Prevention Act (UAPA), 1967. Those arrested comprise human rights activists from around the country whose work combines the strands of Dalit activism critical of Hindutva; legal activists seeking to make the State accountable for encounter deaths, illegal land acquisition for corporate interests, and many other State excesses; those defending Adivasi rights, including the right to land and against torture and rape; those challenging State repression in regions such as Kashmir, the Northeast and Chhattisgarh; and those practising progressive politics in universities, bringing together activism and the academia.

The BK-16 arrest playbook has also been used to deal with those in Delhi who protested against the Citizenship (Amendment) Act (CAA), protesters against the Farm Bills, 2020, and many other dissenters who critiqued State action, all of whom were tarred as anti-national by the State, arrested and subjected to a vicious media campaign. There is a roll call of such arrests, be it that of twenty-one-year-old activist Disha Ravi who tweeted in support of the farmers' protests, or twenty-three-year-old Dalit and labour activist Nodeep Kaur who was tortured and beaten up for daring to protest the Farm Bills, or twenty-eight-year-old comedian Munawar Faruqui who 'dared' to make fun of the home minister. All of these arrests were designed to chill the right to dissent and produce a more conformist society aligned with the State.

While one can point to arbitrary arrests throughout the history of independent India, the systematisation of the arrests of those who express dissenting views and the creation of a climate of fear against freely expressing one's opinion, calls to mind one moment from Indian history—the Emergency of 1975–77 during Indira Gandhi's prime ministership.

The declaration of Emergency on 25 June 1975 resulted in the suspension of fundamental rights, including the right to freedom of speech and expression and the right to move the courts for the enforcement of fundamental rights. This enabled the State to increase its power over its citizens to unprecedented levels. The horrors of the Emergency included 110,000 persons being locked up, 161,000 sterilised, many of them forcibly, and over seven lakh displaced in Delhi alone.[1] Essentially, the rule of law was suspended and the judiciary in effect gave the State carte blanche for an executive rule unfettered by the Constitution.

The Emergency posed the most serious threat to the Indian democratic project. In fact, the *Times of India* mourned the death of democracy through an obituary notice on 28 June 1975: 'D'ocracy, D.E.M., beloved husband of T. Ruth, loving father of L.I. Bertie, brother of Faith, Hope, and Justicia, expired on 26 June.'[2]

However, democracy was not quite dead and the Emergency faced a growing resistance among people, and when the opportunity came, they overwhelmingly voted out the Indira Gandhi regime in the elections of

1977 to resuscitate democracy. Acts of resistance both small and large, ranging from protests to underground literature to judicial dissents to a father searching for justice for his disappeared son, fed into the narrative of the illegitimacy of the Emergency and eventually contributed to its withdrawal and the announcement of elections. The Shah Commission, which was established post the Emergency, exposed the torture, arbitrary arrests, illegal demolitions and mass sterilisations during the era and, by telling the truth of what had happened, embodied the hope that never again would India witness such horrors. The political class took action through the 44th Amendment enacted in 1978, which, among other things, and most crucially, limited the Union government's power to declare an emergency and to suspend all fundamental rights. Human rights groups, such as the People's Union for Civil Liberties (PUCL), which were formed during the Emergency, continued to work to protect the fundamental liberties of the citizen even after 1977.

Although the post-Emergency era witnessed a return to the forms of democracy to which India had grown accustomed, this did not mean the end of State violence, including torture, illegal detentions and other forms of violence. After 1977, in fact, the human rights situation deteriorated in Kashmir, the Northeast and Punjab, all of which suffered mini-emergencies and authoritarian rule.

However, these rights violations never approached the scale, gravity and systematic nature of the kind during the Emergency, that is, until Modi's ascendency. PUCL said in a press statement in 2018 that Modi's regime had given way to a completely new order of rights violation, which it called an 'undeclared emergency' where the rights of the citizens were 'being snatched away under the guise of "Patriotism and cultural nationality"'. It added that freedom of speech, writing and expression were banned everywhere.[3] This systematic assault on free speech is what brings to the fore the collective memory of the Emergency.

The Emergency era is also invoked because the subtle mood which envelops the nation now, as it did then, is one of fear of expressing one's opinion and of arrest as a consequence. During the Emergency era, it was the local police in each state or the Central Bureau of Investigation (CBI) which often arrested persons after the proverbial midnight knock on the door. The police emerged as the symbol of the Emergency. Under Modi's rule, although the police continue to be an instrument of the regime, the National Investigation Agency (NIA), which functions under the direct control of the home ministry, has emerged as the main instrument of the government to investigate UAPA offences. Many NIA accused never come out on bail and their trial is never conducted with a sense of urgency. Such long periods of unjust incarceration are enough to perpetuate a climate of fear.

While the law of choice during the Emergency to curtail dissent was the Maintenance of Internal Security Act (MISA), 1971, and the rules under the Defence of India Act, 1915, today it is the UAPA. UAPA case data is available only since 2014 and shows a steady uptick in figures under Modi's rule, including for periods when there were no actual terrorist attacks in the country, to address which the law is supposed to have been made.

Lying hidden under the statistics are the stories of individuals who are still in jail, including journalists, lawyers, artists, activists and intellectuals who have been critical of the Modi government. Emblematic of this unconscionable use of the law is the continued detention of journalist Siddique Kappan under the UAPA for the 'mere fact of trying to go to Hathras to report on the infamous caste atrocity' in the village, as journalist Mrudula Bhavani writes.[4]

The Emergency witnessed an attack on the rule of law, using the instrumentality of constitutional amendments. The passing of the 39th and 42nd amendments were brazen attempts to convert a culture of rule of law into one of arbitrary force. The 39th Amendment prohibited any challenge to the election of the prime minister and made the change retrospective, protecting Indira Gandhi's prime ministership, while the 42nd Amendment brought in wide-ranging changes to the Constitution. Among the critical modifications which enhanced executive power were those which sought to limit judicial power to adjudicate on the constitutional validity of legislations. These amendments were a 'constitutional outrage', as the eminent jurist H.M. Seervai writes in *The Emergency*.[5]

There is a similar process of degradation of the rule of law during the Modi era. This cannot, however, be captured in a narrative of brazen constitutional amendments but is rather what legal scholar Tarunabh Khaitan describes as 'killing the Constitution with a thousand cuts'.[6] According to Khaitan, the BJP has 'incrementally, but systematically' sought to 'undermine or capture mechanisms that seek executive accountability'. The institutions that can hold the executive accountable, be it the Election Commission, Parliament, media, civil society, political opposition or the judiciary, have been methodically weakened and undermined. This is the kind of capture of the Constitution that might be harder to pinpoint but could have equally, if not more, dangerous consequences for India as a democracy. Khaitan writes:

> ... two vertical lines mark the lead up to two periods of consistent decline across most markers of the health of a democracy in India: Gandhi's Emergency in 1975 and Modi's premiership in 2014. During the Emergency, democratic decline in India was ... stark along all markers. In the Modi years, the decline has generally been less spectacular (barring the rapid decline in the independence of the Election Commission and campaign finance transparency), and evidences his incremental, but systemic, undermining of India's democracy.

The attack on rule of law during the Emergency was not only through constitutional amendments but also through the bypassing of established rules, norms and conventions to centralise power in the hands of the regime. The Shah Commission, which was appointed post the ouster of the Emergency regime, documented that right from the appointment of judges to the appointment of the Reserve Bank of India's governor, decision-making bypassed established norms.[7] At its heart, the Emergency was a centralised administration with all decisions ultimately flowing from the mother–son duo of Indira and Sanjay Gandhi.

Similarly, in the current BJP government, there is a bypassing of established norms and conventions, resulting in the concentration of power in the hands of Modi. This was apparent during Modi's first term when the cabinet system, the federal system and all other conventions of the working of a constitutional democracy were given the go-by and power was concentrated in the prime minister's office. This centralised concentration of power is captured in the resignation letter of a disgruntled minister in the Modi Cabinet. Though a disgruntled former minister is not likely to say complimentary things about his former boss, what is important to note is the nature of the complaint. As Upendra Kushwaha, who resigned in 2018, put it:

> It is not just your attitude towards Bihar which has pained me a lot but your opaque style of functioning and non democratic leadership style has left me disappointed and dismayed. You have systemically dismantled the functioning of the cabinet of the government that is mandated in our constitution. The Union Cabinet has been reduced to a mere rubber stamp, simply endorsing your decision without any deliberation. Ministers and officers posted in ministries have become figureheads as virtually all decisions are taken by you, your office and the BJP President. (Which is anti-constitutional).[8]

The second Modi government followed in the tracks of the first in its impulse to centralise power. Though this time around, it had two men at the top—Narendra Modi and Amit Shah.

One significant check on any authoritarian tendencies of a government is the media, which can, by casting a searching spotlight on governmental actions, ensure accountability. However, during the Emergency, the pressure of the State succeeded in producing a largely pliant, uncritical media. This is captured succinctly by BJP politician L.K. Advani, who said, 'You were asked only to bend, but you crawled.'[9] While there is no declaration of Emergency today, the State censors the media, directly and indirectly, through both overt and covert acts, producing a largely conformist media, no less pliant than its counterpart during the declared Emergency of 1975.

In a situation rife with unconstitutional actions, the judiciary has a grave responsibility. But the judiciary, one of the most important institutions of accountability, failed to live up to its constitutional mandate of being a check on executive lawlessness during the Emergency. The Supreme Court during that period held that once the presidential order issued under Article 359 suspended fundamental rights, the high courts could not entertain habeas corpus petitions.[10] (The only voice to the contrary was Justice H.R. Khanna's luminous dissent.)

Today as well, we witness a situation in which the judiciary stands mute in the face of constitutional violations. The court has failed to hear and decide matters of undeniable constitutional importance. It has so far failed to decide on pressing issues such as the abrogation of Article 370, the constitutionality of the CAA and the case on electoral bonds. Among the cases that it has heard, in *Anuradha Bhasin v Union of India*,[11] though it noted that total communication blackout of over five months in Kashmir was a disproportionate measure, it did not provide any effective relief, thus sanctifying executive supremacy.

If, during the Emergency, the Supreme Court shut its doors to thousands of persons unlawfully detained by the State under MISA and other laws, in 2020 the court failed to hear habeas corpus petitions in Jammu and Kashmir. As of October 2021, the BK-16 continue to languish in jail, even though three years have passed since some of them were arrested.[12] Most of the anti-CAA protestors too continue to be in jail.

Though those arrested during the Emergency era numbered over a lakh, while those arrested during the undeclared emergency of today may still be only in the thousands, the comparison between the two eras is apposite when it comes to the intent of the two regimes in shutting down dissent using preventive detention laws (both de facto and de jure), centralising power in the cult of a 'supreme leader', blurring the distinction between the executive and the judiciary, clamping down on media, and bypassing the Constitution—through amendments to it in the Emergency era and the undermining of democratic institutions during the Modi rule.

The features both regimes have in common call to mind Spanish political scientist Juan Linz's description of an authoritarian regime. Drawing on the work of Linz, political scientist Christophe Jaffrelot argues in his book *India's First Dictatorship*, co-authored with Pratinav Anil, that we must understand the Emergency as a species of authoritarianism. Linz defines an authoritarian regime as a 'ruler-centered regime'.

> [The] ruler exercises his power without restraint at his own discretion and above all unencumbered by rules or by any commitment to an ideology or value system. The binding norms and relations of bureaucratic administration are constantly subverted by personal arbitrary decisions of the ruler which he does not feel constrained to justify in ideological terms.[13]

The Emergency regime was based on the arbitrary and personalised rule of the Gandhis and had no deep ideological allegiances, argues Jaffrelot. The regime's ideological justification for the imposition of Emergency was the Twenty Point Programme, which included measures such as 'reducing the price of essential commodities, implementing land ceiling legislation, housing the landless and making debt bondage illegal'.[14] Indira Gandhi boasted a day into the Emergency, '... some people talk of revolution. Our government has already begun one.'[15] However, Jaffrelot points out that the programme 'only served to provide some post hoc economic ballast'[16] for a decision which was rooted in the fear that the government was losing its grip on power. As such, the programme was 'ideologically schizophrenic' and was never implemented with the seriousness of a regime committed to ideological and material transformation. In fact, some way into the Emergency, the Twenty Point Programme was supplanted by Sanjay

Gandhi's Five Point Programme, with the focus narrowing to just two of the points in the latter: family planning and urban renewal. Today, the Emergency is largely remembered for mass sterilisations and slum demolitions, both difficult to characterise as pro-people or socialist.[17] As the Shah Commission documented, the mass arrest of trade unionists under MISA further punctured any serious claim to a socialist direction.

The main rationale for the priorities of the regime shifting to these two points lay in the quirks of Sanjay Gandhi's leadership and preferences. The fact that the government's policy priorities depended so much on his proclivities meant that the nature of the regime could be best understood through the sociologist Max Weber's characterisation of 'sultanism'—'a regime marked by the extreme development of the ruler's discretion'.[18]

Crucially, the Emergency regime never succeeded in building a level of popular support for its programmatic thrust. Jaffrelot argues that the policy of the State during the Emergency was not to activate the support of the people and make changes in favour of 'pro poor policies', but rather to 'encourage the depoliticization of society—of universities, factories and the countryside'.[19] The response of the citizens to the Emergency 'was sullen, not enthusiastic', as historian Gyan Prakash notes in *The Emergency Chronicles*.[20]

Clearly, the Modi regime too has 'sultanist' characteristics, illustrated in the arbitrariness of the decision to impose demonetisation in 2016 and a hasty and unplanned nationwide lockdown during the COVID-19 pandemic in 2020. The regime is also based on a cult of personality centred on Modi. Images of the prime minster dominate most advertisements issued by the Central government and BJP-led state governments, as do references by the BJP to the 'able, sensitive, committed and visionary leadership of Prime Minister Shri Narendra Modi' on many issues, including containing the COVID-19 pandemic.[21]

However, there are at least six factors which mark Modi's rule as inaugurating a new kind of State, going beyond the 'authoritarian' or 'sultanist' features that it shares with the Emergency period.

Firstly, unlike the Emergency rule which had only a flimsy

ideological commitment to socialist revolution, there is a clear thread unifying the actions of the Modi government—its ideological moorings in Hindutva are absolutely key to understanding the regime. In his book *Bunch of Thoughts*, the prominent Hindutva ideologue M.S. Golwalkar points out that the essence of the nation is 'the Hindu race with its Hindu Religion, Hindu Culture and Hindu Language (the natural family of Sanskrit and her offsprings) . . . In Hindustan exists and must needs exist the ancient Hindu nation and nought else but the Hindu Nation. All those not belonging to the national i.e. Hindu Race, Religion, Culture and Language, naturally fall out of the pale of real "National" life'.[22] In Golwalkar's terminology, the three internal threats to the Hindu nation are Muslims, Christians and Communists. Hindutva ideology at its core strives to unite and strengthen the Hindu community, demonise and stigmatise the enemy and assert the superior national rights of Hindus in India.[23]

Secondly, the Modi regime draws its support from the vast civil society networks of the Rashtriya Swayamsevak Sangh (RSS), unlike Indira Gandhi's rule, which was largely dependent on the coercive power of the State alone to take forward its objective. A right-wing volunteer network, the RSS is reputed to be the largest civil society organisation in the world. Andersen and Damle in their book *Messengers of Hindu Nationalism* document the extent of the RSS's spread. They note the presence of platforms and organisations for different spheres of social, cultural, political and professional life—there is the Akhil Bharatiya Vidyarthi Parishad for students, Akhil Bharatiya Adhivakta Parishad for advocates and the judiciary, Arogya Bharati for public health, Bharatiya Mazdoor Sangh for labour, Bharatiya Kisan Sangh for farmers, Bharat Vikas Parishad for social service, Bharatiya Itihas Sankalan Yojana for history, Balagokulam for children's cultural organisation, Gau Samvardhan for cow protection, and so on.[24]

Thirdly, the Modi regime is genuinely popular among the people, as seen by the BJP's back-to-back electoral victories. This was not true of the Indira Gandhi Emergency regime, support for which 'was sullen, not enthusiastic'. In India, images of people queuing up uncomplainingly outside dysfunctional ATMs after demonetisation or of people obediently and jubilantly banging pots during the COVID-19 lockdown on the prime minister's command have underscored Modi's popularity and are testament to his mass base and ability to control and dominate societal ways of thinking.

This form of domination over the social common sense has been achieved through most of the mainstream media becoming a platform for lauding the prime minister and remaining faithful to his rule rather than to democratic principles. The media also helps in the spread of the Hindutva ideology by enabling hate speech against minorities and crystallising and deepening the 'communal common sense'[25] that Muslims are outsiders to the Indian nation and not entitled to the right to equal citizenship. The deleterious effects of this societal transformation are already beginning to show—from 'social and economic boycotts' of Muslim businesses and small vendors to calls for the physical elimination of the Muslim community,[26] all of which presage a dangerous phase more reminiscent of Nazi Germany than the period of Emergency.

Fourthly, the popularity of the regime is supplemented by the power of the mob in Modi's India. In contemporary India, the images of the lynching of Mohammed Ashfaq in his own house on the suspicion of eating beef in 2015, the lynching of Pehlu Khan on the 'suspicion of smuggling cattle' and the knifing of Junaid Khan after an argument on seat-sharing in a train in 2017[27] are only the tip of the iceberg of hate crimes against minorities. The lawless mob that has arisen during the Modi regime attacks those who are perceived as not belonging to a nation based on a Brahmanical Hindutva—in particular, Muslims, Dalits and Adivasis. The participants in mob violence see themselves as nationalists and, in their self-perception, what others call their crimes are nothing other than service to the nation.

Fifthly, while the power of the mob is one way through which conformity is manufactured, there is now a brazen attempt to make Hindutva ideology a part of Indian law, even if it violates the Constitution. The enactment of the CAA marked a moment when legislative change emerged as a viable route to take forward the ideological vision of the regime. Apart from the CAA, the tightening of the anti-cow slaughter laws in Maharashtra and Karnataka as well as the anti-conversion and anti-'love jihad' laws enacted in Uttarakhand, Uttar Pradesh and Madhya Pradesh and on the cards in Haryana and Karnataka indicate an emerging legal framework which puts in place second-class citizenship for both religious and caste minorities.

Sixthly, the regime has also not been shy of its nakedly pro-corporate agenda. The pandemic is being used to push through far-reaching changes in areas of social, economic and political life, which would not have been possible without strong pushback if the institutions of democracy were able to function. These changes—be it the farm laws which benefit corporations, or the dilution of environmental laws, or the further dilation of labour laws—have further marginalised the concerns of labour, environment and public health. According to Oxfam, '... the wealth of [Indian] billionaires increased by 35% during the lockdown'. The study showed that what 'Ambani earned during the pandemic would keep the 40 crore informal workers that are at risk of falling into poverty due to covid-19 above the poverty line for at least 5 months'.[28]

To summarise, the six factors which mark the Modi regime as inaugural in India's independent history are its rooting in the ideology of Hindutva, the support of the RSS, which has a vast network of on-the-ground volunteers, the undeniable popularity of the regime, the role of the mob in actively destroying rule of law, legal changes that seek to entrench Hindutva and bypass the Constitution, and the naked privileging of the rights of capital over labour and the rights of future generations. In Jaffrelot's understanding, as he writes in a *Scroll. in* article, the 'Hindu nationalist movement has a long-term perspective and is changing India more than any other political force since Mahatma Gandhi's Congress'.[29]

These six factors which define the current regime call to mind Linz's description of totalitarianism, distinct from authoritarian rule by 'dictators', 'military juntas' and 'Caesaristic leaders', as he writes in *Totalitarian and Authoritarian Regimes*. Under totalitarian rule, 'power is exercised in the name of an ideology', there is 'some form of mass organization' and there is the 'participation of members of the society' in the legitimisation of the regime. Totalitarian rule is not based solely on the power of the 'armed forces' and 'police' but also on the support of 'mass organisations'. It has the ambition of remaking society in its image, and elections have a different but high significance for totalitarian rulers, as they serve an important 'integrative function', when the public's 'visible and joyous identification with the regime' is on display.[30]

It is undoubtedly true that the Modi regime has all the hallmarks of an authoritarian regime founded on the absolute power of the leader around whom a personality cult has been manufactured. However, Modi's reign goes beyond these and is a regime with clear totalitarian ambitions. This distinction is important to understand because an authoritarian regime, being founded on an individual leader's cult, may eventually flounder, but a totalitarian State, based as it is on popular support with an ideological objective, will not collapse so easily.

The totalitarian ambitions of the Modi regime are understood by the main political opposition. The Left has regularly characterised it as fascist, and even Rahul Gandhi, a leader of a centrist party which was responsible for the Emergency, has alluded to the distinction. When asked about the Emergency, Rahul Gandhi said, 'I think that was a mistake.' He went on to differentiate between the two regimes by stating that 'the Congress Party at no point attempted to capture India's institutional framework' and that his party's 'design does not allow us [to do] that'. According to him, the BJP functions less like a political party and more like a part of a larger movement, to which electoral loss is irrelevant. He recalled that in Madhya Pradesh, between December 2018 and March 2020, when the Congress was in power, it was difficult for the party to rule as the then chief minister Kamal Nath told him that 'senior bureaucrats in his government would not listen to him as they were RSS people and would not do things they were asked to do'.[31]

The danger of totalitarianism goes beyond just a threat to political parties and spans the diversity of India. Those who are in favour of a federal polity, those in favour of an Ambedkarite ideology, those who want to protect personal liberties of food, clothing, marriage and worship, those of minority faiths and other minority communities, those who are opposed to the pro-corporate tilt of government policy, be it farmers or workers, those who are concerned about the serious threat posed by environmental changes to the Adivasi population of India, all these affected groups face an existential threat from totalitarianism.

India is indeed inching towards totalitarianism. But is that the inevitable future? Is an analysis of the present merely to proclaim, 'Abandon hope all ye who enter here?' Is there a midpoint between what one of the most influential political philosophers of the twentieth century, Hannah Arendt, and one of the few to 'philosophize systematically about politics against the background of Nazi totalitarianism',[32]calls a mood of 'reckless optimism' on the one hand, and on the other, a 'belief in unavoidable doom' in *Origins of Totalitarianism?*[33] A mood of 'reckless optimism' would arise from a form of utopian thinking unmoored from the realities of the present—a bit like the fervent belief of Voltaire's Candide in the face of all evidence to the contrary that 'all is for the best in this best of all possible worlds'.

In India today, where the dominant mood in progressive circles is hardly one of 'reckless optimism', what one is left with is 'reckless despair'. To find hope in the midst of this despair is difficult. Hope cannot be a Panglossian utopianism, based on nothing other than a groundless conviction that things will be better.

For Arendt, who survived the Nazi Holocaust, '... the Achilles heel of totalitarian evil was the being it sought so completely to transform— homo sapiens itself'. This was not because human beings, under the Nazi rule, were good by nature but because they 'were inherently contingent and innovative'. One can never predict the way each person would respond under given conditions because the human race is 'infinitely plural'. For Arendt, '... every birth is a new beginning' and 'so long as people were born and inhabited the earth, their capacity to break out of totalitarian conditions, and to create a world worthy of plural human beings, could not be eliminated'.[34]

Keeping Arendt's invocation in mind, one way forward is to have a concrete analysis of how human beings have resisted oppression in history. By telling of stories of courage in difficult times, out of the potentialities of the past, a future of possibilities could emerge.

This book is divided into five sections.

The first chapter will examine the Emergency period from 1975–77. As noted, this is the period to which we can most profitably compare the current moment to be able to better understand how power operates and how resistance can be enabled. During the Emergency era, the executive sought to increase its power through preventive detentions of its critics, control of the media, prohibition of protests and demonstrations and intimidation of the judiciary. While most people capitulated to the demands of the executive, all did not and the exemplary resistance of people—right from judges like Justice H.R. Khanna, who refused to sanctify the state's actions to T.V. Eachara Varier, who fought for justice for his disappeared son, twenty-one-year-old engineering student, Rajan—continues to speak to the future.

The second chapter looks more closely at the history of preventive detention in the country. Both the Indira Gandhi regime during the Emergency of 1975–77 and the Modi regime during the contemporary era have a ready-made tool to deal with dissent—preventive detention which is authorised by the Indian Constitution in its fundamental rights chapter as Article 22. The colonial origins of preventive detention, though challenged, were ultimately sanctified by the Constituent Assembly. While its presence in the fundamental rights chapter is anomalous, the intent of the drafters was to read preventive detention narrowly and to limit its use to narrowly defined circumstances. The power of preventive detention and its constitutional limitations was interpreted by the Supreme Court in the famous A.K. Gopalan v State of Madras decision. While the majority sanctified the State's power to preventively detain in this case, Justice Fazal Ali chose to read the power of the State to preventively detain more narrowly to ensure conformity with fundamental rights. The question, of course, is how can Justice Fazal Ali's dissent become a basis for challenging existing preventive detention laws?

The third chapter examines the contemporary period of undeclared emergency when a powerful executive uses repressive laws to check dissent. In particular, the law that has become the symbol of the undeclared emergency is the UAPA, under which thousands have been arrested and are languishing in jail. Another symbol of repression is the powerful NIA, which again has been used to keep high-profile critics in jail and create a climate of fear. Ordinarily, in a constitutional democracy, the power of the executive is kept in check by the media, civil society and the judiciary. Modi's India has seen the judiciary, in many key situations, abdicate its constitutional responsibilities and the mainstream media largely toes the State's line, while civil society has been harassed and intimidated by the agencies of the State.

The fourth chapter argues that though the Modi regime has all the hallmarks of an authoritarian regime founded on a personality cult, it goes beyond and is a regime with clear totalitarian ambitions. This section documents the vast effort by the ruling regime to harness the instrumentalities of both State and civil society in aid of this project of societal transformation. As in most totalitarian regimes, the power of the State is supplemented by the power of the mob that enforces its will, regardless of the constitutional requirements of rule of law. This project of societal transformation is also instrumentalised through fake news and hate speech that aim to alter societal common sense in accordance with Hindutva. The fact that the Hindutva movement is in power means that the law can now be instrumentalised to change a secular framework to a Hindutva framework. Today, there are laws like the CAA that set in place unequal citizenship, or the ones on cow slaughter that interfere with the freedom to eat the food of one's choice and the freedom of profession and trade as well as laws such as the anti-conversion ones, which dictate which faith you can follow and who you can marry.

The last chapters, though titled 'What is To Be Done?', rather than lay out a plan of action documents what is already being done. What is apparent is that the actions of the regime have invited acts of resistance both big and small. This section draws on comparative experiences, activist experiments and historical analogies to attempt some answers on how to confront a totalitarian future. There are creative ways in which a voice of resistance is being both manifested and amplified, using the resources of Indian history and culture, taking inspiration from activisms in other parts of the world as well as drawing from global histories of resistance. This section documents some of these traditions and histories of resistance and argues that out of these multiple streams, it is essential that a strong and united resistance to totalitarianism emerges.

1

Authoritarian Rule

The Emergency (1975-77)

Comprehension does not mean denying the outrageous, deducing the unprecedented from precedents, or explaining phenomena by such analogies and generalities that the impact of reality and the shock of experience are no longer felt. It means, rather, examining and bearing consciously the burden which our century has placed on us—neither denying its existence nor submitting meekly to its weight. Comprehension, in short, means the unpremeditated, attentive facing up to, and resisting of, reality—whatever it may be.

– Hannah Arendt[1]

UNDERSTANDING A CONTEMPORARY MOMENT IS ALWAYS CHALLENGING, as being in the middle of the flow of history can rob one of perspective. But seeing the present moment as part of a longer history offers a vantage point. The closest parallel to the situation in India today is the Emergency of 1975–77, when the right to expression and association were curtailed, dissenters were arrested on a mass scale and a climate of fear pervaded all sections of State and society. This ubiquitous fear, in turn, led to the judiciary forgetting their constitutional responsibilities and ceding full authority to the executive. The media too surrendered its independence. But equally, part of the history of the Emergency includes the roles played by those who fought against it, seeking to preserve the values of the Constitution in difficult circumstances.

To recall that historical period—not by way of easy analogy, but as a way to begin a process of reflection about the current time—could be a step towards what Arendt calls 'comprehension'.

Emergency had been declared on two previous occasions, following the Chinese aggression of 1961 and during the war with Pakistan in 1971. Both proclamations invoked the ground of 'external aggression'. However, it was the declaration of Emergency on 25 June 1975 by Indira Gandhi, which invoked the ground of 'internal disturbance', that posed the most significant challenge to the Indian democratic experiment.

Article 352 of the Constitution gives the president the power to declare an emergency if the president 'is satisfied that a grave emergency exists whereby the security of India ... is threatened whether by war, external aggression or internal disturbance'. The presidential proclamation made it clear that the Emergency was warranted because of 'imminent danger to the security of India being threatened by internal disturbance', as author Venkat Iyer notes in *States of Emergency*.[2] Prior to the proclamation, the country had witnessed peaceful protests led by Jayaprakash Narayan (JP) against Indira Gandhi, with JP calling for 'total revolution', which was painted by the prime minister as an 'internal disturbance'.

Although this shocked the nation, the framework for this was already written into the Constitution. Through its emergency provisions, the Constitution provides for the suspension of three of its important features—the federal character of the State, the fundamental rights guaranteed to citizens and the right to constitutional remedies.

Firstly, the federal structure becomes unitary, with the executive power of the union extending to 'giving of directions to the state as to the manner of the exercise of executive power' and with Parliament assuming the power to legislate on matters in the state list.[3] As Ambedkar put it, '... once the President issues a proclamation ... the whole scene can become transformed and state becomes a unitary state. ... Such a power of converting itself into a unitary state no federation possesses'.[4]

Secondly, the suspension of all rights under Article 19—freedom of speech and expression, assembly, association and movement—is authorised by Article 358 and can be restricted by the State by either 'law' or 'executive action'.[5]

Thirdly, the president has the power during the period when the emergency is in force to declare that 'the right to move any court for the enforcement of rights under Part III ... shall be suspended'.[6]

Once an emergency is proclaimed under Article 352, it is the powers conferred by Articles 353, 358 and 359 that allow a government to rule India by executive fiat unchecked by either Parliament, judiciary or the media. Under Article 353, the Union is given the power to direct state units to function in accordance with the instructions of the Central government. Article 358 gives the Union the power to override the limits imposed by Article 19, thereby silencing the media. Article 359 suspends the right to move any court for the enforcement of fundamental rights.

At the time of the drafting of the Constitution, these provisions had alarmed some members of the Constituent Assembly. H.V. Kamath noted that the emergency powers were more 'drastic' than the 'extensive powers to the executive' granted by the Weimar Constitution of post-First World War I Germany. He appealed to the House to ensure that the 'liberty of the individual' and the 'freedom and powers of the constituent units are not suppressed'.[7] K.T. Shah expressed 'deep misgivings' about 'the worst features of centralised authority' proposed in the emergency provisions.[8] He divined a 'desire' to 'arm the executive, arm the Centre, arm the Government against the legislature against the units and even against the people' on the possibility of 'threat to internal peace'.[9]

However, the provisions were not without their supporters. T.T. Krishnamachari forcefully argued that the 'clothing' of the Constitution with 'extraordinary powers' was necessary, as people who may be in power in the future must be 'empowered' to 'save the Constitution' and the emergency provisions were a 'safety valve' to do so.[10]

The immediate cause for the imposition of the 1975 Emergency lay in the challenge posed by the JP movement and the judiciary to Indira Gandhi's total supremacy. The agitation led by JP with a call for 'total revolution' to replace parliamentary democracy with a 'communitarian or partyless democracy', as Christophe Jaffrelot and Pratinav Anil note in *India's First Dictatorship*, was able to bring thousands on to the street demanding Indira Gandhi's resignation.[11] JP's strategy was to paralyse the working of the government, including a call to the army and the police to disobey the State. This was seen to pose a threat to the survival of the Congress government.

Parallel to the struggle with JP, Indira Gandhi was also engaged in a struggle to limit the powers of the judiciary. The final straw that broke the camel's back came from this quarter with the unprecedented decision of the Allahabad High Court to set aside the election of the prime minister on grounds of electoral malpractice. When Indira Gandhi went to the Supreme Court on appeal, the court only granted 'a conditional stay' on the judgement which denied her the 'right to speak or vote in parliament'.[12] This finally provoked Indira Gandhi into declaring the emergency.

Initially, the Emergency was an extraordinarily successful gambit, and Indira Gandhi herself is reputed to have said, 'Even I was astonished' by 'the public reaction to the declaration of Emergency,' as activist Balraj Puri notes in an article in the *Economic and Political Weekly (EPW)*. Indira Gandhi further observed, 'When the Emergency was declared there was not a murmur at all. There was not a case where the police had to be used.' The silence was in stark contrast to the fact that just the previous day, 'lakhs of people' had turned up to listen to JP and were 'determined to bring down the Prime Minister'. The declaration of emergency along with the arrest of 'all top leaders of the political parties including JP left the nation cool. There were no spontaneous strikes, no demonstrations, no uprooting of rails'. As the then defence minister Bansi Lal is supposed to have boasted, '... not a dog barked'.[13]

With the people of the country shocked or terrorised into silence, the stage was set to tighten the grip of the Emergency regime by a range of actions. In shocking factual detail, the 'truth' of what happened during the Emergency was laid out in the reports of the Shah Commission, set up by the post-Emergency Janata Party government.

The seminal reports submitted by Justice J.C. Shah, who chaired the committee, were vital in moving the excesses of the Emergency from the realm of conjecture to fact and from the domain of individual knowledge to collective history.

As per the commission, the four broad areas in which legislative power was exploited during the Emergency were: misuse of the power of arrest, abuse of authority, forceful family planning and unauthorised demolitions.

Preventive Detention and the Emergency

Preventive arrests are perhaps the central image of the Emergency and the signature tune of the Indira Gandhi regime. The Maintenance of Internal Security Act (MISA), 1971, amended in 1975 and 1976 to support the Emergency regime, became emblematic of the police excesses during the period.

MISA had its precursor in the form of the Preventive Detention Act, 1950, whose constitutionality had been upheld in *A.K. Gopalan v State of Madras* and which continued in the statute books up to 1969 due to its validity being extended every two years by Parliament. Then, with the passing of the Unlawful Activities Prevention Act, 1967, the government dropped the idea of further extending the life of the Preventive Detention Act, as it felt that UAPA 'could effectively take its place'.[14]

However, the political exigencies of the 1970s, which included an economic crisis, war with Pakistan as well as the emergence of anti-government movements such as the one led by JP and the Navnirman Andolan, were seen by the Indira Gandhi regime as threats to its rule. In response, the government brought into force another iteration of a preventive detention law, namely, MISA.[15]

MISA, 1971

MISA, passed during the Indo–Pakistan War of 1971 and the subsequent formation of Bangladesh, authorised pre-trial detentions based on the 'satisfaction' of the Central or state government. It allowed for a person to be detained if the State was 'satisfied' that it would prevent the person from acting in a manner prejudicial to, among other things, 'the security of the state or the maintenance of public order'.

Despite certain procedural safeguards in MISA,[16] abuse was built into the very structure of the act, argued the Shah Commission. Opposition leaders from the Left as well as the Right—including two stalwarts of the Jan Sangh, precursor to the Bharatiya Janata Party (BJP)—were clear even when MISA was tabled for debate in Parliament that the law was fraught with troubling implications for Indian democracy:

Atal Bihari Vajpayee of Jan Sangh said:

> This is the beginning of a police state and a blot on democracy. It is the first step towards dictatorship … These powers will not be used against foreign spies but against political opponents.

L.K. Advani of Jan Sangh said:

> I assure you that this preventive detention law of MISA will be used against Shri Morarjee Desai, Shri Shyam Dhar Mishra and Shri Gurupadswamy.

Piloo Modi of Swatantra Party said:

> I am more than ever convinced that this Government and this Party cannot be entrusted with the powers that it is demanding today … If you were to read the history as to how democratic movements have grown throughout the century, it has been by this one principle of habeas corpus that all democratic societies are evolved. What does this Bill do? … It snuffs out Habeas Corpus in the middle of the 20th century after 25 years of independence. … To deny this country habeas corpus is to rejuvenate the Star Chamber … without habeas corpus there is no democracy.

Somnath Chatterjee of Communist Party of India (Marxist) said:

> It is a shameless exhibition of hunger and greed for more power. They are taking upon their hands this Black Act, this piece of legislation which does not provide even the semblance of security to an individual in this country. In the name of refugee influx, in the name of the security of the State, which all remains undefined, this power has been given in the hands of an ordinary petty bureaucrat who is prone to act at the behest of the party in power.

The opposition to MISA spanned the political spectrum from the Left to the Right—all were convinced that MISA was a threat to democracy. Vajpayee's statement that a law such as MISA would not be used against 'foreign spies' but against 'political opponents' was prescient about how MISA would be used by the Indira Gandhi regime, and cautioned against the role that such laws would play in India's democracy.

The MISA Amendments During the Emergency

Among the legislative measures undertaken by the State during the Emergency were amendments to MISA that sought to further whittle down the procedural safeguards available to persons detained under the law.

Under the newly introduced Section 16A of the Act, the existing procedural safeguards were done away with. The section begins with the ominous words, 'notwithstanding anything contained in this Act or any rules of natural justice', thereby doing away with any form of even semi-independent scrutiny of orders of preventive detention. In place of the advisory board recommended in the original Act, which would comprise of judicial members or those who were qualified to be judges,[17] the 'appropriate government' was given the power to reconsider whether 'the detention of the person' is 'necessary for effectively dealing with the emergency'.[18] The detainee had no right to either know the grounds for detention or to make any representation against the detention order according to Section 16A(5). Detention under MISA was not subject to the right to personal liberty of the individual 'by virtue of natural law or common law' under the newly introduced Section 18. This provision made explicit the fact that as far as the drafters of this amendment were concerned, whatever rights the individual had were solely at the behest of the State. There was no question of the individual claiming that they had the right to know the grounds of detention or make representations against their detention or to be free from torture by anchoring those rights in natural law. If these rights were not explicitly recognised, they did not exist.

In the Shah Commission's analysis, 'These amendments completely metamorphosed the character of MISA.'[19] The commission concluded, 'The freedom of the executive from all restraints of judicial scrutiny led directly to the large-scale abuse of authority and misuse of powers during the Emergency.'[20]

The amendments were supplemented by directives from the Central government, which, though they may not have had the sanction of law, functioned to coerce obedience. Even if a state government was satisfied that the detenu posed no danger and could be released, it ran up against the obstacle of the 'suggestion' by the Central government that 'all state governments [were] to obtain the advice of the Central Government before releasing the detenu'. It is interesting that the 'advice' by the then home secretary in a letter dated 3 January 1976 did qualify itself by stating that 'it is true that this procedure is not a legal requirement but the matter has to be viewed in the overall context of the emergency'.[21] In the context of the Emergency, where the Centre was all powerful, merely adding that the permission of the Centre was not a legal requirement did nothing to empower state governments to make independent decisions on detention. As the Shah Commission concluded,

> Though this was only an advice but in practice, it had the effect
> of an order and state governments started following the practice

of referring all cases of release of MISA detenu to the Central Government from January 1976 onwards ... By these directives, the Central government in an executive manner restricted the legal right of the state governments to revoke the orders of detentions passed under MISA.[22]

The Targets of MISA

The Shah Commission classified the detentions under MISA during the Emergency under four categories:

1. Members and associates of Opposition Political Parties
2. Members and associates of banned organisations, viz., RSS, JEI, Anand Marg and CPML
3. Criminals
4. Anti-social elements and economic offenders.[23]

'Out of approximately 35,000 persons detained under MISA throughout the country during the emergency,' the commission noted, 'about 13000 were those alleged to be connected with political parties including the banned organisations'.[24]

In a majority of the states, a large number of persons belonging to Opposition parties were detained on the grounds of alleged participation in one or more 'secret meetings in which the imposition of the Emergency and government policies were opposed or criticised'.[25] Almost the entire parliamentary Opposition was rounded up and put in jail, including the elderly JP; other stalwarts of the socialist, Lohiate and communist parties, such as Sitaram Yechury and Pinarayi Vijayan; and leaders of the Jan Sangh. The members of the Communist Party of India, which supported the Emergency, were excluded.

The police were liberal in construing who the 'associates' of banned organisations were. As the Shah Commission noted, though the Central government notification banned only certain organisations like the RSS, Jamaat-e-Islami, Anand Marg, CPML, the state governments 'acted almost in a frenzy', and detained persons on the 'slightest suspicion of association with these organisations', even if there were 'no reasonable grounds to detain them'. The state governments were 'goaded' by the Centre through periodic 'directives' to launch a 'vigorous drive against these organisations'.[26]

The Shah Commission has documented many egregious examples of how MISA was misused by the State against political activists. One such case was that of Bhim Sen Sachar, aged eighty-two, veteran freedom fighter, first chief minister of Punjab and former governor of Andhra Pradesh. He was also the father of Rajinder Sachar, the chief justice of the Delhi High Court. Bhim Sen Sachar, along with several other activists, had written an open letter to the prime minister in July 1975, critical of the Emergency from the point of view of 'the freedom and dignity of the individual':

> Apart from your political supporters, the common people of Delhi now talk in hushed tones as they do in communist societies; they do not discuss politics in the coffee house or at the bus stand and look over their shoulders before expressing any opinion. An atmosphere of fear and political repression prevails and politically conscious citizens differing from your viewpoint, prefer to observe a discrete silence, with some of them afraid of the mid-night knock on their door. [...]
>
> The present situation looks every citizen in the face and the old surviving freedom fighters in particular. We must respond to the call. Accordingly, we propose, with effect from August 9, 1975 and regardless of consequences to ourselves, to advocate openly the right of public speech and public association and freedom of the Press for discussing the merits and demerits of the Government arming itself with extraordinary powers.[27]

Following this letter, Sachar was detained along with seven others, and as per the testimony of one witness, Sushil Kumar, who was the district magistrate of Delhi, a decision had been taken to arrest Sachar and others under MISA, following the receipt of a 'communication to the Prime Minister'. On being asked by the commission as to who took the decision to arrest Sachar, the witness replied that it was the prime minister.[28] The grounds for detention were lifted verbatim from the open letter, making it clear that it was Sachar and other political leaders' opposition to the Emergency which was indeed the provocation for detaining them.

The Shah Commission noted that Sachar's detention was a 'classic example of the misuse of the provisions of MISA'. What also emerged was how the entire administration gave up any pretence of following the rule of law to implement the will of the prime minister. This story should be a 'warning to any Government against giving such vast and arbitrary powers in the hands of authorities without providing effective and compelling safeguards against their possible misuse'. The commission aptly pointed out that 'the undesirable trend in the administration of Maintenance of Internal Security Act' was that, at the behest of the prime minister, detention orders were being issued by additional district magistrates even though they were not themselves 'personally satisfied either about the need for detentions of the individual concerned or the adequacy of grounds for their detention'.[29]

Apart from political activists, students were also targeted through MISA arrests. The Shah Commission classified the student detainees into two categories. The first comprised those who were involved with 'opposition political parties like the Jan Sangh' and 'RSS'. The second included 'student leaders', who took part in 'agitations in educational institutions', though they may not have 'indulged in political activity'.[30]

While some were detained and released after the Emergency was lifted, some never made it back. Emblematic of this are the stories of Prabir Purkayastha and P. Rajan. Purkayastha was detained under MISA and was released after the Emergency was lifted, while Rajan, who was abducted by the police, was killed in custody.

Purkayastha was a student of Jawaharlal Nehru University (JNU) and a member of the CPI(M)'s student wing, the Student Federation of India (SFI). On the morning of 25 September 1975, plain-clothes policemen in a black car arrived in JNU, accosted Purkayastha and started pushing him towards the car. Though his friends rushed to stop this, 'the policemen beat back the students, lifted Prabir off his feet, and shoved him into the rear seat', as historian Gyan Prakash documents in *Emergency Chronicles*. One of his friends rushed to 'the driver's seat and tried to snatch the car keys from the ignition. ... But the police officer Bhinder, came from behind, grabbed her hair, and hurled her to the ground.' Purkayastha was taken to the Hauz Khas police station and then transferred to Tihar Jail.

The additional district magistrate issued a warrant for arrest under MISA post the arrest, without any material before him. The police report which should have been the basis of the arrest warrant was only prepared five days after the arrest. The habeas corpus petition filed on Purkayastha's behalf was dismissed. He was finally released after a year of imprisonment by the Delhi administration on 20 September 1976.[31] Today, he continues his activism as the editor of the online news portal NewsClick, which has been subjected to raids by the Enforcement Directorate, a reminder that an emergency regime cannot be thought of as a phenomenon of the past alone.[32]

The story of Rajan, a twenty-one-year-old student of the Regional Engineering College, Calicut, Kerala, was one of the many individual tragedies of the Emergency era. Rajan too was abducted by the police from his hostel, but was tortured and killed in police custody.

His father, T.V. Eachara Varier, narrates in his memoir, *Memories of a Father*, how he ran from pillar to post to get news of his son, sending a number of representations right from the level of the director general of police to the chief minister, the home minister and even the prime minister.[33]

This public activity of seeking accountability during the Emergency was a lonely enterprise. People around Varier were afraid of being seen with him. His associates started to avoid him, viewing him as the 'father of an extremist'. Varier describes a pervasive climate of fear which enveloped him, and he too 'was scared to talk to people'. He began to feel like he was a 'character in a story by the great Indian writer Premchand', and imagined himself as 'the freedom fighter in his short story, "The Examination"', because 'people had started to reject' him.[34]

Varier carried on with the search for his son. He was 'one of the few' who were 'left with little alternative' and were 'bold enough' to keep searching.[35] He met various State authorities, including the then chief minister of Kerala K. Karunakaran, but to no avail.

The truth of what happened to Rajan only emerged post the lifting of the Emergency, when Varier filed a habeas corpus petition before the Kerala High Court. In an exceptional procedure, the high court conducted an inquiry into what had happened by examining witnesses, and came to the conclusion that Rajan was taken by the police and was tortured by them in custody.[36]

The court's finding compelled the Kerala government to order an inquiry, which too acknowledged that Rajan was detained and tortured in police custody. Following this, on the order of the high court, two prosecutions were initiated, one against those who tortured and murdered Rajan and the other against those who committed perjury by lying on affidavits submitted to the court. However, in the course of the two trials, all those standing trial were acquitted because of witnesses turning hostile and a lackadaisical prosecution by the State.[37]

The harassment of student activists during the Emergency was a way of targeting independent thinking critical of the State. As Varier observes, the torture of his son Rajan was akin to 'the torture at Hitler's concentration camps' and was 'an experiment, undemocratic and heartless, to find out whether the intellectual honesty and sense of justice of a generation could be destroyed by the power of an iron fist'.[38]

The other group targeted under the MISA regime was trade union leaders. This was ironical as the self-justification of the Emergency was to bring about a socio-economic transformation, including the enhancement of workers' participation in industrial management. To indicate the regime's commitment to workers' participation, Article

43-A was introduced as part of the Directive Principles of State Policy, which enjoined the State to secure participation of workers in the management of industry. The arrest of trade union leaders, however, exposed the hollowness behind this pretend ideological justification for the Emergency. As the Shah Commission noted:

> MISA was also used in a majority of the states to curb trade union activities. Several workers working in factories and trade union leaders were detained on the ground that in the past they had participated in agitations against the management. There were cases when even a single incident of pressing the authorities for meeting the demands of workers were made the basis of a detention order.[39]

The Arbitrariness of Arrests

While there were specific groups who were arrested under MISA, not all arrestees fitted the description of being political activists, trade unionists or student leaders.

'In a large number of cases, the grounds given for detention merely alleged that the person concerned was a member or sympathiser of a named banned organisation without mentioning any activity on his part,' the Shah Commission noted. The commission was highly critical of this expansive approach, observing, 'Many such detentions were bad in law and disclosed a total lack of application of mind by the detaining authority.'[40] It also noted that the standards laid down by the Supreme Court in *Khudi Ram Dass v State of Bengal* for 'subjective satisfaction' were completely ignored by the executive in its arbitrary use of MISA.[41]

State authorities misused the power of arrest at every level based on individual biases and predilections, and 'MISA was used as a weapon against all kinds of activities; not even remotely connected with the security of the state, public order or maintenance of essential supplies.' Those arrested included 'those contesting government decisions in a civil court', 'Government servants accused of corruption', 'petty traders violating licensing conditions', 'persons involved in land disputes', as well as those 'alleged to be opposed to family planning or not actively cooperating with the programme of family planning'. The commission concluded, 'MISA was used for purposes totally beyond the purview of Section 3(1) of the Act.'[42]

The prime minister herself and the government were fully aware of these exigencies and that the 'powers under MISA were being misused on a considerably large scale'.[43] Indira Gandhi had, in fact, written a letter to the chief ministers in which she noted, '... let it not be said that this amending ordinance is in any way being misused or misapplied. It is of the essence that the powers under this amendment should be used only to the extent necessary to meet the situation of the emergency'.[44]

But this was at best lip service as the government continued to 'misuse' MISA. In case after case, the State proceeded to arrest persons under the Act without complying with the statutory requirements. As the Shah Commission documented, many of the arrests under MISA never met the requirement of the 'subjective satisfaction of the detaining authority' and did not fulfil the requirements of Section 3 of the Act.

Censorship of the Media

One of the significant dimensions of the Emergency was the curtailment of Article 19(1)(a) and (b), the twin rights to 'freedom of speech and expression' and to 'assemble peacefully and without arms' guaranteed by the Constitution.

Censorship was imposed under Rule 48 of Defence and Internal Security of India Rules (DISIR). This allowed the government to censor or pre-censor matters related to the 'defence of India', 'public safety' and 'maintenance of public order'.[45]

The 'capriciousness of the Censor authorities' and 'their arbitrariness' was criticised by many leading media editors. Cho Ramaswamy, editor of *Tughlaq* magazine, noted how 'jokes, cartoons, and satirical articles' were all 'subjected to censorship without their being even remotely concerned with the Defence and Internal Security of India'. Some of the material censored included quotations from Mussolini, Hitler and even excerpts from Nehru's writings. Journalist Nikhil Chakravarty testified to the Shah Commission that Information and Broadcasting Minister V.C. Shukla had objected to quotations from Rabindranath Tagore and Mohandas Gandhi. A.D. Gorwala, editor of *Opinion*, attested that quotations from the Gita were censored.[46]

Censorship was to be 'carried out through a set of guidelines issued by the Chief Censor'. These guidelines 'exceeded the scope of Rule 48 of DISIR insofar as it prevented Editors leaving editorial columns blank or filling with quotations from national leaders like Tagore and Gandhi'.[47] The actual work of censorship on a day-to-day basis also went beyond the scope of any guidelines. 'Orders were arbitrary in nature, capricious and were usually issued without any relation to the provisions of Rule 48.' The chief censor had explicitly prohibited oral orders, but as the testimony of the chief censor to the government, H.J.D. Penha, before the Shah Commission revealed, '... reducing orders into writing would have defeated the very purpose of censorship and hence from almost the very beginning directions on subjects to be censored were issued orally'.[48]

The government also classified newspapers as 'friendly, neutral and hostile', allowing for 'political considerations' to determine which newspapers could carry and hence gain revenue through government advertisements.[49]

Censorship rules under DISIR also oversaw the media reporting of parliamentary proceedings. The chief censor's guidelines, among other things, allowed for statements made on behalf of the government to be published on certain conditions but 'nothing else was allowed to be published except the names and party affiliation of the Members speaking on a subject in support or against the subject. The result of voting could be factually reported'.[50]

Reporting on court proceedings too fell within the purview of DISIR. The media were allowed to publish 'only the operative part of the judgment ... in appropriate language' and were banned from publishing anything that would 'infringe censorship laws'.[51] Apart from this, the government also gave instructions on how certain judgements were to be reported on. In fact, on covering Indira Gandhi's appeal to the Supreme Court in her election petition case, '... a series of directions were issued by the Chief Censor on what aspects of the case should be given publicity and what aspects of the case should not be played up at all'. Once the judgement came, the newspapers were instructed to 'play up' the fact that her appeal had been upheld and 'that the cross appeal of Shri Raj Narain was dismissed'.[52]

The other egregious example of the censorship of court proceedings was seen in the reporting of the *ADM Jabalpur* judgement, as the jurist and constitutional scholar H.M. Seervai notes in *The Emergency, Future Safeguards and the Habeas Corpus Case*. Newspapers were commanded not to report the dissent by Justice Hans Raj Khanna, who thought it unwise for individuals to be detained under MISA without judicial oversight.[53] If more people had known about Justice Khanna's dissent, it could have given them the hope of resistance by highlighting a fearless anti-establishment viewpoint even during the height of the Emergency. But as the media stayed mum on this, the counter viewpoint was consigned into what Arendt calls 'holes of oblivion' and cemented the power of the regime.[54]

While the censorship regime's own guidelines were often supplanted by 'oral orders', there was also an attempt to institutionalise this regime and make it 'part of the ordinary law of the land'. The government passed the Prevention of Publication of Objectionable Matter Act, 1976. 'Objectionable matter' included 'representations and words' which were 'defamatory' of the president and the prime minister as well as 'exciting disaffection against the Government', allowing the government to classify a wide range of things, including criticism of the State, as 'objectionable'. Moreover, the Press Council of India—an institution that provides an organised forum for journalists and among its mandates includes 'preserv[ing] the freedom of the press' and 'help[ing] newspapers and news agencies maintain their independence'—was abolished by an ordinance. The Parliamentary Proceedings (Protection of Publication) Act, 1956, was repealed, ensuring that the protection guaranteed to any person who published 'substantially true report of any proceedings of either House of Parliament' was done away with.[55]

These steps, according to journalist B.G. Verghese, were carried out to 'institutionalise the emergency'.[56]

Use of Force in Family Planning

A significant change during the Emergency was the shift in the family planning programme from a largely voluntary scheme to a coercive one. The reasoning for this change is outlined in a communication by the Union Health Minister Karan Singh to Indira Gandhi regarding the population problem:

> The problem is now so serious that there seems to be no alternative but to think in terms of introduction of some element of compulsion in the larger national interest. ...The present emergency and the declaration of the 20-point programme by the Prime Minister have provided an appropriate atmosphere for tackling the problem.[57]

And then the prime minister herself reinforced this shift:

> We must now act decisively and bring down the birth rate speedily to prevent the doubling of our population in a mere 28 years. We must not hesitate to take steps which might be described as drastic. Some personal rights have to be kept in abeyance, for the human rights of the nation, the right to live, the right to progress.[58]

An example of how the Central government set in place coercive population control measures is the instruction issued to the principals of all Kendriya Vidyalayas: 'Children of parents who have two or more children and have not undergone sterilization of either parent should not be entitled to seek admission in Kendriya Vidyalayas.'[59]

A key element of the coercion envisaged in the family planning programme was the stress on sterilisation as the chosen technique of family planning. States were given sterilisation targets by the Centre, but the states, in a bid to please the Centre, 'decided to give themselves a higher target'. This despite the states being 'advised from time to time not to indulge in excesses and not to overstrain themselves' as per Health Secretary Gian Prakash. The states were also 'warned' that 'there should be no excess or coercion of any type in the promotion of family planning'.[60] However, the warning was not not intended to be seriously followed. The Shah Commission noted that there was never any evidence that the health ministry wrote to the states against 'upward revision of targets'. In fact, the health ministry told the states that 'a watch should be kept to ensure that after the sowing and harvesting … [the] daily average goes up' when it felt that there was a downswing in the number of sterilisations performed.[61] The states seemed to have correctly understood what the Centre actually wanted and went ahead with an upward revision of sterilisation targets.

To achieve these often self-imposed targets, the states used a mixture of incentives and disincentives, resulting in a wide variation in policies across the country. State governments also competed with each other, both in sterilisation targets as well as the kinds of measures instituted.

Himachal Pradesh introduced the Himachal Pradesh Government Servants (Special Provisions Relating to Family Planning) Rules, 1976, incorporating disincentives such as disqualification from earning increments, medical reimbursement, promotion, allocation of government housing, etc., for an 'eligible person', if he or his spouse did not undergo sterilisation within three months of the commencement of the rules. These rules were described by the prime minister herself as 'rather harsh'.[62]

Maharashtra had an even more cruel legislative response when it introduced the Maharashtra Family (Restriction on Size) Bill, 1976, which planned to compulsorily sterilise all adults who had more than three children. This bill was withdrawn after the Centre felt that the Act, in language and substance, went against the voluntary emphasis of the family planning programme.[63]

However, despite the Centre expressing its apprehensions about the measures undertaken by Himachal Pradesh and Maharashtra, the coercive structure of the family planning programme remained intact, with other state policies continuing to be in operation. The Shah Commission report provides numerous examples, such as the Uttar Pradesh Government Servants (Special Provisions relating to Family Planning) Rules, 1976, which laid down that it was the 'duty' of every government servant to 'motivate' others to get sterilised, failing which, the government employee would be penalised through his salary or his annual increments or both.[64]

It was not only government servants but also the public who were targets of the family planning programme. Himachal Pradesh formalised the withholding of essential commodities through fair price and ration shops to individuals with more than two children, unless they underwent sterilisation.[65] The Central government seems to have frowned on this order, which led to it being rescinded, only to give way to a new directive which stated that people with more than two children had to be sterilised to be eligible for 'any public office or grant of house site or scholarship/fee concession for their children, etc'.[66]

In Karnataka, 'stringent action was to be taken against those who carried on organized opposition to family planning programme'.[67] Uttar Pradesh produced information of the arrest of persons who opposed the scheme, with sixty-two detained under MISA, 1,159 arrested under the DISIR, 1971, 303 arrested under the Indian Penal Code (IPC), 1860, and twenty arrested under the Criminal Procedure Code (CrPC), 1973.[68] The Madhya Pradesh government, in effect, admitted to the commission that people were forcibly sterilised. In response to a questionnaire by the Shah Commission, the Madhya Pradesh government replied that 'it is common knowledge that people were forcibly taken away from houses and other public places but no record of these instances is available'.[69]

Apart from these, the policy responses of states as diverse as Bihar, Haryana, Rajasthan, Andhra Pradesh, Assam, Gujarat, Karnataka, Orissa, Punjab and Delhi, as the Shah Commission report shows, clearly demonstrated the coercive nature of the programme, far from the rhetoric of 'voluntariness' deployed by the prime minister.

The family planning programme was also perceived as targeting individuals from a certain religion. Opposition by Muslims to family planning on grounds that it was prohibited by their faith was contested by the State, which said that '... the family planning programme is a national programme. It has nothing to do with religion and is a purely economic programme'.[70]

However, the facts documented by the commission seem to belie this protestation of neutrality. On 6 November 1976, Uttarwar village in Haryana, inhabited mainly by Muslims belonging to the Meo community, was raided by a large police force armed with rifles and tear gas. After the raid, the police carried away in trucks about 550 villagers to the police station for interrogation. Of these persons, later on, 180 were taken to nearby family planning centres at Nuh and Mandkola and sterilised. 'This raid on village Uttarwar,' concluded the Shah Commission, '... was planned deliberately by the state officials because of the opposition to the sterilization programme of the State Government.'[71] After the raid, electricity to the region was disconnected and FIRs were registered against villagers for possession of arms and for carrying on propaganda against the family planning programme.[72]

The infamous atrocities at Turkman Gate in Delhi where Muslims resisting demolitions and sterilisations were shot down also show the anti-minority bias. In *For Reasons of State*, John Dayal and Ajoy Bose document the happenings preceding the massacre. A family planning camp was set up at Dujana House, two kilometres from Turkman Gate, but the government was not successful in 'motivating' the men of the locality to get sterilised. Even when the government rounded up alms seekers from around the area and forcibly sterilised them, it was strongly resisted by the women of the locality. The inhabitants of Turkman Gate went to meet Jagmohan Malhotra (known widely by his first name Jagmohan), the vice chairman of the Delhi Development Authority (DDA), to ask that they be rehabilitated. To this, Jagmohan is reported to have said: 'Do you think we are mad to destroy one Pakistan to create another Pakistan?'[73] Scholar Emma Tarlo details the happenings of the day in *Unsettling Memories*. All attempts to save the locality at Turkman Gate failed, with the DDA sending in bulldozers. When people resisted, they were shot down and the bulldozers ran over people in their homes. The number of people who were killed is still unknown and the Turkman Gate massacre remains one of the forgotten tragedies of independent India with not even a 'simple memorial plaque' to commemorate it. [74]

Demolitions

Although demolitions were undertaken even before the Emergency, the Shah Commission noted that in the past 'attempts were made to ensure that nobody was shifted unless some arrangement for his rehabilitation was already made'. However:

> ... the entire concept ... suffered a drastic change after the emergency was imposed and demolitions by bulldozers of slums and the encroachments came to acquire the blessings of the Governments concerned. The speed and scale of work in this direction surpassed all precedents and dwelling houses, shops, temples and places of worship and homes of the poor were destroyed. There was a phenomenal increase in the number of demolitions during the period of emergency compared to the number of demolitions in the years preceding it.[75]

The reason for the demolitions was 'beautification', removal of encroachments, and so on, which were priorities of governments in India even prior to the Emergency. Earlier, protests against demolitions, media reporting and political pressure exerted by local politicians acted as a check against unrestrained demolitions. But in the absence of these pushbacks against unrestrained demolitions during the Emergency, the Central government began 'taking advantage of the fear psychosis generated by the proclamation of emergency' and using the police force to 'unlawfully and arbitrarily' demolish many structures.[76]

As with family planning measures, the number of demolitions varied from state to state. The maximum complaints before the Shah Commission with respect to demolitions were from Delhi (1,248), followed by Madhya Pradesh (628), and Uttar Pradesh (425).[77] The Shah Commission concluded that 'a majority' of the demolitions in Delhi were 'undertaken under the orders of Shri Sanjay Gandhi' and the demolitions in other states were 'undertaken to please Sanjay Gandhi'. This might account for the fact that Delhi, with its relatively smaller population and size, topped the list of demolitions. The influence of Sanjay Gandhi in the nationwide demolition drive is indicated by the resident commissioner of Uttar Pradesh in his communication to another government official:

> As desired by the Chief Minister, I called upon Shri Sanjay Gandhi and showed him the various plans for urban development of Agra. Shri Gandhi appreciated the programme and expressed the view that with immediate effect the State Government should endeavour to remove cattle from the streets, unauthorized structures and beggars … within the next six months.[78]

Some states passed laws to facilitate demolitions. Bihar, for example, passed the Bihar Public Land Enforcement (Amendment) Ordinance, 1975, which authorised the 'removal of temporary structures etc from the public land forthwith without the formality of advance notice and also use of force in cases where such structures were deemed prejudicial to public safety'. This ordinance also barred civil courts from 'interfering with demolition operations'. When the demolitions began, 'there was no advance notice'. Instead, announcements on public address systems asked 'encroachers' to voluntarily remove their structures within a given time, 'failing which the government agencies were to start demolition operations at the encroachers cost on penal rate basis'.[79]

In some cases, the courts intervened to grant stays, but to no avail. The Punjab and Haryana High Court in *Deepak Nanda v State of Haryana*,[80] granted a stay against demolitions and passed strictures against the 'arbitrary and high handed' manner in which they were carried out in the night hours. The court noted that 'it is well settled that even the peaceful possession of a trespasser cannot be disturbed except by due process of law' and agreed that the petitioners were in 'peaceful possession' of the land. However, a large number of shops were still demolished 'in utter disregard' of the stay order.[81]

Supplanting the Rule of Law

It is widely known that the Indira Gandhi regime used constitutional amendments, legislation and executive actions to supplant the rule of law.

One of the significant ways in which rule of law was supplanted was through the law itself. In particular, Indira Gandhi chose to attack it through the mode of constitutional amendments. The 38th, 39th and 42nd amendments transformed the intricate system of checks and balances into a framework in which the executive could rule untrammelled.

The 38th Constitutional Amendment made the declaration of the Emergency non-justiciable. The 'satisfaction' of the president was to be 'final and conclusive' and could not be 'questioned in any court on any ground'. Thus, the jurisdiction of the courts was definitively ousted.

The 39th Constitutional Amendment vested the power to decide disputes with respect to the election of the prime minister in a body determined by Parliament and the jurisdiction of the court was ousted here too. In a blatant attempt to declare the election of Indira Gandhi valid regardless of the judgement of the Allahabad High Court, which had convicted her of electoral malpractice and debarred her from holding any elected post for six years,[82] Article 329A(4) was introduced. It stated that even if a court had declared the election of a prime minister or Speaker to have been void, 'notwithstanding any such order ... such election shall continue to be valid'.[83] While piloting the bill, notes senior advocate Prashant Bhushan in *The Case That Shook India*, Law Minister H.R. Gokhale sought justification for it on the grounds that 'since the Prime Minister had not only been elected by a vast majority but is also recognised throughout the length and breadth of the country as the undisputed leader, she should not be subjected to the process of judicial scrutiny where the election could be set aside even on the flimsiest ground'.[84]

The 42nd Constitutional Amendment was unapologetic in its aim to further strengthen the executive at the expense of the other arms of the State. The 'statement of objects and reasons' to the amendment bill stated quite unambiguously that 'parliament and the state legislatures embody the will of the people and the essence of democracy is that the will of the people shall prevail'.

This also had the logical corollary of limiting the power of the judiciary by taking away the 'jurisdiction of High Courts with regard to determination of constitutional validity of central laws' and conferring such jurisdiction exclusively on the Supreme Court.[85] The amendment also sought to limit judicial power to strike down legislation by laying down that the 'minimum number of judges who could determine the constitutional validity of any central or state law was seven' and that two-thirds of the judges must concur for a legislation to be declared invalid.[86]

Among the provisions which inordinately increased the power of the executive was the introduction of Article 31D, which provided that a law 'prohibiting anti-national activities' cannot be 'deemed to be void on grounds that it abridges Article 14, 19 or 31'.

Apart from constitutional amendments, the Indira Gandhi regime also amended a number of laws such as the Election Law (Amendment) Act, 1975—which retrospectively legitimised the 'corrupt practices' on the basis of which Indira Gandhi was disqualified by the Allahabad High Court—and MISA, and passed legislations such as the Prevention of Publication of Objectionable Matter Act, 1976.

The executive too deviated from lawful processes and established conventions. Such departures from established procedures are not often easy to prove, but because of the documentary access enjoyed by the Shah Commission, it was able to systematically record the abuse of power and authority starting from the very top.

One such abuse of power of the executive was R.N. Agarwal, an additional judge of the Delhi High Court, not being appointed a permanent judge, as recommended by the chief justice. Although this recommendation was accepted by the Union minister of law and justice, it was overruled by Indira Gandhi. The prime minister's grudge against the judge can be traced back to a judgement he presided over.

Kuldip Nayar, editor of the Express News Service who was detained under MISA, had filed a petition for habeas corpus, which was heard by the MISA Bench of the Delhi High Court comprising Justices Agarwal and S. Rangarajan. Sensing that the mood of the court was in favour of the petitioner, the administration represented by the additional district magistrate of Delhi revoked the detention of Nayar. However, the court went on to pass orders in which it was critical of Nayar's detention. The court said, '... we have been at pains to explain' that 'the rule of law will not permit arbitrary executive action'. The judgement recorded the fact that the detaining authority did not even know Nayar was a journalist nor had any material before it to come to an 'assessment that the detenu would act prejudicially to the maintenance of public order'.[87]

The Shah Commission noted, '... the orders of the Government were set aside [by the court] and the attitude of the Government's decision was criticised, especially the manner in which the orders were passed'. The commission concluded that it was this decision of Justice Agarwal which led to the recommendation for his permanent judgeship being overturned by the prime minister herself. This was 'prima facie, in the nature of an order of punishment for participating in the hearing in Kuldip Nayar's case and passing an order which tarnished the image of the Government in the public eye. ... The commission is therefore of the view that a case of misuse of authority and abuse of power is disclosed in this case against Smt. Gandhi.'[88]

If authority was used to weed out those against the government, it was also used to appoint and promote those the prime minister favoured. K.R. Puri, for instance, was appointed governor of the Reserve Bank of India, in spite of his lack of qualifications being flagged by the finance minister himself. This too was done on the directions of the prime minister.[89]

This was not the only instance, and the Shah Commission documented in detail how there was a 'subversion of lawful processes and well established conventions and deviation from administrative procedures and practices' when it came to other high-level appointments, including the appointment of T.R. Varadachary as chairperson of the State Bank of India. [90]

The abuse of the rule of law formed the backbone for a whole range of other abuses during the Emergency. Once departures from established procedures become the norm, arbitrariness—the whim of administrators—becomes the rule of administration and then the law. The findings of the Shah Commission demonstrate in shocking detail the extent to which India had become a centralised polity with all power vesting in the supreme leader, Indira Gandhi. It was her will or whim which decided if a person was to be preventively detained or if an appointment to a higher office was to be confirmed or if a periodical was to be censored. At its heart, the Emergency was a centralised administration with all power ultimately flowing out of the duo of Indira and Sanjay Gandhi.

Role of the Supreme Court: Executive Supremacy and a Dissent for the Ages

After the declaration of the Emergency and the arrests of thousands under MISA, the executive moved to immunise itself from judicial scrutiny by promulgating a presidential order under Article 359(1) of the Constitution, suspending the right of any person to move any court with respect to orders of detention under MISA for the enforcement of rights conferred by Articles 14, 21 and 22.

Consequently, some of those who were arrested under MISA challenged their detention by way of habeas corpus petitions in the high courts. Nine high courts came to the conclusion that the 'petitions were maintainable if the orders of detention were not authorized by law or were contrary to law or were mala fide'. [91]

The high courts, in effect, held that even if fundamental rights were suspended, they could still test the validity of the detention order against the statutory provisions of MISA. Thus, if the detention was based on an unsigned order or the detention order did not specify any of the prescribed statutory grounds, it could be struck down and the detainee released, even during a period of emergency. The high courts gave effect to the principle that 'though the emergency barred the enforcement of certain fundamental rights, it did not abrogate the rule of law, or the obligation to obey the law'.[92]

These nine high court judgements were appealed by the Union of India in the Supreme Court in *ADM Jabalpur v Shivakant Shukla*.[93] The argument of Attorney General Niren De in the court was that 'Article 21 is the sole repository of the right to life and personal liberty' and 'if the right to move any court for the enforcement of that right is suspended', the writ petitions of the detenu must be dismissed 'without any further inquiry'. The fact that the detention was based on irrelevant grounds or the detention was not 'bona fide' was of no consequence.

The detenus were represented by senior advocates Shanti Bhushan, Soli Sorabjee, V.M. Tarkunde, Anil Divan, Ram Jethmalani, C.K. Daphtary as well as other advocates.[94] Seervai notes that the counsel for the detenu sought to bring to the attention of the court the stakes of the matter by 'remind[ing] the Supreme Court of the most shameful episode in human history—the extermination of 6 million people in the gas chambers of Nazi concentration camps, and pointed out that if courts abdicated their duty to see that the law was obeyed, the infamies of Hitler could take place in India'.[95]

Granville Austin, a historian of the Indian Constitution, details the arguments of the court in *Working a Democratic Constitution*. Bhushan argued that 'detentions could be questioned, even if the courts were not to look into the grounds of them'. 'If a a district magistrate through a telegram orders the detention of three hundred persons', Bhushan asked rhetorically, 'could there have been any application of mind or satisfaction in making the detentions?'[96] That 'the executive could not interfere with an individual's liberty unless it could support the legality of its argument in a court of law' was Sorabjee's point. Tarkunde argued that 'the onus for proving the legality of a detention order shifted to the government once a habeas corpus petition was filed'. Divan referenced a precedent which had held that 'a detenu could challenge his detention on the ground that it was illegal in terms of the Defence of India Act'.[97]

The arguments of the respondents were paraphrased by Justice Khanna when he put it to the attorney general that 'Article 21 pertains not only to liberty but also to life'. Justice Khanna then went on to give an example: 'Supposing some policeman, for reasons of enmity, not of state, kills someone, would there be a remedy?'

De replied, 'consistent with my position, My Lord, not so long as the Emergency lasts.' And he added, 'it shocks my conscience, it may shock yours, but there is no remedy.'[98]

By a majority of four to one, the court came to this conclusion:

In view of the Presidential Order dated 27th June 1975 no person has any locus standi to move any writ petition under Article 226 before a High Court for habeas corpus or any other writ or order or direction to challenge the legality of the order of detention on the ground that the order is not under or in compliance with the Act or is illegal or is vitiated by malafides factual or legal or is based on extraneous considerations.[99]

The high courts, against whom the Supreme Court was hearing the appeal, had asserted their right to test the detention order against the statutory framework provided by MISA. It was this bare compliance with a minimum legality which the majority bench of the Supreme Court denied to all the detainees, granting a total prohibition on any form of judicial scrutiny of a detention order during the period when the Emergency was in force.

The court felt that in extraordinary times, the executive must be deferred to.

As Chief Justice A.N. Ray put it:

While the courts of law are in normal times peculiarly competent to weigh the competing claims of individuals and government, they are ill equipped to determine whether a given configuration of events threatens the life of the community and thus constitutes an emergency.

Justice Y.V. Chandrachud cited precedents from the United Kingdom to make the point that a 'jurisdiction of suspicion is not a forum for objectivity'. He added, 'Those who are responsible for national security must be the sole judges of what the national security requires.' He indicated that 'perhaps' the only argument which the court could entertain was whether the 'authority which passed the order of detention is duly empowered to pass it, whether the detenu is properly identified and whether on the face of the order the stated purpose of detention is within the terms of law'. But, he went on to add, 'These questions, in almost all cases, will have an obvious answer.' Finally, he concluded:

> Counsel after counsel expressed the fear that during the emergency, the executive may whip and strip and starve the detenu and if this be our judgment, even shoot him down. Such misdeeds have not tarnished the record of Free India and I have a diamond-bright, diamond-hard hope that such things will never come to pass.

Justice P.N. Bhagwati observed:

> The maxim salus populi suprema lex esto, that is public safety is the highest law of all, must prevail in times of crisis and the people must submit to temporary abdication of their constitutional liberties in order to enable the government to combat the crisis situation which might otherwise destroy the continued existence of the nation.

The Supreme Court went on to overrule the nine high courts and hold that the presidential order was constitutionally valid. And so, the right of persons to move the court for enforcement of fundamental rights and statutory rights stood suspended by a majority of four is to one. The majority concluded that when the Emergency was in force, the executive's decisions to detain a person would not be subject to any judicial oversight. In effect, the judges ruled that a declaration of emergency was not only enough to set aside fundamental rights but also the requirement that statutory law be complied with.

Justice Chandrachud's 'diamond-bright and diamond-hard hope' and Justice Beg's conclusion that the State was bestowing 'an almost maternal ... care and concern' upon the detenus was belied by what was going on. As Seervai notes, 'Even before Justices Chandrachud and Beg had awarded good conduct certificates to the Union and State Governments, a grim tragedy had been enacted in the Kakayam Police Camp', referring to Rajan's capture, torture and murder in police custody.[100] Seervai rightly asks:

> Before the untimely grave of Rajan, and the desolate home of his father, the words of Justices Chandrachud and Beg, quoted earlier, seem a cruel mockery. How many Rajans have perished in detention? How many have come out maimed in mind and body?[101]

As Rajan's poignant case reminds us, under the Emergency regime, there were abductions, preventive detentions, torture and murder. Due to the censorship of the media and the arrest of Opposition politicians and activists, there was no forum to air these grievances, and those who would have naturally made a public issue of these injustices were in jail. In this context, the Supreme Court was the last port of call. 'Coming at the darkest period in the history of independent India', the ADM Jabalpur judgement 'made the darkness complete'.[102]

However, *ADM Jabalpur* was not a unanimous judgement, with a brave dissent by Justice Khanna, who forcefully asserted the role of the judiciary even in a time of national emergency. There are four dimensions to his dissent which are important in the contemporary context.

Firstly, Justice Khanna was fiercely critical of the attorney general's submission that Article 21 was the sole repository of the right to life.

He held that the protection of the right to life and personal liberty is the 'essential postulate and basic assumption of the rule of law'. As such, the 'right not to be deprived of one's life or liberty was not the creation of the Constitution. Such right existed before the Constitution came into force'. He said:

> ... this sacred land shall not suffer eclipse of the rule of law and that the Constitution and the laws of India do not permit life and liberty to be at the mercy of absolute power of the executive, a power against which there can be no redress in courts of law, even if it chooses to act contrary to law or in an arbitrary and capricious manner.

Secondly, his dissent can be read as a forceful critique of the formalist understanding of the rule of law on which the majority opinion was based. Justice Khanna held that just because a law is passed, it cannot deprive a person of judicial redressal against threat to right to life and liberty. As he noted, there is a difference between 'the reality of rule of law' and 'illusion of the rule of law'. In a formalist understanding of law, 'based on a hierarchy of orders', even 'the organised mass murders of Nazi regime qualify as law'. As he put it, however, 'this argument cannot disguise the reality' that 'hundreds of innocent lives have been taken because of the absence of rule of law'.

Thirdly, Justice Khanna held that 'the executive can never go against the provisions of the Constitution or any law'. He went back to the words of Ambedkar before the Constituent Assembly, who had said that 'constitutional government' cannot function unless the 'constitutional authority remembers the fact that its authority is limited by the Constitution'. Justice Khanna concluded that the high courts had the power of 'issuing appropriate writs in case it is found that the executive orders are not in conformity with the provisions of the Constitution and the laws of the land' and 'judicial scrutiny of executive orders' is an 'integral part of our constitutional scheme' and that it was impermissible to 'exclude judicial scrutiny'.

Fourthly, his dissenting opinion was a ringing affirmation of the judiciary's role in a time of emergency. 'Even in an emergency when the state is threatened the courts must speak,' he noted.

The question is not whether there can be curtailment of personal liberty when there is threat to the security of the State. I have no doubt that there can be such curtailment, even on an extensive scale, in the face of such threat. The question is whether the laws speaking through the authority of the courts shall be absolutely silenced and rendered mute because of such threat.

Justice Khanna was conscious that his was a voice in the wilderness and that his colleagues on the bench were not with him. He ended his dissenting judgement by invoking the words of the former US chief justice Charles Evans Hughes: 'A dissent in a court of last resort, is an appeal to the brooding spirit of the law, to the intelligence of a future day, when a later decision may possibly correct the error into which the dissenting judge believes the court to have been betrayed.'

However, such was the censorship regime surrounding the decisions of the court that Justice Khanna's heroic dissent was not allowed to be published during the Emergency.[103] There were personal consequences for Justice Khanna too. Although he was in line to be the next chief justice, in January 1977, nine months after he delivered his dissenting judgement, he was unjustly overlooked. On being superseded, Justice he resigned from the Supreme Court. One of India's most eminent lawyers, Nani Palkhivala, penned a moving tribute in the *Sunday Standard* on Justice Khanna's resignation, saying that the judge would be remembered for 'his historic judgment' in the habeas corpus case, which was a 'shining example of judicial integrity and courage'. He concluded: 'to the stature of such a man, the Chief Justiceship of India can add nothing'.[104]

In 2017, the Supreme Court in *Puttaswamy v Union of India* (the case in which privacy was declared to be a fundamental right), excoriated the majority decision in *ADM Jabalpur* as a 'discordant note' in the evolution of a jurisprudence which 'places the dignity of the individual [at] the forefront'.[105] The majority said that the *ADM Jabalpur* judgement would 'have to be consigned to the archives, reflective of what was, but should never have been'. The Supreme Court overruled *ADM Jabalpur*, with

Justice D.Y. Chandrachud noting that 'the view taken by Justice Khanna must be accepted, and accepted in reverence for the strength of its thoughts and the courage of its convictions'. Justice S.K. Kaul said that the *ADM Jabalpur* judgement was 'an aberration in the constitutional jurisprudence of our country' and expressed the 'desirability of burying the majority opinion ten fathom deep, with no chance of resurrection'. The overruling of *ADM Jabalpur* means that it is not the law of the land anymore and can no longer be cited as a precedent.

Justice Khanna's dissent kept alive the possibility of justice and became a beacon of inspiration in Indian history. The fact that today the judge is a byword for judicial courage can be seen in a valedictory address for judges by a former chief justice of the Chhattisgarh High Court, Yatindra Singh, who in 2014 referenced the dissent as the 'silver lining in the failure of the rule of law during the emergency'. He compared it to the great dissent of Lord Atkin in *Liversidge v Andersen*,[106] during which Justice Atkin had famously said that when it came to the 'liberty of the subject', judges should not become 'more executive-minded than the executive'.

Justice Singh went on to say, 'With one judgment, Justice Khanna became more famous, more respectable, more celebrated than any judge to have ever adorned the bench in our judiciary,' and told the assembled judges, 'May you go on to follow "rule of law" and become a judge like Justice H.R. Khanna.'[107] It is precisely when the executive overreaches in contemporary times that such dissent moves from being a part of the judicial archive to becoming a conversation about the future of Indian democracy.

Fighting to Preserve Democracy: Lessons of the Emergency

Perhaps the most well-known face of the resistance to the Emergency was Janata Dal leader and trade unionist George Fernandes, who went underground and kept the spirit of resistance alive through 'feisty bulletins and open letters' to Indira Gandhi, which accused her of being a 'fascist dictator', writes Gyan Prakash in *Emergency Chronicles*.[108] But his family had to pay the price for this. To get information on Fernandes's whereabouts, his brother Lawrence was picked up and tortured by the police.[109] Finally, Fernandes was apprehended, and at his trial, he held up his hands restrained in cuffs and proclaimed, 'The chains we bear are symbols of the entire nation which has been chained and fettered by dictatorship, a symbol of the infamy which has been perpetrated on our country.'[110]

Other citizens, in big ways and small, contributed to keeping alive the spirit of democracy.

As Balraj Puri, one of the followers of JP, writes in the *Economic and Political Weekly*:

> The urge for freedom, a basic human urge, further inspired and institutionalised by the illustrious leaders of India could not be easily banished from the minds of the people. When the opportunity came to choose between freedom and bondage, their choice was obvious and unmistakable. The common man demonstrated, what the intellectual had not appreciated, that he valued freedom no less than bread.[111]

The ideological scaffolding of the Opposition, based as it was on the legacies of the freedom struggle—like the open letter by Sachar and others—was what the regime found most difficult to stomach. 'The greatest handicap of the authors of the Emergency', writes Puri, 'was their inability to disown Gandhi and Nehru for obvious reasons. That they were a source of inspiration to the opposition and embarrassment to the ruling party.' This led to Jawaharlal Nehru's own paper, *National Herald*, being either persuaded or stopping of its own volition the publication of 'his famous quotation on its masthead which read, "Freedom is in peril, defend it with all your might"'.[112]

When grave acts of injustice were perpetrated, individuals leading ordinary lives sometimes took on extraordinary mantles of courage. As a profile in courageous perseverance, the struggle of Varier, who fought against all odds to ensure that the State was made accountable for the abduction, torture and murder of his son Rajan, should be remembered.

Even if Varier did not get final justice in the form of the conviction of those who committed the torture and murder of his son, his struggle was not in vain. A movement for justice for Rajan was born. When the writ petition was filed after the Emergency was lifted, it was carried by 'all the major newspapers in Kerala' and 'the news spread through Kerala like wild fire', notes Varier. There was also a 'huge crowd in the High Court on the day the writ was considered', and 'Rajan's case was being felt among the people'.[113] This was a seismic shift from Varier's initial lonely battle when public support was not forthcoming.

The high court verdict itself was a victory as the State's lies and evasions were exposed, and it was forced to admit that Rajan was tortured and murdered by its officials. The then chief minister of Kerala, K. Karunakaran, was forced to resign following the Supreme Court verdict upholding the finding of the high court. This had its impact on national politics as well, with Rajan's case becoming a 'topic of discussion across the country'. Varier also succeeded in his civil case for damages, with the judge ordering a compensation amount of Rs 600,000.

Varier's love for his son and the desire to keep his memory alive found expression through the building of a memorial. In fidelity with his son's ideals, instead of constructing a conventional memorial, he decided to fund the building of a wing of the Ernakulam General Hospital dedicated to patients in need of critical care. Varier notes in his autobiography, 'This is still the only ward in the general hospital where the beds are not empty; it is always crowded with patients.'[114] The students of the Regional Engineering College (now called National Institute of Technology, Calicut) where Rajan studied also seek to keep his memory alive through an annual cultural festival called Ragam. The college has installed a bust of Rajan in its compound, which serves to remind students of the ideals that he stood for.[115]

Despite this incredible life's work of striving for justice for his son and keeping alive his memory, Varier movingly concludes in his book:

My son is standing outside, drenched in rain. I still have no answer to the question of whether or not I feel vengeance. But I leave a question to the world: why are you making my innocent child stand in the rain even after his death? I don't close the door. Let the rain lash inside and drench me. Let at least my invisible son know that his father never shut the door.[116]

The judiciary too played its role in enabling resistance to the Emergency. Nine high courts entertained petitions of habeas corpus till the Supreme Court ruled otherwise. The majority in *ADM Jabalpur* did not stand up to the Emergency, but when the darkness seemed absolute and the Supreme Court set the final seal of imprimatur on extinguishing the right to liberty, we had the luminous dissent of Justice Khanna, whose words spoke to the future.

The fact that Justice Khanna's opinion was delivered regardless of personal consequences opened out the space for ethical action among the legal fraternity. Till today, his dissent continues to inspire all those who feel that the law cannot be synonymous with tyranny and the right to personal liberty cannot be extinguished by law.

There are many complex reasons for the lifting of the Emergency, including possibly Indira Gandhi's certainty of victory in the ensuing elections. However, undoubtedly, the resistance to the Emergency made clear that there would be costs to her regime, in terms of adverse international opinion as well as the loss of democratic legitimacy. The image of the political opposition and of student leaders in jail, censorship of the press and the horrors of demolitions and mass sterilisations made the government unpopular.

These acts of resistance both small and large, ranging from protests to underground literature to judicial dissents to the courage of a father to keep looking for his son, fed into the narrative of the illegitimacy of the Emergency and eventually contributed to its withdrawal and the announcement of elections. In the elections, Indira Gandhi was comprehensively defeated, and her electoral defeat was akin to a referendum on the Emergency, with people rejecting the authoritarian regime.

The formation of the Janata Party government post the Emergency led to the restoration of liberal democracy, reversal of some of the egregious constitutional amendments, and change of policies and repeal of legislations that went against the Constitution, including MISA. It also, importantly, set up the Shah Commission to uncover the excesses of the Emergency regime. In particular, the 44th Amendment to the Indian Constitution passed in 1978 based itself on the understanding that 'Recent experience has shown that the fundamental rights, including those of life and liberty, granted to citizens by the Constitution are capable of being taken away by a transient majority.' It sought not only to reverse some of the egregious wrongs of the Emergency but also to 'provide adequate safeguards against the recurrence of such a contingency in the future and to ensure to the people themselves an effective voice in determining the form of government under which they are to live'. [117]

One of the important dimensions of this amendment was the changes made to Article 352 to introduce safeguards against its misuse. The phrase 'internal disturbance', which was used to declare the Emergency by Indira Gandhi, was replaced by 'armed rebellion', which makes the threshold upon which an emergency can be invoked highly specific.

The amendment also details a series of procedural safeguards against the declaration of an emergency. While previously, an emergency could have been declared on the sole advice of the prime minister, now such advice has to be based on 'the decision of the Union Cabinet' and must be communicated to the president in writing. The level of parliamentary control over the decision to impose emergency has also been increased. While before, Parliament had to approve the decision to impose emergency within two months if it was to continue, now, the time period has been reduced to one month. Also, the approval has to be by both houses of Parliament, with a majority of half the membership of each house and a further majority of at least two-thirds of those present and voting.

Article 359 was amended to include a 'non derogation clause', providing that even during an emergency, the right to move the courts for enforcement of Articles 20 and 21 could not be suspended. The amendments to Article 359 nullified the *ADM Jabalpur* judgement as the Constitution now guaranteed that even during an emergency, no presidential order could take away the right to life under Article 21.[118]

However, the 44th Amendment remained an incomplete victory as the important amendments to Article 22 were never notified and hence never came into force. The amendment changed the period of preventive detention from not longer than three months to two months unless an 'Advisory Board constituted in accordance with the recommendations of the Chief Justice of the appropriate High Court has reported before the expiration of the said period of two months that there is in its opinion sufficient cause for such detention'. The amendments also sought to build a level of independence for the advisory board from the executive by providing that 'the Chairman shall be a serving Judge of the appropriate High Court and the other members shall be serving or retired Judges of any High Court'.[119]

The fact that the Janata government did not notify these amendments leads one to speculate that once it was in power, it was loath to introduce any checks to its own power to preventively detain its opponents. The failure to notify the amendments was litigated before the Supreme Court by A.K. Roy, who was a Marxist member of Parliament (MP). In *AK Roy v Union of India*,[120] the petitioner argued that a mandamus should be issued to the executive to implement the will of Parliament. The court held that '... it is difficult to appreciate what practical difficulty can possibly prevent the Government from bringing into force the provisions of Section 3 of the 44th Amendment, after the passage of two and half years. But the remedy, according to us, is not the writ of mandamus'. The court was clear that it was 'not for the Court to compel the Government' and that 'the executive is responsible to the Parliament and if the Parliament considers that the executive has betrayed its trust by not bringing any provision of the Amendment into force, it can censure the executive'.

It is important to note that Justice A.C. Gupta and Justice V.D. Tulzapurkar dissented from the majority judgement authored by Justice Y.V. Chandrachud. Justice Gupta held that a reading of the 'Objects and Reasons' of the Constitution (44th Amendment) Act, 1978, disclosed 'a sense of urgency' as Parliament was concerned about 'providing safeguards' to ensure that 'life and liberty' of the citizen are not taken away by a 'transient majority'. He found it difficult to believe that the executive had the power to 'scotch an amendment of the Constitution passed by Parliament and assented to by the President'. Based on this reasoning, he went on to 'issue a writ of mandamus directing the Central Government to issue a notification ... bringing into force the provisions of Section 3 of the Act within two months from this date'.

However, forty-six years after the Emergency, this dissent too awaits what Justice Khanna would have called the 'intelligence of a future day' to resurrect it and make it the law of the land. This incomplete victory of the 44th amendment, meant to ensure that what happened during the Emergency would not happen again, only underlines the resilience of the 'institutionalised emergency' of preventive detention, which seems to have a life of its own regardless of the fact that the Emergency era constitutional outrages were otherwise overturned.

Even as the struggle against the Emergency, leading to its withdrawal and the reversal of many of its policies, is rightly seen as something to be celebrated, it behoves us to adopt a position towards it, that is somewhere 'between reckless optimism and reckless despair', as Hannah Arendt warns in *The Origins of Totalitarianism*.[121] For, in the end, not even the shock over the excesses of the Emergency could overturn the executive writ with respect to preventive detention.

2

Roots of the Emergency

Preventive Detention

JUST LIKE THE INDIRA GANDHI REGIME DURING THE EMERGENCY of 1975–77, the current Modi regime has a readymade tool to deal with dissent: preventive detention, which is authorised by the Indian Constitution in its Fundamental Rights chapter as Article 22.[1] This provision has been referred to as the 'undemocratic heart of the Indian Constitution' by former politician P. Padmanabhan.[2]

Article 22 on 'protection against arrest and detention in certain cases' begins promisingly enough by setting out the rights of the accused person under 22(1) and (2). As per the first clause, an arrested person has the right to be informed 'as soon as may be' of the grounds of arrest, the right to 'consult' and 'to be defended by a legal practitioner of his choice'. The second clause directs that the arrested person be produced before a magistrate within twenty-four hours of arrest, and no person shall be detained beyond twenty-four hours without the authority of a magistrate.

However, under 22(3)(b), both the rights detailed above will not apply to a person detained under a law providing for preventive detention, such as the Preventive Detention Act, essentially nullifying the important protections on arrest guaranteed by the first two clauses.

Although Article 22 provides limited safeguards such as detention beyond a period of three months to be authorised by an advisory board and provides for the right of the arrested person to make a representation against such detention, both these limited rights are subject to further qualifications, rendering them illusory.[3]

How did Article 22 become a part of the Indian Constitution?

Ironically, the provisions authorising preventive detention made their way into the Constitution in response to the severe criticism of the anaemic nature of the right to life guaranteed under Article 21, the then draft Article 15.[4]

The relevant part of draft Article 15 reads: 'No person shall be deprived of life or personal liberty except by procedure established by law...'[5] Many members of the Constituent Assembly felt that this provision gave the State the power to deprive an individual of the hard-won right to personal liberty, merely by passing a law and without empowering the judiciary to examine whether the law violated the right to life.

To the members of the Constituent Assembly, the role of the British in suppressing individual freedom was a painful memory. Pandit Thakur Das Bhargava drew attention to the history of the freedom struggle and how 'laws such as XIV of 1908 called the Black Law' were used to arrest 'thousands, if not hundreds of thousands of Congressmen'. Under Act XIV of 1908, the British government arrogated to itself the power to declare any organisation illegal merely by notification. This Act was passed in the 'teeth of full opposition', even though it was 'condemned by the whole of India'. The courts did not have the power to hold that 'the notification of the Government was wrong'. Based on this history, Bhargava argued that draft Article 15 should encompass within itself the power of the judiciary to examine legislation on the anvil of fundamental rights. To do so, he argued, the phrase 'procedure established by law' in the draft Article 15—which read, 'No person shall be deprived of life or personal liberty except by procedure established by law'—should be replaced by 'due process of law'.[6]

K.M. Munshi too had the experience of the British Raj in his mind when he made a plea for having 'due process in Article 15'. As he put it, '... there is a tendency to pass legislation in a hurry which gives sweeping powers to the executive and the police'. There will be no 'deterrent, if these legislations are not examined by a Court of law'.[7]

'Due process of law' was preferred to 'procedure established by law' because the former had 'acquired a certain fixed meaning both in England and in America, as a result of the struggle for liberty against the Executive which went on there for centuries'.[8] Bakhshi Tek Chand summarised the 'three essentials' of due process: 'you will not condemn a person before hearing him; you will not proceed against him without enquiry; you will not deliver judgment against him without trial'.[9]

In response to this impassioned plea for introducing 'due process of law' into draft Article 15, B.R. Ambedkar confessed that he was torn between two viewpoints, which he characterised as having to sail between 'Charybdis and Scylla'. He was cognisant of the 'possibility of a Legislature packed by party men making laws which may abrogate or violate what we regard as certain fundamental principles affecting the life and liberty of an individual', yet, at the same time, he said that he did not see how 'five or six gentlemen sitting in the Federal or Supreme Court examining laws made by the Legislature … can be trusted to determine', based on their 'individual conscience', 'biases' or 'prejudices', 'which law is good and which law is bad.' He said that he would 'leave it to the House to decide in anyway it likes'.[10]

However, nine months after the conclusion of the debate on draft Article 15 of the Constitution, Ambedkar came back with another proposal that he thought would take care of some of the concerns of those who felt that 'we were giving a carte blanche to Parliament to make and provide for the arrest of any person under any circumstances as Parliament may think fit'. To address these concerns, draft Article 15A (now Article 22) was introduced, 'making compensation for what was done then in passing article 15. In other words, we are providing for the substance of the law of "due process" by the introduction of article 15A'.[11]

Article 15A, while recognising the rights of an accused person to legal representation and to know the grounds of arrest as well as to be produced before the nearest magistrate within twenty-four hours, went on to authorise preventive detention. The reason for the preventive detention provision was because, in Ambedkar's opinion, the 'exigency of the liberty of the individual' should not be above the 'interests of the State'.[12]

There was even more severe criticism for Article 15A than for Article 15. Jaspat Roy Kapoor said that the 'whole article is jarring to the ear and is one more illustration of the conservatism which characterises the chapter on Fundamental Rights'.[13] Bakhshi Tek Chand scathingly observed that its inclusion would 'disfigure the Constitution'.[14] Pandit Thakur Das Barghava called it a 'blot on the Constitution'.[15]

Even those who recognised that a modern State had to have preventive detention laws, such as Bhargava, argued that they must be regulated by law and that at 'least the barest demands of justice be secured to a person who is a detainee'.[16] H.V. Kamath concurred and opined that 'a man is detained on suspicion only. It is but fair that our Constitution should lay down specifically that no detenu will be subjected to physical and mental ill-treatment'.[17]

M.A. Ayyangar did not hesitate to point out that the chairperson of the drafting committee, Ambedkar, had no experience of jail, because of which he was not alert to the 'hardships suffered by others'. Kapoor recalled how when Congressmen had been detained during the Satyagraha movement under the preventive detention laws, they had waited 'anxiously' for a review of their detention. One of the remedies pressed by both Kapoor and Ayyangar was a periodic, rather than a one-off, review of detentions.[18]

Members articulated the incongruity of preventive detention with the Fundamental Rights chapter as well as its lack of fidelity to the ideals of the Independence struggle. Mahaveer Tyagi asked: '... what relevance is there for a detention clause in the Constitution which is meant to guarantee fundamental rights to the citizens?' He argued that the clause authorising preventive detention 'changes the chapter of fundamental rights into a penal code worse than the Defence of India Rules of the old government'. He poignantly added:

How I wish Dr. Ambedkar was with me in jail after being arrested and hand-cuffed for a whole night? I wish he had had my experience. If he had been hand-cuffed along with me, he would have experienced the misery. I fear, Sir, the provisions now proposed by him would recoil on himself. Sir, as soon as another political party comes to power, he along with his colleagues will become the victims of the provisions now being made by him.[19]

Kamath rounded off his critique of the provision by gesturing to the future use of this clause:

Has anybody considered how some other persons, possibly totally opposed to our ideals, to our conceptions of democracy, coming into power, might use this very Constitution against us, and suppress our rights and liberties? This Constitution which we are framing here may act as a Boomerang, may recoil upon us and it would be then too late for us to rue the day when we made such provisions in the Constitution.[20]

However, in spite of the strong criticism, the preventive detention clause—now Article 22—was finally passed without providing for the minimal protection urged by some of the members, such as protection against torture and constitutional recognition of periodic review of preventive detention.

In Ambedkar's closing address on draft Article 15A, he defended the article from the charge that it should not have been enacted at all, on the grounds that since the lists contained in the Seventh Schedule of the Constitution authorised both the Centre and the states to enact preventive detention laws,[21] this article 'put a limitation upon the exercise of making any law which we have now given both to the Centre and to the Provinces' and hence was necessary from the point of denying 'complete liberty' to the governments to make just 'any law' on preventive detention.[22] He was clear that the intent behind Article

15A was to 'curtail' the 'power' of both the Centre and the provinces and to 'put a limitation upon it'.[23]

Based on this final summation by Ambedkar, the vote on Article 15A took place, and it was passed with the acceptance of a few important amendments proposed by the members, such as the right of the person being detained to know the grounds of detention and the right to make a representation against the detention order. Some of the questions raised by the members of the Constituent Assembly were left to Parliament to decide, such as the requirement of periodic review and the prescription of a maximum period of preventive detention. Other questions, such as the right to cross-examination, were, according to Ambedkar, implicit in the right to make a representation. Unfortunately, other issues, such as the right to be free from torture, were not addressed in Ambedkar's closing statement.

The question which troubled many members was how a rights-loving person such as Ambedkar could have proposed this article. In Alladi Krishnaswami Ayyar's opinion, the legitimacy of Article 15A vested in the fact that Ambedkar, who was undoubtedly 'keen' on 'the problem of personal liberty', had 'thought fit to bring forward this amendment' and desired that 'this article must find a place in the Constitution'.[24] Another member, P. K. Sen, speculated that Ambedkar was 'overborne' by 'extraneous forces', and that there were two Ambedkars in the Constituent Assembly. The 'one Dr. Ambedkar, plain and simple as he is intensely in sympathy with the individual as regards rights and liberties and the other somewhat like the ghost of himself, as it were, like the perturbed spirit in Hamlet hovering about and over his innate love of freedom and yet being overborne by other forces'.[25]

Ambedkar himself defended his commitment to liberty by invoking his record in the viceroy's cabinet, where he, along with another European member of the cabinet, had 'fought for' the introduction of a rule 'regarding review' of preventive detention. He specifically referenced the accusation that he had no feeling for the detenus as he had never been to jail and said, '… it is not necessary to go to jail to feel for freedom and liberty'.[26]

He disagreed with the critics of Article 15A that it was antithetical to freedom and, in fact, argued that it served to protect rights. If this debate is to be seen from this perspective, the then Article 15A and the now Article 22 must be interpreted as a safeguard of personal liberty, as that was the intent of the members of the Constituent Assembly.

The first occasion to interpret the meaning of Article 22 came when the veteran communist leader A.K. Gopalan challenged his detention under the Preventive Detention Act as violative of Articles 19, 21 and 22 of the Constitution.

An old adversary of the British Raj, Gopalan had been imprisoned repeatedly by them. However, even the provincial government headed by the Congress just prior to Independence continued to imprison him for protesting against its policies. The dawn of Independence saw the Madras government release all political prisoners, except Gopalan.

In his autobiography, *In the Cause of the People*, Gopalan points to the irony of being a prisoner not of the British government but of the Congress government in spite of being part of the movement for Independence. Hearing cries of 'Mahatma Gandhi ki jai' and 'Bharat Matha ki Jai' 'reverberate' through the jail on the eve of Independence Day, he decided to celebrate even if in jail. So, on the morning of 15 August 1947, he marked the day by walking the length of the jail compound carrying the national flag, accompanied by other prisoners, after which he hoisted the flag on the roof. The jail authorities were not happy with this, but instead of dispersing the gathering with a 'lathi charge', they arrested Gopalan on the charge of sedition and produced him before the magistrate, before whom he made this statement:

I am proud that I am being tried for creating enmity against the legally constituted Emperor of British India. All freedom lovers in this country and the leaders of the freedom movement from its birth, like Nehru, Gandhi and such leaders, have tried to create enmity against the Emperor's government. ... As a result of all of this, his Majesty's government and British India have ceased to exist today. Many of my colleagues who committed the same crime along with me have become Ministers and Governors. There is some incongruity in bringing me to trial at this time when on the face of it we have just achieved freedom. I am sorry that things have come to such a pass.[27]

The 'incongruity' pointed out by Gopalan, however, did not seem to trouble the new government in power. As well-known human rights lawyer K.G. Kannabiran writes in *The Wages of Impunity*:

For the magistrate and the public prosecutor, nothing appeared incongruous. They were not able to see any break. Governance for them was a continuous process and the principles of governance set up by the British in India were seen as appropriate and relevant for free India. The advent of independence was just an event which did not disturb continuity.[28]

Citizens were, however, disturbed by the continued detention of Gopalan in independent India and 'agitations broke out throughout Kerala' in September of 1947, as Gopalan notes, with 'public meetings, demonstrations, deputations, telegrams, letters' pressing for his release. He undertook a fast in prison and wrote to the Madras ministry, saying, 'I was a political prisoner from 1930 to 1945 in the eyes of a foreign government. Under today's popular government I am branded a criminal. The only reason I can find for this is that I am a Communist.'[29]

It was only following this agitation that he was finally released from prison on 12 October 1947, almost two months after Independence. On being released, Gopalan joined another agitation against the Congress government and was arrested again on 17 December that year. This time, he was held under the preventive detention law in Madras, which continued to be valid because the various state governments had promulgated Preventive Detention (Extend the Duration) Orders to ensure the continuance of the 'public safety and security measures' enacted by the British government. When these orders were challenged, the high courts of Patna, Calcutta, Orissa and Hyderabad struck down the orders applicable to the respective states as invalid.[30] To cope with this striking down of state-level preventive detention laws, less than a month after the Constitution came into force on 26 January 1950, the Union government enacted the Preventive Detention Act on 15 February 1950. Gopalan's detention was now under the authority of the Preventive Detention Act of 1950.

Gopalan challenged his detention by way of a writ petition to the Supreme Court under Article 32, which allows citizens to move the apex court for violation of fundamental rights. It was the first writ petition which was heard on a fundamental rights claim in independent India and was heard by the full bench of the Supreme Court, consisting of all six judges. Gopalan challenged the constitutionality of the Act under Articles 19 (freedoms of speech, expression, association, movement, etc.), 21 (right to life) and 22 (preventive detention provisions).

The case, *A.K. Gopalan v State of Madras*,[31] provided the court an opportunity to affirm the rights-protecting nature of the Constitution by examining the preventive detention provisions on the anvil of fundamental rights. All six judges went on to write six separate opinions making the judgement difficult to decipher. However, four of the six judges upheld the constitutionality of the Preventive Detention Act as a whole. The only point on which all six judges were in agreement was that Section 14 of the Act, which barred a court from requiring the production of grounds of detention, be struck down. The case was important for the ratio it laid down, particularly with respect to the interpretation of articles 21 and 22. With respect to Article 22, the only question was whether the procedure prescribed in the statute conformed to Article 22, with the majority holding in the affirmative. (Save Section 14, which all agreed violated Article 22 and had to be struck down). With respect to Article 21, the interpretation hinged on the meaning of the phrase 'procedure established by law'.

Chief Justice H.J. Kania put forward the understanding that 'if the legislature prescribes a procedure by a validly enacted law and such procedure in the case of preventive detention does not come in conflict with the express provisions of Part III or article 22(4) to (7), the Preventive Detention Act must be held valid notwithstanding that the Court may not fully approve of the procedure prescribed under such Act'. Justice Bijan Kumar Mukherjea observed, '... even if the procedure is not exhaustive, it is not permissible to supplement it by application of the rules of natural justice'.

When it came to Article 21, the majority rejected the argument of the petitioner that 'procedure established by law' included within it the principles of natural justice. As Chief Justice Kania formulated it, the question was whether law was 'lex i.e., enacted law or does it mean "jus", i.e., law in the abstract sense of the principles of natural justice'. For the majority, the 'law' under Article 21 was lex, not jus.[32]

This distinction between lex and jus is vital. If the law is lex, then as long as it is validly passed under Article 21, even if it deprives a person of fundamental rights, it is still valid, as it conforms to the test of a 'procedure established by law', and so the State can deprive a person of 'life or personal liberty'. However, if the law means jus, then the procedure has to also conform to the principles of natural justice, even if it is otherwise validly enacted by the legislature.

The majority in the bench held that since the law meant by Article 21 was lex and the Preventive Detention Act was validly passed by Parliament, it could not be subject to challenge. As Chief Justice Kania said, the Preventive Detention Act 'must be held valid notwithstanding that the Court may not fully approve of the procedure prescribed under such Act'.

Even as the majority upheld the act as a whole, all six judges expressed a sense of disquiet with the preventive detention provisions. As Justice Mehr Chand Mahajan put it, 'Preventive detention laws are repugnant to democratic constitutions.' He also observed, 'Curiously enough, this subject has found place in the Constitution in the chapter on Fundamental Rights.' Justice Mukherjea was also forthright in expressing his discomfiture and stated that preventive detention 'cannot but be regarded as a most unwholesome encroachment upon the liberties of the people'. In Justice M. Patanjali Shastri's opinion, preventive detention was a 'sinister-looking feature, so strangely out of place in a democratic constitution' and 'incompatible with the promise of the Preamble'.

Despite voicing their discomfiture with the Preventive Detention Act, the furthest the majority was prepared to go was to strike down Section 14 of the Act, which prohibited the disclosure of the grounds of detention before a court.[33] This was held to be a 'drastic provision'. Chief Justice Kania disagreed with the submission of the attorney general that the 'whole object of the section was to prevent ventilation in public of the grounds and the submissions' and held that it violated Article 22(5), which mandates that a person has the right to be told of the 'grounds' of the detention and the right to representation against the order.

The discomfiture with the preventive detention provision seems to have led Justice Mahajan to pass on the responsibility of protecting fundamental rights from the judiciary to the public. He observed that 'our protection against legislative tyranny, if any, lies in ultimate analysis in a free and intelligent public opinion which must eventually assert itself'.

The decision in *A.K. Gopalan* was widely seen as a big disappointment by the human rights community. Kannabiran describes the judgement as 'the first Indian made foreign judgement'. In his opinion, Parliament's power under Article 22(7) to legislatively sanction preventive detention beyond a period of three months without authorisation by an advisory board was a 'drastic power' and should have been treated as an 'exception'. By not doing so, 'legal grammar ... abrogated liberty' and 'the court endorsed as valid the incarceration of political dissidents without any accountability'.[34]

For Kannabiran, the decision in *A.K. Gopalan* completely bypassed the spirit of the Constitution and instead chose to engage in 'the pettifogging of the law'. He borrowed the phrase 'pettifogging of the law' from Justice Vivian Bose's dissent a year earlier in *S. Krishan v State of Madras*, in which the majority upheld the constitutional validity of the Preventive Detention (Amendment) Act, 1951. Justice Bose observed that one must 'look past the mere verbiage of the words and penetrate deep into the heart and spirit of the Constitution', which was about a 'way of life,' and 'the right to individual freedom'. Justice Bose went on to hold:

> Is not our Constitution in violent contrast to those of States where the State is everything and the individual but a slave or a serf to serve the will of those who for the time being wield almost absolute power? I have no doubts on this score. I hold it therefore to be our duty, when there is ambiguity or doubt about the construction of any clause in this chapter on Fundamental Rights, to resolve it in favour of the freedoms which have been so solemnly stressed.[35]

The majority in *A.K. Gopalan*, according to Kannabiran, failed to interpret the Constitution as a product of a historic Independence struggle. To him, 'Bose alone understood that words were mere symbols and indeed a gloss, and that the prolonged struggle for independence should form the key to understanding the Constitution and the laws affecting freedom.'[36]

However, it is interesting to note that Gopalan himself was more sanguine. In his autobiography, he draws attention to the fact that the Supreme Court did hold Section 14 unconstitutional. This was important because, as political scientist George Gadbois notes in *Supreme Court of India*, 'due to Section 14, Gopalan did not know the grounds of his detention and had to challenge the constitutionality of his detention in the abstract without being able to provide a particularized case as to why his detention was bad in law'.[37]

Gopalan further notes in his book that the judgement helped safeguard the fundamental rights of those detained under the act. The important argument put forward by his counsel, M.K. Nambiar, that the Preventive Detention Act itself was unconstitutional, was 'hotly debated by judges and legal experts' post the judgement. He concludes that 'although that law-suit failed to bring about my release, it was a great achievement in the sense that it raised an important constitutional issue'. His long-term perspective on the judgement is all the more remarkable as post the judgement 'he returned to jail under police escort'.[38]

The small window kept open by the Supreme Court through the striking down of Section 14 allowed Gopalan to approach the Madras High Court for his release, based on the argument that the grounds on which he was detained did not conform to the Preventive Detention Act. Thus Gopalan found himself before the Madras High Court in a writ which he argued himself. He notes that 'large crowds came to hear the argument'. He was set free on the last date of the hearing by the court, but in a travesty of the judicial proceedings, was re-arrested outside the court and 'escorted back to Cuddalore Jail'. He had to file another writ petition before the Madras High Court, which was heard two days after his re-arrest, and he was again released with specific directions to the police 'not to touch [him]'. The police did not 'dare to disobey this injunction', and he was finally released after spending four years in jail from December 1947 to 1951 under an Indian government.[39]

Even in the *A.K. Gopalan* judgement, the possibility of the Supreme Court deciding differently was kept alive through the forceful dissent of Justice Fazl Ali. The minority opinion of Justice Ali went much further than expressing disquiet or hope in an awakened citizenry; he struck the act down in its entirety. His reasoning was based on the notion that law could not mean mere 'lex', but had to be 'jus'. In his reasoning, the principle that 'no person can be condemned without a hearing by an impartial tribunal which is well-recognized in all modern civilized systems of law' has to be a part of the word 'law'. 'Law' had to mean more than 'statute law'.

Justice Ali's dissent was based on the thinking that though preventive detention was authorised by the Constitution, the court had the obligation to narrowly interpret the power to make a law on preventive detention to ensure conformity with fundamental rights. He argued that even the power of Parliament under Article 22(7) to authorise preventive detention beyond three months without producing the detenus before an advisory board had to be read strictly and the Preventive Detention Act failed to 'prescribe either the circumstances or the class or classes of cases in the manner required by the Constitution'. Thus, in Justice Ali's opinion, the power to preventively detain was limited by the framework of both Articles 21 and 22.

His dissent also took inspiration from the British judge James Atkin's dissent in *Liversidge v Anderson*, in which the majority upheld the legality of preventive detention during the Second World War. Drawing upon the courageous dissent of Lord Atkin, Justice Ali observed that it 'is difficult to say that there is not a good substratum of sound law in the celebrated dictum of Lord Atkin' that 'even amidst the clash of arms the laws are not silent' and 'that they speak the same language in war as in peace'.[40]

Seventy-seven years later, Justice Rohinton Nariman, in *Puttaswamy v Union of India*,[41] held that Justice Ali's dissent was one of the three great dissents in the jurisprudence of the Indian Supreme Court. He approvingly cited Justice Ali's 'foresight', which 'simply takes our breath away', on two important points:

Firstly, Justice Ali was a far-sighted critic of the viewpoint that each fundamental right was 'a code by itself' and 'independent of the others'. In his judgement, he held that 'it cannot be said that Articles 19, 20, 21 and 22 do not to some extent overlap each other', and in doing so, he anticipated the later wisdom of the Indian Supreme Court. Secondly, he provided a viewpoint on how to understand the word 'law' in its 'wider meaning' and 'abstract' formulation, thereby providing a critique of the idea that law is 'nothing more than statute law'.

Both these points anticipated the future decisions of the Indian Supreme Court, and Justice Nariman saw this dissent through the lens of the US jurist Charles Evans Hughes as an 'appeal to the brooding spirit of the law, to the intelligence of a future day, when a later decision may possibly correct the error into which the dissenting judge believes the court to have been betrayed'.[42] The judgement of Justice Ali was a 'cry in the wilderness' till the decision of the Supreme Court in *R.C. Cooper v Union of India* twenty years later.

In 1970, the Supreme Court, in *R.C. Cooper v Union of India*,[43] hearing a petition against bank nationalisation, held that fundamental rights were not 'mutually exclusive' and that the nationalisation of the banks could be challenged not only under the right to property under Article 31(2) but also under the right to freedom of trade and profession under Article 19(1)(f).

Eight years later, in *Maneka Gandhi v Union of India*,[44] the Supreme Court read the word 'law' more expansively to mean not just 'lex' but 'jus'. Gandhi's passport had been impounded, and when she had asked for the reasons, the Central government told her that it was not in the public interest to disclose these. Gandhi challenged this State action, and the judgement ruled that she could be deprived of her passport not by any enacted law but by a law which was 'just, fair and reasonable'. As Justice P.N. Bhagwati held, 'Procedure in Article 21 means fair, not formal procedure. Law is reasonable law, not any enacted piece.' Post *Maneka Gandhi*, law under Articles 14, 19 and 21 is no more just 'lex' but 'jus'.

However, if the 'intelligence of a future day' demands that preventive detention laws will be found to be violative of the right to life, liberty and equality, that day has not yet arrived. In fact, the Supreme Court has upheld the constitutional validity of the National Security Act (NSA), 1981.[45] Later laws which were not enacted as preventive detention laws but have de facto functioned as preventive detention laws are anti-terrorism laws, including the Terrorist and Disruptive Activities Act (TADA), 1994[46] and the Prevention of Terrorism Act (POTA), 2003,[47] both of whose constitutional validity has also been upheld. Thus, there is a constitutional sanction to both de jure and de facto preventive detention, putting the hard-won liberties of the citizen under perpetual risk from capricious, arbitrary and vengeful State action. It is in this sense that, ever since Independence, India has been under an institutional emergency in which the hard-won liberties of the citizens are perpetually under risk.

This state of affairs has also drawn the attention of the United Nations Human Rights Committee, which, on examining India's human rights record, described the rule by the police under anti-terror laws such as TADA and the Armed Forces (Special Powers) Act (AFSPA), 1958, as having established 'a continuing state of emergency' without it being declared as such and without it being subjected to any time limit.[48]

Neither international scrutiny nor the broader interpretation of *Maneka Gandhi* as well as *R.C. Cooper* has made a dent in the edifice of laws authorising preventive detention. As Kannabiran notes:

> In the matter of personal liberty, the courts have by and large, as a matter of policy validated the conferment of vast power to the executive. … The legislative and interpretive history of the more than fifty years after independence has been one of curtailing personal liberties.[49]

Kannabiran's point regarding the failure to protect personal liberty raises more fundamental questions. While this is undoubtedly a story of legislative and judicial failure, do the roots go deeper? Is the problem really that the idea of democracy as encompassing the freedom of speech and expression one which has yet to put deep roots in Indian society? Would the path to a judicial and legislative protection of personal liberty lie in the emergence of a wider societal consciousness of the value of protecting personal liberty?

3

The Modi Era

The Undeclared Emergency

To my friends, colleagues and family—I cannot thank you enough for standing by me through this period. I remain in your debt.

Do please listen to Leonard Cohen sing the Anthem and remember to:

Ring the Bell,

Which still can ring

Forget your perfect Offering

There is a crack,

A crack in everything

That's how light gets in.

– Gautam Navalakha quoting a verse of *Anthem*
in a note before his arrest[1]

AFTER THE LIFTING OF THE EMERGENCY IN 1977, INDIA RETURNED to functioning functioning as a '50-50 democracy', as historian Ramachandra Guha describes his book *India After Gandhi*. The parts that make India a functioning democracy include holding of periodic elections with smooth transfer of power; not being a 'Hindu nation' with a de jure discrimination against religious minorities despite being a Hindu majority country; the vigorous exercise of freedom of speech and expression and the right to association by its citizens; the largely free media; and the functioning of the judiciary as a sentinel to safeguard fundamental rights.[2] On the debit side is the fact that minorities face 'prejudice and hostility', with Muslims being 'one of the poorest and most vulnerable communities in India'.[3] He also points to the problem of corruption, criminality of the political class, failure to provide justice, as seen in the corruption of the police and the plight of undertrials, and the imperfect protection of the right to freedom of speech and expression from vigilante attacks.[4]

The credit side of the 50-50 democracy has faced further attenuation ever since the election of the Modi government in 2014 and its re-election in 2019. The transfer of power through free elections may have continued, but other characteristics of a democracy have been further diluted. The government's suppression of dissent using repressive laws and the media, and the judiciary's silence in the face of this executive action, recall the fear and helplessness which characterised the Emergency era. The freedom of thought, assembly and association, which are essential features of Indian democracy, face their most serious challenge since 1975.

As one of India's oldest and most-respected civil liberties organisations, People's Union for Civil Liberties (PUCL), which was born during the Emergency era, put it, 'Today in the year 2018 "Undeclared Emergency" has been clamped all throughout the country' and 'rights of the citizens are being snatched away under the guise of Patriotism and cultural nationality', 'freedom of speech, writing and expression are being banned' and 'systematic efforts are being made to harass the activists who are struggling for defending, preserving and promoting the human rights. Any voice of dissent is being repressed in the name of treason or sedition'.[5]

The PUCL, through its invocation of an undeclared emergency, is speaking of the far greater intolerance for dissenting voices than in any other time in the recent past. Though not all previous administrations were tolerant of dissent, there were still checks and balances to safeguard the right to dissent through the media, civil society and the judiciary, even when the government in power was intolerant of dissenters. It is in this failure of the system as a whole to protect the right to dissent that we see the long shadow of the Emergency years.

Some of the country's best-known intellectuals such as Pratap Bhanu Mehta have also argued that the undeclared emergency of today seems to be as 'insidious and far-reaching'[6] as the Indira Gandhi regime of 1975–77. One of the essential characteristics of a period of emergency is the centralisation of power. Guha argues in an article for NDTV that for both Indira Gandhi and Modi, the 'party', 'government', 'administration' and 'country' are but an 'extension' of their personalities. The structural similarities between the two eras, in Guha's terms, is that, yet again, 'one party', 'one ideology' and 'one leader' are attempting to 'impose their will on our gloriously heterogeneous Republic'.[7] As Christophe Jaffrelot argues in an interview to the *Wire*, in the current Modi regime, power is concentrated in the hands of two people, Narendra Modi and Amit Shah, closely resembling the power duo of Indira and Sanjay Gandhi during the Emergency era.[8]

But, alongside an all-powerful leader, it is the unrestrained use of repressive laws to check dissent that puts today's India in a state of undeclared emergency. The current Modi government, similar to the Emergency regime, keeps critics in check by using the instrumentalities of the State such as the CBI, the NIA, the Enforcement Directorate, the tax authorities and 'anti-terror' laws such as the UAPA.

Ordinarily, in a constitutional democracy, the power of the executive is kept in check by the media, civil society and the judiciary. Many, including former judges Justices Lokur and Shah, have voiced their discomfort with the abdication of the judiciary's responsibility to ensure that the executive functions with the limits of the Constitution. The mainstream media has largely toed the line of the State, as media observer Sevanti Ninan observes. As far as civil society is concerned, the arrest of the BK-16 is a paradigmatic case of an attempt to intimidate and harass civil society into silence.[9]

Another, more subtle but significant dimension of both emergencies, the declared and the undeclared, is the climate of fear. In the Emergency of 1975–77, octogenarian freedom fighter Bhim Sen Sachar, father of Justice Rajinder Sachar, a former chief minister of Punjab, was thrown into jail for opposing the Emergency regulations muzzling the freedom of speech and expression. He was arrested after he wrote an open letter to Indira Gandhi, severely criticising the decision to impose the Emergency. The letter is quoted both by the Shah Commission as well as by Justice Rajinder Sachar in his book *In Pursuit of Justice*. In the open letter, Bhimsen notes and criticises the atmosphere of fear that the declaration of Emergency generated:

> … the common people in Delhi now talk in hushed tones as they do in communist societies; they do not discuss politics in the coffee houses or at bus stands and look over their shoulders before expressing any opinion. An atmosphere of fear and political repression prevails.[10]

In the contemporary era, well-known industrialist Rahul Bajaj, in a function attended by Home Minister Amit Shah, claimed that there was a 'climate of fear' in the country. 'Nobody from our industrialist friends will speak, I will say openly,' he said. 'When UPA II was in power, we could criticise anyone. You [the government] are doing good work, but despite that we don't have the confidence that you will appreciate if we criticise you openly.'[11] His comments about the business industry could equally apply to the intelligentsia, civil society, media and judiciary.

A centralised, authoritarian government unafraid to use repressive laws and unchecked by any constitutional and institutional restraints coupled with a widely prevalent feeling of fear are what characterise today's undeclared emergency. An undeclared emergency is insidious because it goes under the radar of international law and the scrutiny of international organisations, local and international media as well as agencies of the United Nations.[12]

The UAPA: A Symbol of the Undeclared Emergency

The UAPA began as a law that criminalised both 'unlawful activity' and 'unlawful associations' in 1967. It added terrorism-related offences in 2004, making terrorism a permanent part of the legal regime. The 2008 procedural amendments made bail all but impossible, giving the law the character of a preventive detention act. Thus, according to Senior Advocate Mihir Desai, today, the UAPA serves three distinct but related ends, namely the criminalisation of unlawful activity / association, the criminalisation of terrorist acts and preventive detention.[13]

One important parallel between the two eras is the use of preventive detention laws such as MISA during the Emergency and the use of the UAPA as a de facto preventive detention law in the contemporary era. MISA was a preventive detention law under which persons could be detained prior to committing an offence. The UAPA functions as a de facto preventive detention law as most of those charged under it are usually not released on bail and have to await the end of the trial and an acquittal in order to leave prison. The trial is rarely completed expeditiously, and the accused often have to suffer imprisonment for many long years, only to be eventually acquitted.

The story of Srinagar resident Bashir Ahmad Baba, who spent eleven years in jail before being acquitted of terrorism charges when he turned forty-four, is only one among many such cases of wrongful arrest and incarceration. Baba was detained in Gujarat in 2010 on the accusation of recruiting Muslim youth and sending them to Pakistan to undergo terrorism-related training, all of which turned out to have no substance. However, the legal system took eleven years to finally establish that Baba was innocent.[14] Similarly, Mohammed Ilyas and Mohammed Irfan were thirty-eight and thirty-three years of age when they were acquitted by a special court of charges under the UAPA and released in June 2021 after nine years of imprisonment.[15]

These are not statistical anomalies. Justice Aftab Alam, a former judge of the Supreme Court, presented his analysis of the National Crime Records Bureau (NCRB) data of UAPA cases in a webinar. He demonstrated that the NCRB data showing the conviction rate under UAPA as 29.2 per cent was meaningless as it was calculated on the basis of the 113 cases disposed of in 2019, of which there were 33 convictions. The story that had been omitted was that there were 2,361 UAPA cases pending trial. If this figure of 33 convictions was measured against the 2,361 pending cases, then the conviction rate came down to 2 per cent with a pending rate of 98 per cent. The 'police disposal rate'—the rate at which investigations were completed—for UAPA offences was at 42.5 per cent and pendency rate was at 77.8 per cent. Justice Alam concluded that with 'such low rates of disposal and such high pendency both at the investigation and trial stages it is no surprise that though the case might finally fail, the accused would come out of incarceration only after 8,10 or in some cases even after 12 years'.[16] Thus, the story of the UAPA is really the story of prolonged detention without trial, i.e. a de facto preventive detention law.

Under MISA during the Emergency, as per the Shah Commission, over 100,000 were arrested. The number of arrests under the UAPA is estimated to be in the thousands with a 72 per cent increase in arrests in 2019 as compared to 2015.[17] Data for UAPA cases registered by the NCRB has been recorded only since 2014. The cases booked have shown a steady uptick since then—976 cases in 2014, 897 in 2015, 922 in 2016, 901 in 2017, 1,182 in 2018 and 1,126 in 2019.[18] The figures for 2019, according to the Union minister of state for home, G. Kishan Reddy, mark a 72 per cent increase in the number of persons arrested under the anti-terror law—1,948 persons were arrested under the UAPA in 1,226 cases that were registered across the country.[19] Former IPS officer N.C. Asthana scathingly observed in the *Wire* that 'No other country of the world registers so many cases against its own citizens for allegedly having committed offences against the state.' He sees this as an anomaly, especially when there was 'not a single genuine terrorist attack' which had taken place 'anywhere in the country' in that time period.[20]

The UAPA was introduced by the Congress administration in 1967 as a law to penalise membership of 'unlawful associations', which were loosely defined as engaging in an activity that 'supports secession', 'disrupts sovereignty of India' or 'causes disaffection'. These terms are at best vague, and the law has ended up restricting the constitutional right to speech and association under the overarching rubric of whatever the State deems to be in the interest of national security.

This law was amended in 2004, 2008, 2013 and 2019. The 2004 amendments introduced offences related to terrorism into the UAPA after the repeal of the Prevention of Terrorism Act (POTA), 2002. The 2008 amendments after the deadly Mumbai terror attacks overhauled the act drastically. Among the many changes making the act more stringent were the modifications in sections 43A to F, which further diluted the procedural protections of the CrPC. Significantly, Section 43D(5) was introduced, which made bail next to impossible, giving the law its preventive detention character. In 2013, the definition of a terrorist act under Section 15 was further broadened to include 'damage to the monetary stability of India'. Companies as well as trusts and societies were made liable for offences under the Act. In 2019, under the BJP government, the Act was again modified to empower the Central government to designate individuals as terrorists. Speaking in the Lok Sabha, MP Asaduddin Owaisi argued that this power to designate an individual as a terrorist was arbitrary as the government could act without 'any bonafide' to designate a person as a terrorist on a 'whim'. He, in effect, pointed out that this notification of an individual as a terrorist is an arbitrary executive action where the government acts on the 'basis' of 'feeling', and which moreover is not subject to judicial scrutiny.[21]

While the 2004 amendment introduced the 'terrorist act' into the law, the 2008 amendments also criminalised being a member of a terrorist gang, harbouring a terrorist, conspiracy to commit a terrorist act and raising funds for terrorism. This resulted in the criminalisation of a range of acts which may only be indirectly connected to the main act of terror. The 'terrorist act' itself was based on the 'intent' to 'threaten the sovereignty of India' or 'likely to threaten the sovereignty of India' and included acts ranging from the 'use of bombs', 'damage to property', 'kidnapping of persons' and 'disruption of essential supplies' to a broadly defined catch-all category—'any other means of whatever nature'—allowing the law to capture within its sweep a range of activities which may have nothing whatsoever to do with terrorism.

The conversion of the UAPA into a progressively more stringent anti-terror law was rife with serious implications for the human rights of the accused, as could have been prophesied by an analysis of the history of previous anti-terror legislation in India. One of the earliest anti-terror laws was TADA, 1985, under which 67,059 persons were detained, 8,000 were tried and 725 convicted by 1994. The conviction rate was 1.25 per cent. However, most TADA accused would have 'spent between 5 years to 10 years in jail' because of the restrictive bail provisions, notes the general secretary of PUCL, V. Suresh, in a publication from the organisation.[22]

POTA too put thousands in prison, and they were forced to spend many years in jail because of restrictive bail provisions. Congress MP Manish Tewari pointed out in the Lok Sabha that, of the 1,031 people arrested in POTA's 4,349 cases, only 13 were convicted by the time it was repealed in 2004. Tewari noted that the statistics he was quoting in 2019 were those tabled by the then home minister Shivraj Patel in the Rajya Sabha. The conviction rate then was a mere 1.26 per cent.[23]

The constitutional validity of both TADA[24] and POTA[25] was challenged in the Supreme Court, and the court upheld both laws. However, the public campaign against these laws met with greater success, as TADA was allowed to lapse and POTA was repealed.

Both TADA and POTA were anti-terror laws meant to address an extraordinary situation and hence departed from the ordinary protections of criminal law for a fixed period of time. For this purpose, both Acts had sunset clauses with TADA set to lapse in two years and POTA in three years, unless renewed by Parliament. TADA, which was enacted in 1985, was renewed in 1987, 1989, 1991 and 1993.

The fact that the laws would expire unless explicitly renewed gave additional momentum to the campaign against them. The sustained public campaign resulted in the National Human Rights Commission

(NHRC) writing to each MP, asking them to let TADA lapse.[26] It was finally allowed to lapse in 1995, following this vigorous public campaign. POTA was repealed by Parliament in 2004, even before the three-year period could elapse, again the result of a public campaign.[27]

The UAPA has no such provision and the extraordinary departures from the ordinary criminal law which it enables do not require periodic justification before Parliament. They have become a permanent part of the legal regime, not subject to a regular parliamentary audit. The idea of a periodic audit was also part of POTA as it had a provision for the constitution of Review Committees to be headed by a retired judge who had the power to review orders passed under the Act.[28] Again, as far as the UAPA is concerned, there is no designated judicial authority who can review orders passed under the statute, making the UAPA that much more of an unaccountable legislation.

However, what gives the UAPA its truly deadly character are the amendments to the procedural provisions made in 2008, which were introduced in the light of the terror attack in Mumbai. These changes made the anti-terror law into a de facto preventive detention law.

Similar to the changes in remand provisions brought about in TADA and POTA, Section 43D(2) of the UAPA provides that the police remand period is extendable from fifteen days to thirty days, while the time for submitting the chargesheet can extend to 180 days from 90 days. This has only to be contrasted to anti-terror laws in other democracies to get a sense of the extraordinary power vested in the police in India. In the United Kingdom, a similar change was mooted post the London terror attack of 2007, when the British Parliament proposed an increase from fourteen days to ninety days for the permissible length of pre-trial detention of terror suspects. However, this bill was defeated in Parliament with its members finally agreeing to a period of twenty-eight days. Even this was a temporary measure which was annually reviewed, and the period for which pre-trial detention can be authorised reverted to fourteen days by 2012.[29]

Section 43D(5) of the UAPA, again similar to TADA and POTA, states that no person shall be released on bail for terrorism-related offences under Chapter IV and VI of the Act if the court 'on perusal of the case diary or the report made under section 173 of the Code is of the opinion that there are reasonable grounds for believing that the accusation against such person is prima facie true'.

As Suresh, the general secretary of PUCL argues, 'What this means is that the accused/arrested person cannot apply for bail until the chargesheet is filed, which, in cases where UAPA is applied, can be extended to a period of 180 days.' Even after six months have elapsed, the court can still deny bail, if it forms the opinion that there are 'reasonable grounds' for believing that the accusation against such person is 'prima facie true'.

He concludes that:

> The law is construed in such a manner that it will be impossible to obtain bail. For the first 180 days, the accused may not even know what the case is against him. Thereafter, the release of the accused on bail is dependent on the Court's subjective satisfaction that the accusation is not prima facie true. [30]

This provision is a departure from bail jurisprudence under ordinary criminal law. In the bail law for general offences, the denial of bail is not a form of punishment but rather a decision the judge arrives at if there is a reasonable basis to conclude that releasing the accused would result in them fleeing, tampering with evidence or intimidating witnesses. These standards for the grant of bail are statutorily abandoned when it comes to anti-terror laws, and the UAPA is no exception. Like all other terror laws, in UAPA too, bail is made a distant possibility as the considerations for release on bail under ordinary criminal law are substituted by Section 43D(5), which mandates that the court shall not release the accused on bail if it is of 'the opinion that there are reasonable grounds for believing that the accusation against such person is prima facie true.'

The stringency of the bail provision in UAPA stands out starkly as compared to the bail provision in its predecessor legislation, POTA. As per the Supreme Court's interpretation, the stringent bail provision under POTA would not apply after one year, as then 'the accused can be released on bail after hearing the Public Prosecutor under ordinary law without applying the rigour of Section 49(7) of POTA.'[31] This vital safeguard is not there in the UAPA, making it a de facto preventive detention law.

Compare the preventive detention dimension of the UAPA to de jure preventive detention laws. The maximum period of detention under the NSA,[32] the now repealed MISA[33] and the lapsed Preventive Detention Act of 1950 is a year.[34] Under the colonial government, detention under the Rowlatt Act was for a maximum period of two years.[35] Under the UAPA, as we have seen, detentions of ten years before acquittal are not uncommon, making it a de facto preventive detention law of far greater stringency than any de jure preventive detention law enacted by the Indian Parliament or even the draconian Rowlatt Act enacted by the colonial authorities.

That being said, even if the threshold for release on bail under Section 43D(5) of the UAPA is very high, that threshold can still be met, as was demonstrated by a division bench of the Delhi High Court headed by Justice S. Muralidhar in 2018 in the case of *Zahoor Ahmad Shah Watali v National Investigation Agency*.[36]

Watali is a Kashmiri businessman who was accused of 'acting as a conduit to transfer funds from terrorist organisations operating out of Pakistan and from other sources to India to fuel violence in J&K'. In a well-reasoned judgement, the Delhi High Court asked whether the material gathered by the NIA was enough for the trial court to conclude that there were 'reasonable grounds to believe that the accusation against the respondent was prima facie true'. The high court held that the material before it did not meet this threshold. It also concluded that there was no document before it proving that Watali had met someone from the Pakistan High Commission, as alleged in the charge sheet, and there was no evidence that the money in question was 'passed on to the Hurriyat leaders'. Similarly, it decided that there was 'no prima facie material to show the involvement of the Appellant in any criminal conspiracy with the other accused'. The court also did not take into account the Section 161 statements before investigating officers, as they were not provided to the accused as mandated by law. Similarly, 164 statements before judicial magistrates were disregarded by the court as these were not 'discussed in the chargesheet, not examined by the trial court and not given to the appellant'.

The high court released Watali on bail, holding that it was a 'settled legal position that as far as the statute concerning the serious offences inviting grave consequences are invoked, the trial court will scrutinise the material with extra care'. The court forcefully observed that 'the trial court should certainly not ... proceed merely on the statements of the investigating agency because if it does so, it would be acting merely as a post office of the investigating agency and this would do more harm to meet the challenge arising out of terrorist activities rather than deterring terrorist activities'. This was an important reading of the law as the court in no uncertain terms laid down that it would independently scrutinise the material before it to see if it 'prima facie' led it to the 'reasonable' conclusion that the accusations were true.

However, the Supreme Court overruled the high court judgement and held that the lower courts could not go into the veracity of the material against the accused. As the apex court put it, the question of 'discarding the document at this stage, on the ground of being inadmissible in evidence, is not permissible. For, the issue of admissibility of the document/evidence would be a matter for trial. The Court must look at the contents of the document and take such document into account as it is'. It also held that 'the materials/ evidence collated by the Investigating Agency in reference to the accusation against the concerned accused in the first information report, must prevail until contradicted and overcome or disproved by other evidence.'

The effect of the Supreme Court judgement was to demote every trial court adjudicating UAPA cases into nothing more than a 'post office of the investigating agency', as Justice Muralidhar had apprehended. This dilution of the trial courts' adjudicatory role through the Supreme Court's interpretation of Section 43D(5) of the

UAPA in *Watali* has had a devastating impact at the ground level. As Suresh of PUCL put it:

> What the Watali ruling has now established as law for the entire country is that until the trial concludes, no court can ever consider any application seeking bail filed by any person accused of committing an UAPA offence under Chapters IV ('Punishment for Terrorist Activities') and VI ('Terrorist Organisations and Individuals'). Even the possibility that this process may take years cannot be a ground urged for the court to consider bail. All that is required is a charge under the UAPA and some material implicating the accused person. Thereafter, until the conclusion of the trial, the accused persons cannot even dream of obtaining bail.[37]

However, the harshness of the apex court's ruling in *Watali* was diluted to some extent in *Union of India v K.A. Najeeb*,[38] a judgement authored by Justice Suryakant in a bench with justices Aniruddha Bose and N.V. Ramana, delivered less than two months before Justice Ramana became the chief justice of India in April 2021. The NIA had filed an appeal against an order granting bail to K.A. Najeeb, who was accused of offences under the UAPA. The Supreme Court judgement diluted the absolute prohibition in Section 43D(5) against the grant of bail to anyone accused of terrorism-related offences under the UAPA. The court held that 'statutory restrictions like Section 43D(5)', do not 'per se oust the ability of Constitutional Courts to grant bail on grounds of violation of Part III of the Constitution'. In the Supreme Court's opinion, '... the rigours of such provisions will melt down where there is no likelihood of trial being completed within a reasonable time and the period of incarceration already undergone has exceeded a substantial part of the prescribed sentence'.

Thus, the appeal by the NIA against the grant of bail to Najeeb by the Kerala High Court was dismissed as he had been in jail for 'more than five years' and 'there were 276 witnesses still to be examined'. As the Supreme Court observed, 'the appellant NIA' had 'shown no inclination to screen its endless series of witnesses'. The court held that Najeeb was entitled to a speedy trial as part of his rights under Article 21 and as a 'timely trial was not possible and the accused had suffered incarceration for a significant period of time, courts would ordinarily be obligated to enlarge them on bail'.

While this is an important judgement that grants some measure of relief to those arrested under UAPA, it still remains limited as the requirement for release on bail is that the accused has suffered incarceration and that the 'period of incarceration already undergone has exceeded a substantial part of the prescribed sentence'. As the Supreme Court itself observed, '... had it been a case at the threshold, we would have outright turned down the respondent's prayer'. The right under Article 21 to bail due to the violation of the right to speedy trial only kicks in once the right has been substantially violated. The judgement did not address what it had observed was the underlying reason for this violation—the fact that 'the appellant NIA' had 'shown no inclination to screen its endless series of witnesses', thereby prolonging the trial.

However, in spite of these limitations, *K.A. Najeeb* has enabled the high courts to take a more rights-affirmative approach. The judgement was cited by the Bombay High Court for the proposition that 'statutory restrictions like Section 43D(5)' do not 'per se oust the ability of Constitutional Courts to grant bail on grounds of violation of Part III of the Constitution' in *Varavara Rao v NIA*. In February 2021, the court went on to release Varavara Rao, arrested under UAPA in August 2018 in the Bhima Koregaon case, on bail for medical reasons, stating: 'The condition of old age, sickness, infirmity and multiple health ailments suffered by the undertrial indicate that his continued custody would be incompatible with his health conditions and that sending him back to Taloja Central Prison would amount to endangering his life, thereby violating his fundamental right under Article 21 of the Constitution of India.'[39]

Three judgements delivered by a division bench of the Delhi High Court comprising Justices Siddharth Mridul and Anup Jairam Bhambhani, which granted bail in June 2021 to the young student leaders Devangana Kalita, Natasha Narwal and Asif Iqbal Tanha, all of whom were accused of offences under the UAPA for their alleged involvement in the 2020 Delhi pogrom, also indicate a different approach. The court in all three cases came to the conclusion that there was no material produced by the prosecution which indicated an offence of the nature of terrorism and hence the bar of Section 43D(5) to granting bail did not apply.

In *Asif Iqbal Tanha v State*,[40] the court analysed in particular what constituted terrorism and concluded that there was a distinction between 'terrorism', 'law and order' and 'public order'. The court noted, 'A "terrorist" activity does not merely arise by causing disturbance of law and order or of public order. The fall out of the intended activity must be such that it travels beyond the capacity of the ordinary law enforcement agencies to tackle it under the ordinary penal law.' Terrorism cannot be equated to peaceful protest or even to a disturbance of the public order. It must be of such a gravity as to threaten the security of the State. The court concluded that the accused was engaged in 'protest', a constitutional right which cannot be tarred as terrorism.

The court went on to say in *Natasha Narwal v NIA*[41] that 'in its anxiety to suppress dissent, in the mind of the State, the line between the constitutionally guaranteed right to protest and terrorist activity seems to be getting somewhat blurred. If this mindset gains traction, it would be a sad day for democracy.'

In *Devangana Kalita v NIA*,[42] the court held that 'We are afraid, that in our opinion, shorn-off the superfluous verbiage, hyperbole and the stretched inferences drawn from them by the prosecuting agency, the factual allegations made against the appellant do not prima facie disclose the commission of any offence under sections 15, 17 and/or 18 of the UAPA.'

However, these judgements are being appealed in the Supreme Court as of August 2021. The apex court, while not staying the judgement, has observed that 'the impugned judgment shall not be treated as a precedent and may not be relied upon by any of the parties in any of the proceedings'.[43]

The other inroad into this otherwise impregnable wall of non-release on bail has emerged through the Supreme Court's interpretation of the rights of UAPA-accused to be released on statutory bail. As per Section 43-D(2) of the UAPA, the charge sheet should be filed within ninety days. However, the court has the authority to extend this period up to 180 days. If a bail application is not filed within 90 days, or within 180 days (assuming the court has extended the time period for filing the charge sheet), the accused must be released on bail. This is the right to default bail or statutory bail. In *Bikramjit Singh v State of Punjab*, which was a case involving an accused under the UAPA, the question before the Supreme Court was whether the magistrate was a court under the UAPA and NIA Acts and hence had the authority to extend the period within which the charge sheet could be filed from 90 days to 180 days. In a judgment authored by J. Rohinton Nariman, the Supreme Court held that the 'Magistrate has no power to remand a person beyond the stipulated period of 90/60 days' and since the charge sheet had not been filed within 90 days, the accused was entitled to the 'indefeasible right' to default bail.[44]

The court reasoned that the 'right to default bail' was not 'a mere statutory right under the first proviso to Section 167(2) of the Code', but rather a 'part of the procedure established by law under Article 21 of the Constitution of India, which is, therefore, a fundamental right granted to an accused person to be released on bail once the conditions of the first proviso to Section 167(2) are fulfilled'.

This reading of the law was applied by the Karnataka High Court, which also upheld the rights of UAPA-accused to be released on default bail, observing that 'Once the UA(P) Act is invoked, the learned Magistrate has no power to extend beyond 90 days and only the Special Court has power to extend the detention beyond 90 days.'

What also came as a sign of hope were the judgements of the NIA court delivered in June and July 2021 discharging Assamese activist Akhil Gogoi in two cases in which the UAPA was invoked, allowing him to walk free after one and a half years in jail. Both FIRs were lodged with respect to alleged violence following an anti-CAA protest, and once the

NIA took over the investigation, provisions of the UAPA with respect to terrorism offences were added. In both cases, the NIA court held that 'if there was no prima facie case against the accused', he was entitled to be discharged.

In the case decided in June 2021, the NIA court observed, 'Protests in a democracy are sometimes seen to take the form of blockades also, even causing inconvenience to citizens. However, it is doubtful whether such blockades for temporary periods, if unaccompanied by any incitement to violence, would constitute a terrorist act within the meaning of Section 15 of the UA (P) Act. That in my mind, is beyond the intention of the legislature. There can be other laws to address that.'[45] In the second case decided in July 2021, the court reasoned that the material before it 'prima facie' showed that the acts of the accused did not amount to 'a terrorist act done with the intention of threatening unity, integrity, sovereignty and security of India or a terrorist act done with the intention to strike terror in the people'.[46]

However, even as the above judgements provide some reprieve, there are still thousands in jail under the Act. An online PUCL conference held in January 2021 had victims and activists testifying from twelve states across the country on how the UAPA continues to be invoked to criminalise dissent, be it of speech, association or assembly.[47] It should be noted that even this conference was a preliminary effort to map the countrywide effects of the UAPA and information is still partial and incomplete.

In Delhi, the UAPA has been the preferred tool to target supporters of democratic protests against the CAA held in December 2019–February 2020 and the farmers' agitation against the farm laws which began in December 2020. Testimonies collected by the PUCL from Andhra Pradesh and Telangana indicate that both the Telangana Rashtra Samithi and the YSR Congress used the UAPA to target human rights activists as well as ordinary Adivasis. Madhavrao Gorrepati from the Human Rights Forum shared how, in the border districts with Chhattisgarh, the UAPA was invoked against Adivasis who had fled the terror of the Salwa Judum in Chhattisgarh and come to Telangana.

He made the point that the modus operandi in the UAPA cases was to register an FIR against some Adivasis, make them sign a confession statement implicating a range of persons and arrest those persons. The idea was to keep the investigation pending by not filing a charge sheet and arresting anyone else the police deemed inconvenient. In his words, the arrested included those from 'farmers' organisations, womens' organisations, rights' organisations' and 'anyone who feels some responsibility to the Constitution'.[48] Kranti Chaitanya from the Civil Liberties Committee of Andhra Pradesh made the point that after the BJP came to power in the Centre, the state started to make more use of the UAPA against Adivasi people.[49]

In Punjab, in the opinion of senior criminal lawyer R.S. Bains, 'Under UAPA, you do not need to commit an offence. Just having documentational literature means that you can be easily labelled a terrorist.' He referred to the arrest of three young men for the possession of literature on Khalistan and Naxalism. They were charged with offences of waging war against the state as well as UAPA offences.[50] Finally, they were convicted under the IPC provisions and sentenced to life imprisonment, for the offence of possession of literature. Bains argued that the criminalisation of the possession of literature targets lawyers, journalists as well as any curious person. The law has also been used in recent times to target leaders of the Kisan Andolan. According to Bains, the striking thing about the misuse of the UAPA in Punjab is that at the ground level there is no armed struggle and the police are misusing the UAPA against any person who has literature which is not proscribed but which may speak about issues such as Khalistan. [51]

In Maharashtra, activists spoke about how the law was used against trade union activists, workers, Adivasis and Muslims. Trade union leader Vasudevan Nambiath shared how the UAPA was invoked in 2018 against four contract workers with Adani. The reasons the UAPA was invoked included stopping of work, which affected the supply of electricity by Adani Electricity, providing shelter to a person alleged to be a Naxalite and pressurising workers to make a contribution to the banned CPI

(M). What was missing in the 6,500-page charge sheet was any charge of terrorist activity. This, according to Nambiath, was a clear case of misuse of the UAPA against workers. Another activist, Jagdish Meshram, spoke about how the UAPA was falsely invoked against poor Adivasis in Gadchiroli, especially those who opposed the unbridled mining in the area. When they applied for bail, the sessions court judges invariably said that bail was not possible and asked them to go to the high court or Supreme Court. Meshram said that the Adivasis were so poor that they did not have the money to come to the Gadchiroli sessions court from their villages, let alone go to the higher courts.[52]

A fact-finding report by Karnataka civil society organisations , titled 'Communalising Violence in D.J. Halli', documents the state response to the incident of a mob ransacking the house of an MLA whose nephew had published a derogatory post on Facebook in August 2020.[53] The way the State responded to a law and order issue was to convert it into a communal incident. As per a report in the *Leaflet*, 'people were given a terrorist profile under UAPA' by the state government. 'For the first time in the country 180 people were arrested with no history of terrorism whatsoever and were termed terrorist.' Those arrested included children aged twelve to seventeen years.[54] In Assam, the law was invoked against Akhil Gogoi and many other activists who were a part of the anti-CAA protests in late 2019 and early 2020. In both Karnataka and Assam, the investigations were taken over by the NIA.

Uttar Pradesh under the Yogi Adityanath government has also seen the use of the UAPA against dissenters and those the state sees as inconvenient. One of the most shocking incidents—testified to by his advocate Wills Matthews—was the invocation of the UAPA against Siddique Kappan, a journalist from Kerala, who had gone to Hathras to cover the brutal gang rape and murder of a nineteen-year-old Dalit woman by upper-caste men. He was arrested in October 2020, charged under the UAPA and as of December 2021 is still in jail.[55]

The situation in Kashmir, as testified to by Kashmiri lawyer Mirza Saaib Beg, is one of a permanent state of exception. Beg argues that the justification for extraordinary laws is that the state is facing a situation of 'extreme peril' and hence, for a temporary period in time, the rule of law is suspended. However, as Beg noted, for the whole of his adult life, he has lived under some form of emergency laws and 'constitutional exceptionalism has become a part of daily lives'. In Kashmir, the repressive laws used include the UAPA, the Preventive Detention Act and the AFSPA. There has been an increase in the use of the UAPA in recent times to criminalise 'divergent thoughts'. Beg shared an example—the UAPA was used in September 2020 against ten youngsters in Shopian district who took part in a cricket tournament held in 'memory' of Syed Ruban, a slain militant who was an avid cricket player. Beg argued that while there may be opinions about whether it was right or wrong for the youngsters to commemorate Syed Ruban, this act of commemoration could not in itself qualify as a UAPA offence.[56]

Even in Left-ruled Kerala, the UAPA was invoked in as many as 151 cases between 2014 and 2019.[57] In the January 2021 PUCL webinar, activists from Kerala testified to the use of the UAPA based purely on the possession of literature. Thaha Fasal and Allan Shuhaib were arrested and charged under the UAPA based on the possession of some allegedly Maoist literature in November 2019. After ten months in jail, they were released by the NIA court as it found no evidence against them. The NIA appealed the matter and the Kerala High Court cancelled the bail given to Thaha Fasal but allowed the bail order of Allan Shuhaib to stand based on his age.[58] Advocate K.S. Madhusoodanam shared this narrative to make the point that the UAPA is used to target 'shouting of slogans, distribution of pamphlets and writing of slogans in a banner' and not any act of terror. This, he contended, was not the abuse of the law but the very purpose for which the law was enacted and hence it had to be repealed.[59]

The picture that emerges from this preliminary documentation from across the country is that the UAPA has indeed emerged as a key threat to the right to freedom of expression, assembly and association as well as the right to live with dignity, and has had a devastating impact on those who have been caught within its cross hairs. Prolonged imprisonment under the UAPA has devastated families and destroyed human futures across the country.

The NIA as the Chosen Agent of the State

As noted ealier, the Modi government uses various instrumentalities of the State, such as the CBI, the Enforcement Directorate, the tax authorities and the NIA, to keep its critics in check. What has, however, emerged as its instrumentality of choice in all high-profile cases is the powerful NIA, which should be subject to more serious public scrutiny.

The NIA was created by the National Investigation Agency Act, 2008, again under the UPA dispensation. The statute empowers the agency, which is under the Central government, to investigate and prosecute for offences under the UAPA and the IPC, such as sedition and waging war against the State, as well as other offences specified in the Act, related to aviation, maritime navigation and hijacking. The Central government can direct the NIA to investigate an offence registered under the above-mentioned statutory provisions in any police station in the country.

By statute, the NIA is more powerful than its predecessor, the CBI. The latter was established in 1963 as a central agency to investigate 'not only cases of bribery and corruption, but also violation of Central fiscal laws, major frauds relating to Government of India departments, public joint stock companies, passport frauds, crimes on the high seas, crimes on the Airlines and serious crimes committed by organised gangs and professional criminals'.[60] The CBI derives its powers from the Delhi Special Police Establishment Act, 1946, which mandates that the agency can conduct a probe within a state only after seeking the consent of the state government.[61]

The NIA, by contrast, is not statutorily bound by such federal constraints. In fact, the officer in charge of a police station, on recording an FIR pertaining to the scheduled offences under the Act, is to forward the details to the state government, which, in turn, would have to forward it to the Central government. The Central government has the power to direct the NIA to investigate, if 'it is of the opinion' that a scheduled offence as per the Act has been committed. Once the NIA steps in, the state government is to cease its investigation and turn over all relevant documents to the agency.[62]

Parliamentarians have expressed their profound unease at the usurpation of the state's jurisdiction over law and order by the Union. In the debate in the Rajya Sabha on the NIA amendment bill in 2019, Vivek K. Tankha, Congress MP from Madhya Pradesh, narrated how, when the state's investigation of the murder of an MLA was in an 'advanced stage', it was 'taken away from the hands of the state.' This, he contended, did grave injustice to the 'spirit of cordiality and federalism'.[63]

Dr K. Keshava Rao from the Telangana Rashtra Samiti (TRS) said that 'You are totally taking away the right of the states and you are keeping the states on the sidelines in a federal set-up like India. Second, you are giving to your NIA people the same rights which our police in the states enjoy. It is the same thing. If it is the same thing, then why have them [the state police] at all? Depend on them, have coordination and they will do the job.'[64]

The provisions of the NIA Act depart from ordinary criminal law in substantial ways. Under the CrPC, the trial generally proceeds in the presence of the accused, without any discretionary power given to the judge to dispense with the presence of the accused or his pleader.[65] The CrPC also specifies that the offence will be tried by a 'court within whose local jurisdiction it was committed'.[66] There is no provision for the court to change its place of sitting for all or part of the proceedings of any case. The CrPC mandates that hearings shall be in open court, except in the case of rape trials, when the principle of open court hearings is derogated from to protect the confidentiality of victims.[67] The Act also guarantees the accused a fair trial by granting them the right to effective cross-examination by providing details of witnesses, including their name, address and so on.

The NIA Act, on the other hand, empowers the Central government to constitute special courts to hear cases under it, with procedural protections for the accused being weakened. In a dilution of the adversarial system,[68] the statute authorises the special court 'if it thinks fit and for reasons to be recorded by it' to 'proceed with the trial in the absence of the accused or his pleader and record the evidence of any witness, subject to the right of the accused to recall the witness for cross-examination'.[69] The special court also has the discretion to 'sit for any of its proceedings at any place other than its ordinary place of sitting'.[70] The proceeding may be held in camera if the special court desires it and records its reasons.[71] The special court also has the power to keep the identity and address of witnesses secret if it is 'satisfied that the life of such witness is in danger', hindering the accused's right to cross-examination.[72] The 'measures' the special court can take to protect the life of the witness include a 'decision that it is in the public interest to order that all or any of the proceedings pending before such a Court shall not be published in any manner'.[73] The powers given to the NIA judge to exclude the public read along with the power to exclude both the accused and their lawyers from the proceedings significantly weaken any sort of oversight, with devastating consequences for the accused's right to a fair trial.

The processes laid down for the NIA special court deviate from the basic norms of justice, both procedurally and substantively. As legal scholar Kunal Ambasta notes in an essay on the critique of 'special laws',[74] justice is best served by general criminal laws. He argues that the US legal philosopher Lon Fuller was right in stating that the 'inner morality of law' depends on laws being generally applicable. The 'generality of laws is a recognized feature of a system that purports to have the rule of law'.[75]

The procedural deviations in the NIA Act—from the power to decide where to hold the court sessions to the power to exclude the accused and his counsel from the proceedings—tilt the scale in favour of the State and against the accused.

However, procedural changes in special laws have a way of finding their way back to the general laws. A committee set up in 2020 by the Union home ministry to reform criminal laws, under the chairpersonship of Ranbir Singh, the then director of the National

Law University, Delhi, is a step in this direction. The committee is tasked with a root-and-branch reform of the criminal law comprising IPC, 1860, Indian Evidence Act, 1872, and CrPc, 1973.[76] In an open letter addressed to Ranbir Singh, Guha and others with 'foreboding hazard[ed]' that 'the real intent' of the committee is to 'authorize and legitimize a dangerous new penal system which will see the unconstitutional principles which are the heart of the UAPA become the ordinary criminal law of this land'.[77]

One of the standout features of an NIA investigation is its seemingly high success ratio, with a conviction rate of over 90 per cent as of 2020 as per a home ministry statement in the Rajya Sabha.[78] On the face of it, this is a truly remarkable achievement as the conviction rate achieved by the State under other anti-terror legislation has been minimal. In TADA, it was 1 per cent as of 1994, under POTA it was 1.26 per cent as of 2005 [79] and under UAPA, it was less than 2 per cent as of 2019. What accounts for the NIA prosecutions having a success rate of over 90 per cent?

For one, the over 90 per cent conviction rate is based on an analysis of decided cases in the given year. Out of 62 cases decided in 2020, 56 resulted in convictions, resulting in an over 90 per cent conviction rate. However, if the 56 convictions are measured against the 319 pending cases, the conviction rate comes down to 26 per cent.[80] This is still a very high percentage compared to the conviction figures under TADA and POTA.

A factor that could feed into the higher conviction rate is the utilisation of informal plea bargaining by the NIA. Ambasta writes that the NIA has successfully utilised the 'system of informal plea bargaining ... referred to in Hindi as "Katti"'. The accused changes his plea from 'not guilty' to 'guilty' and 'in many cases, this leads to the trial being concluded at this stage, and the punishment is typically awarded as being the time already served as an under-trial, or a reduced sentence, which can range to several years'. This plea bargaining system, Ambasta reflects, ends up giving the NIA a high conviction rate:

In recent years, there have been several cases that have reached verdicts through the method described above, and it remains an understudied and underreported phenomenon. Even when it does get coverage, the narrative does not count for the actual machinations that have been employed to achieve the result. It is possible that such a change of plea during trial is only made when facilitated by the prosecution agency on the promise that it would not seek a greater sentence for the accused than what they have already undergone. A rationally-thinking accused person would choose to plead guilty when they see the prospect of being confined in prison for the foreseeable future while the trial drags on for years and the remotest possibility of a sentence of life imprisonment at the end of it. This practice also allows the investigative agencies to secure a conviction regardless of the quality of evidence in the given case.[81]

The incentive for the accused to change their plea is the fact that the offence is often under the UAPA, under which bail is almost impossible. Rather than spend long years as an undertrial without the possibility of bail, many prefer to go down the route of informal plea bargaining. For the NIA, it is a win-win situation as it gets to demonstrate that it is an extraordinarily successful investigation agency. As Ambasta notes, this is an understudied phenomenon which requires more empirical substantiation.

The NIA opposes the bail plea of the accused with vigour, going up to the Supreme Court to challenge high court bail orders. However, it has not demonstrated the same vigour when it comes to fulfilling its statutory mandate of ensuring a speedy trial. In the case of *Union of India v K.A. Najeeb*,[82] in which the accused had spent over five years in jail with 276 witnesses still to be examined and charges being framed only as recently as November 2020, six years after Najeeb's arrest, the Supreme Court was constrained to observe that 'two opportunities were given to the appellant-NIA who has shown no inclination to screen its endless list of witnesses'. In the case of those arrested for their alleged connection with the violence at Bhima Koregaon in January

2018, the trial has not yet commenced, as the NIA is yet to complete its investigation three years after the FIR was registered.

The PUCL analysis also indicates that of the 396 cases registered by the NIA, 78 per cent were registered during the NDA government with 22 per cent registered during the UPA government. The failing which afflicts the larger UAPA prosecutions according to Justice Alam is that, even from just a 'purely national security angle', the police disposal rates for UAPA cases stood at '42.5% and pendency rate ... at 77.8%'. The fact that the police were not able to conclude their investigations in spite of having 'extraordinary powers' which went hand in hand with the suspension of 'several fundamental and statutory rights of accused persons' speaks to their ineffectiveness. He notes that this criticism applies to the NIA as well. Although 'the NIA act provides for a dedicated agency, to respond to acts and conspiracies that have a bearing on national security', '... it seems these special laws and dedicated agencies fail to carry out quick and focussed investigations in UAPA cases'.[83]

This delay in commencement of trials due to prolonged or delayed investigations leads to legitimate questions on the strategy of the premier investigating agency, the NIA. Is it, as Ambasta hazards, a way to ensure that the accused remain in jail for as long as possible before an informal plea bargain is presented to them, thereby giving the agency its high conviction rates?

Structurally, the NIA is not designed to function independently as its director is appointed by the Central government and the agency too is under the Centre's superintendence.[84] This contrasts with the appointment of the CBI director, who is chosen by a panel comprising of the prime minister, the leader of the Opposition and either the chief justice or a judge of the Supreme Court nominated by the chief justice.[85] Thus, the NIA is designed to be less independent from political pressures than even the CBI.

This power to choose the chief of the NIA unhindered by any institutional constraints has been utilised by the Modi government to appoint officials who have a track record of satisfying the political executive. Y.C. Modi, the NIA's chief from 2017 to 2021, is from the Gujarat cadre and was a part of the Special Investigation Team (SIT) constituted by the Supreme Court to look into allegations against then chief minister Modi regarding his complicity in the 2002 riots. In '2012, the SIT submitted a closure report to the apex court, stating that the allegations against Modi "are not made out" and that "the allegation about the inaction on part of the State Govt. as well as police department is ... not established."'[86] The *Caravan* notes that the careers of all the officials associated with the SIT have been on an upward trajectory since Y.C. Modi's appointment as the director of the NIA in 2017.

Some of the questions about the NIA's lack of independence from the political executive came to the fore in the agency's investigation of the Samjhauta Express bomb blast. The Samjhauta Express ran between Delhi and Lahore and was the oldest rail link between India and Pakistan after Partition. Bomb blasts in 2007 killed sixty-eight persons on board, forty-four of whom were Pakistani citizens.[87]

The investigation was taken over by the NIA from the Haryana police in 2010. The judgement of the NIA court, delivered in 2019, provides an insight into the manner of the agency's investigation. The NIA special court acquitted Swami Aseemanand and seven other accused. The judge, Jagdeep Singh, was troubled by the acquittal and scathing in his observations on the nature of the NIA investigation. He opined, 'I have to conclude this judgment with deep pain and anguish as a dastardly act of violence remained unpunished for want of credible and admissible evidence. There are gaping holes in the prosecution evidence and an act of terrorism has remained unsolved.'[88]

Justice Singh noted that the NIA failed to adduce any evidence for the alleged meeting during which the blast was planned or to establish the links between the conspirators or to provide call records of the accused. Though the NIA asserted that the motive for the bomb blast was to 'give a befitting reply to the perceived persecution of Hindus by the members of the Muslim community'—theorising it as 'bomb ka badla bomb'—it did not provide any evidence to support this either. The judge listed numerous other flaws in the investigation, including the fact that CCTV footages, 'the best evidence', was withheld by the NIA. The agency also did not conduct a test identification parade, which could have provided 'some vital clue about real culprits', the judge noted.

The acquittals in the Samjhauta bomb blast case followed the acquittal of Swami Aseemanand in the 2007 bombings of Ajmer Sharif Dargah and Hyderabad's Mecca Masjid. These acquittals, too, were the result of the prosecution's failure to prove that the accused committed any offence.[89]

Elementary errors such as not producing CCTV footage and cell phone records do not square up with the self-image of the NIA as a competent investigation agency with an over-90 per cent conviction rate. These failures of the NIA cast a shadow of doubt on its professionalism, integrity and independence. The question, of course, is whether it is sabotaging its own investigations to serve the ends of those in power.

Parliamentarians have expressed their concern over the lack of independence of the NIA from the political executive. Speaking on the NIA amendments in July 2019 in the Rajya Sabha, K.K. Ragesh, CPI(M) MP from Kerala stated:

> Various provisions of this Act are being grossly misused. NIA, unfortunately, has got a dubious record of undermining various terror cases where various groups are involved. Sir, what happened to the Mecca Masjid. ...(Interruptions)...
>
> Sir, what happened to Malegaon blasts case? NIA even discharged the main accused and the court had to intervene. ...(Interruptions)... The court had to reinstate the charges again. ...(Interruptions)... Even the public prosecutor was complaining that NIA is pressuring the public prosecutor to go soft on that case. ...(Interruptions)... Sir, the bail application in the case of the main accused was not even opposed by the NIA...When the question comes to a certain terrorist group then the investigation is getting halted. Investigation is getting diluted. That is why, I am saying, Sir, that NIA is being grossly misused.[90]

Abhishek Manu Singhvi from the Congress expressed similar apprehensions:

You have already given good postings to the NIA head. So, you don't need the power of directing him. In any case, he is going to listen to your bidding because I have yet to see a new NIA head being given extension after extension, and I believe now, enjoy the sinecure even after his retirement. So, you perhaps don't need this power because on a wink and a nod he would do your bidding.[91]

Binoy Visam from the CPI said:

Sir, Samjhauta Express blast case, Malegaon blast case, in all these cases, we have seen that the NIA was not acting in a proper way, it changes the places. Sir, when people at the top level changes, the NIA also changes. So, NIA has such a credibility in this country.[92]

The link between the political executive and the direction taken by the NIA investigation may perforce remain an open secret, incapable of strict proof. However, what is clear is that with respect to the Samjautha blasts, an acquittal was the preferred outcome as far as the Union government was concerned. In Parliament, Amit Shah defended the decision not to file an appeal against the acquittal, stating that the charge sheets filed under the UPA regime did not have any substantial proof, and alleging that the case had been instituted with a political motive.[93] For a government which prides itself on being tough on terror, the decision not to appeal, even making the point that the case itself was 'instituted with a political motive', marks an abdication of the constitutional responsibility to protect the right to life of all persons without discrimination. While the NIA court judge in his judgment recorded his 'pain and anguish as a dastardly act of violence remained unpunished' and went on to make scathing observations about the nature of the 'prosecution evidence',[94] the home minister was content to let an act of terror go unpunished.

The other infamous example of the use of the NIA by the Central government is the takeover of the Bhima Koregoan investigation. The power vested by the NIA statute in the NIA to take over cases in other states without prior sanction by the concerned state, was exploited by the Modi government in the Bhima Koregoan case, which began as an investigation into the violence that broke out after the anniversary celebrations by Dalit groups of the victory of the Mahar regiment at Bhima Koregoan. But it soon became an investigation into an alleged plot hatched by Maoists to assassinate the prime minister. The case was filed in 2018 when the BJP was in power in Maharashtra, by the Pune police. In November 2019, when the Maha Vikas Aghadi alliance came to power under Shiv Sena's Udhav Thackeray, the new government indicated its desire to review the case and began to ask 'questions over the conduct and actions of the preceding government and its police in the Elgar Parishad as well as the Bhima Koregaon cases'. The Central government led by the BJP, in response, ordered the NIA to take over the investigation. The 'hasty transfer' by the Centre was a 'clear bid to keep control' over the investigation and the narrative centred around 'urban naxals', 'Maoists' and a 'plot to assassinate the Prime Minister'.[95]

The PUCL, in its analysis of NIA cases, pointed out that 'in 66 per cent of the cases, there was no terrorist incident as such, with the prosecution depending on the criminalisation of associated activity, be it financial support, conspiracy, etc'.[96] The BK-16 case, which, at its heart, is based not on the prosecution of any terrorism as such but the criminalisation of the freedom of speech and association, is merely one example of this kind of prosecution. The PUCL study also found that the NDA government used the agency more than the previous government, registering 248 cases between 2014 and 2021, as compared to the UPA's 69 registered cases between 2009 and 2014.[97]

The NIA has emerged as the instrument of choice because of the absolute control the Central government can exercise over it. This enables the selection of a pliable officer to head it, ensuring that investigations go in the direction that the government desires. The NIA statute also empowers the agency to disregard India's federal set-up and the rights of states. It provides a statutory framework to enhance the power of the Centre at the cost of the states. The use of the NIA as prosecuting agency also has the unstated but nonetheless very real function of spreading fear in civil society, to deter persons from exercising their right to freedom of speech and expression. The message sent out through the NIA prosecutions is quite clear—those who choose to speak up against the State will suffer detention without end. For all these reasons, the NIA is a policy instrument much favoured by the current regime.

Targeting Civil Society: The BK-16 and Beyond

A template to silence those the State finds troublesome using a fake narrative is visible in the arrest of the sixteen human rights activists, called the 'BK-16' by the media, from around the country in the so-called Bhima Koregaon case.

The fact that all the accused are still in jail—other than the octogenarian poet Varavara Rao, who was released on medical grounds, and Father Swamy, who died in judicial custody—with some of them behind bars for over three years without a trial, speaks to the NIA strategy of indefinite incarceration. Those arrested include lawyers, activists and journalists, and their arrest has sent out a message to the wider civil society—speaking out against the State has enormous consequences.

Unfortunately, the BK-16 template was not unique, with the Modi government following that up with two other rounds of mass arrest. Anti-CAA protestors were falsely charged with violent crimes and arrested for the mere expression of opinion and dissent against a government policy.[98] A similar strategy was followed in Jammu and Kashmir post the revocation of Article 370, which stripped the region of its statehood and autonomy and bifurcated the area into two union territories. In all three waves of arrest, the UAPA was the go-to law for the Modi regime.

The current government used the UAPA as a strategy to shut down dissent for the first time on a large scale in the arrest of the BK-16, and examining this up close provides an insight into what troubles this authoritarian State.

The BK-16

On 1 January 2018, when the Dalit community was commemorating the 200th anniversary of the defeat of the Brahmin Peshwa rulers by the Dalit Mahar soldiers fighting for the East India Company, they were attacked. The news of the incident spread across Maharashtra, and the state witnessed violent agitations in which Dalit groups staged road blocks and demonstrations. A sixteen-year-old boy who was part of the demonstrations was trampled to death when the police chased the demonstrators.[99]

Initially, two FIRs were lodged. The first one was with respect to the attack on Dalits during the anniversary event. Initial investigations revealed the hand of two Brahmin Hindutva leaders—Milind Ekbote, a former BJP corporater, and Sambhaji Bhide, a former member of the RSS—behind the violence. In fact, Ekbote had issued a press release condemning the celebration of the victory of the Mahar regiment, implying that it was anti-national. Both were alleged to have instigated the mob that attacked the Dalit gathering.[100] However, though FIRs were registered against them under IPC provisions, the SC/ST(Prevention of Atrocities) Act, 1989, and the Arms Act, 1954, Ekbote was only briefly arrested before being released on bail, while Bhide was neither detained nor questioned.

A second FIR was registered with respect to the violence which broke out throughout Maharashtra. The FIR indicated that the violence was due to a conspiracy hatched by 'active members of the Communist Party of India (Maoist)' and had the 'potential to destabilize the country'. The police invoked provisions of the UAPA, and on 6 June, they arrested lawyer Surendra Gadling, retired English professor Shoma Sen and human rights activist Mahesh Raut from Nagpur; human rights activists Sudhir Dhawale from Mumbai and Rona Wilson—ironically, a member of the Committee for the Release of Political Prisoners which has campaigned against the UAPA—from Delhi.

The net widened from thereon, and on 28 August, the Pune police placed five more persons under home arrest—trade unionist, activist and lawyer Sudha Bharadwaj and human rights activist Gautam Navlakha in Delhi; human rights lawyer Arun Ferreira and trade union activist, lawyer and academic Vernon Gonsalves in Mumbai; and poet-activist Varavara Rao in Hyderabad. By the end of 2018, all of them were taken into judicial custody. In January 2020, the NIA took over the investigation, and in April 2020, Anand Teltumbde, academic and Ambedkar's son-in-law, surrendered himself to the NIA in Mumbai, in the midst of the pandemic and, ironically, on Ambedkar Jayanti.

Two years after the first arrests, in July 2020, while many of those already arrested still awaited trial, Hany Babu, a teacher of English at Delhi University, was also arrested on the vague charge of spreading the ideology of Maoism/Naxalism and encouraging unlawful activities.[101] In September 2020, Sagar Gorkhe, Ramesh Gaichor and Jyoti Jagtap, activists with the Kabir Kala Manch—a cultural organisation formed in the wake of the 2002 Gujarat pogrom, which works for Adivasi, Dalit and workers' rights—were arrested from Pune. On a later date in October 2020, Stan Swamy, an eighty-two-year-old Jesuit priest and social activist, was arrested from near Ranchi.[102]

Those arrested had no proximate relationship to the violence in Bhima Koregoan, and in fact, the nature of the crime changed from 'inciting the violence in Bhima Koregaon to alleged involvement in a nationwide "Maoist" conspiracy to destabilise democracy, overthrow the government by setting up an "anti-fascist front" and plotting to assassinate Narendra Modi. All of the activists were labelled as "urban Naxalites" and accused of being members of the banned Communist Party of India (Maoist)', as per a report in *Scroll.in*.[103]

A petition filed by eminent historian Romila Thapar in the Supreme Court asked for an 'independent and credible investigation' into the arrest of Bharadwaj, Navlakha, Gonsalves, Ferreira and Rao. However, the majority declined to intervene to set up a court-monitored investigation. The dissenting opinion of Justice D.Y. Chandrachud noted the lack of credibility in the police's allegations. He observed that while the 'investigation commenced as an enquiry into the Bhima-Koregaon violence', it was 'sought to be deflected' by making the 'serious allegation' that 'there was a plot against the Prime Minister'. Justice Chandrachud took exception to the fact that 'such allegations' were 'bandied about by police officers in media briefings' and noted that the 'ASG [additional solicitor general] fairly stated that there was no basis to link the five arrested individuals to any such alleged plot against the Prime Minister'.[104]

This trope of a fabricated plot against the prime minister has an older history. From 2003 to 2006, Gujarat was rocked by a series of 'encounter killings'. Those killed included Sadiq Jamal, Ishrat Jamal, Sohrabuddin and his wife, Kausar Bi. As lawyer and trade union activist Mukul Sinha put it, 'the idea behind the fake encounters was to keep the anti-minority spirit alive. The methodology was to kidnap Muslims from outside the state, bring them to Ahmedabad, profile them as terrorists and then kill them … The Muslims were terrified that one of them could be picked up and the Hindu majority was also terrified. (about its security.) It was a fantastic gameplan.'[105] The charge sheets in all these cases invariably alleged that there was a plot to kill the then chief minister of the state, Narendra Modi. Those eventually arrested for these fake encounters included top police officers of the ATS as well as the then home minister Amit Shah.[106]

Justice Chandrachud's dissent is a field guide to unpacking the Bhima Koregoan case. As he observed, '… the Court has to be vigilant in the exercise of its jurisdiction under Article 32 to ensure that liberty is not sacrificed at the altar of conjectures. Individuals who assert causes which may be unpopular to the echelons of power are yet entitled to the freedoms which are guaranteed by the Constitution. Dissent is a symbol of a vibrant democracy. Voices in opposition cannot be muzzled by persecuting those who take up unpopular causes.'

He was alluding to the falsity of the cases against those imprisoned, their status as dissenters and the importance of dissenters in a democracy. The use of the UAPA in the Bhima Koregoan case has made bail a remote possibility, and the trial is yet to commence as of October 2021.[107]

The other critical method employed in the BK-16 case was the use of malware to implicate them. When the *Caravan* magazine did a 'cyber-forensic examination of the contents of Wilson's hard disk', it found that 'the disk contained malware that can be used to remotely access the computer and plant files'.[108] More recently, Arsenal Consulting, a global expert in digital forensics, analysed Wilson's hard disk and found that 'Rona Wilson's computer was compromised for just over 22 months' and the primary goals of the attacker were 'surveillance and incriminating document delivery'. Arsenal found that there was 'no evidence which would suggest that the top ten most important documents used in the prosecution against Mr. Wilson were ever interacted with in any legitimate way on Mr. Wilson's computer. More particularly, there is no evidence which would suggest any of the top ten documents, or the hidden folder they were contained in, were ever opened'. It also found that 'the incriminating documents were delivered to a hidden folder on Mr. Wilson's computer by NetWire and not by other means'.[109]

A similar analysis of Surendra Gadling's computer revealed that the fourteen documents deemed by the defence to be vital to the case against him were 'delivered to a hidden folder (named "Material") on the tertiary volume of Mr. Gadling's computer by NetWire and not by other means'. Further, Arsenal concluded that on one particular day, 'July 22, 2017 … the attacker was deploying documents to a hidden folder on Mr. Gadling's co-defendant Rona Wilson's computer approximately fifteen minutes prior to deploying documents to a hidden folder on Mr. Gadling's computer. In addition to the attacker's deployment methodology being identical between the two deliveries, one of the deployed documents … was identical'.[110]

Based on the analysis of Gadling and Wilson's computer, Arsenal concluded that 'this is one of the most serious cases involving evidence tampering that Arsenal has ever encountered, based on various metrics which include the vast timespan between the delivery of the first and last incriminating documents on multiple defendants' computers'.[111]

Mihir Desai argues that what makes this regime particularly dangerous is this move beyond surveillance and charging persons on weak evidence to actually fabricating evidence and manufacturing a larger conspiracy.[112] This level of manipulation and fabrication of evidence is, according to Desai, unprecedented in the use of anti-terror laws.

The invocation of the UAPA by the police and the NIA and the painstaking effort to implicate the BK-16 through electronic surveillance and implanting of evidence seems out of proportion to the threat that this disparate bunch of activists, many of them in the evening of their lives, could actually pose to the State. The only way one can make sense of it is by bringing together some of the thematics embodied in the lives of those arrested. All of them are activists engaged in making the State accountable, and they speak on issues that the Central government finds particularly troubling.

The first strand of activism embodied in the work of the BK-16 that the regime finds threatening is the re-imagination of Dalit activism. What unites Dhawale, Teltumbde and the Kabir Kala Manch trio of Gaichor, Gorkhe and Jagtap is that, for them, Dalit activism is about taking on the Hindutva State. Teltumbde in his writings, Dhawale in his activism and Gaichor, Gorkhe and Jagtap in their songs embody Ambedkar's vision that 'Hindu Raj' would be 'the greatest calamity for this country'.[113]

Teltumbde's work aims at explaining the structures of caste oppression, and he finds strong links between the rise of Hindutva and the continued oppression of Dalits. He has written extensively in the *EPW* on contemporary issues and produced scathing critiques of Hindutva and its practitioners. He writes that 'ghar wapsi' is a 'return to the hell hole of Hinduism',[114] about Hindutva's disregard for the scientific temper,[115] the myth of the holy cow,[116] justice for the Gujarat pogrom of 2002[117] and many other crucial issues. The thread running through his writings is both a focus on the concerns of Dalit communities and a broader critique of current political and neo-liberal economic orthodoxies.

Dhawale was arrested for the second time under the UAPA in 2018 under the NDA administration. The real reason for the arrest was Dhawale's resistance to what he described as the 'fascist forces'. Dhawale saw with crystal clarity the fascist project of 'co-opting the leaders of the dalit community' and eliminating the 'contradiction' between Hindutva and Dalit liberation. A key aspect of this 'co-option' was the re-definition of Ambedkar by 'suppressing his principle ideological position'. Dhawale notes the success of this project of co-option when 'leading voices of dalit literature and the Dalit Panthers' including 'Laxman Gaikwad and J.V. Pawar' participated in a convention organised by the government through the Sahitya Akademi. The fact that in the convention itself, J.V. Pawar, who was 'one of the founding members of the Dalit Panthers', went on to 'congratulate Modi' for 'organizing' the Convention indicated the success of the co-option.

Dhawale himself was crystal clear in his ideological opposition to Hindutva and said that it had to be 'confronted' 'through the medium of an ideology, an organization and a concerted struggle'. He went on to say that 'the fight against fascism is a direct and unambiguous fight and that 'fascism attacks us by breaking our strength and dissolving our unity, and its onslaught comes with the full force of repression'. To ensure victory, 'we' will have to 'unite', 'end discord', 'strengthen our ideological position' and 'build and nurture the true aspirations of freedom'. He asserted that 'We will move towards a democratic society and build it with firm foundations' and that 'no one can kill the dream for democracy'.[118]

The Kabir Kala Manch was founded post the Gujarat pogrom of 2002 and works for Adivasi, Dalit and workers' rights.[119] Gaichor, Gorkhe and Jagtap, as part of the Kabir Kala Manch, and through their cultural activism, draw in people from different socio-economic backgrounds with a strong base among Maharashtrian working-class families.[120] They have addressed discrimination based on class, caste and religious ascription and taken Dalit politics beyond 'single-issue activism', embracing a strong critique of Hindutva.[121]

The second strand in the work of the BK-16 that the state finds troubling is of legal activism. Bharadwaj, Gonsalves, Gadling and Ferreira are all lawyers who sought to make the State accountable for its unconstitutional actions, be it encounter deaths, illegal land acquisition for corporate interests, defending those arrested under terrorism charges or protecting labour rights. Lawyering for each of these issues is, in effect, a defence of the constitutional vision against the State's deviations. Through their arrests, the State is sending the message that there will be costs to legal activism in defence of the marginalised.

A well-known criminal lawyer from Nagpur, Gadling is the general secretary of the Indian Association of Peoples' Lawyers (IAPL) and has represented numerous human rights defenders arrested on fabricated charges of being anti-national. He is also a Dalit rights activist. He has represented G.N. Saibaba—arrested in 2014 under the UAPA by the then Congress- and Nationalist Congress Party-led government in Maharashtra for 'his alleged links with the outlawed CPI (Maoist)'[122]— besides Dhawale, Ferreira and Gonsalves, who are now his co-accused. Gadling was also part of a team that visited Kashmir in 2018 to condemn the persecution of human rights lawyers in the state.[123] He has been the go-to lawyer when it comes to stringent laws like TADA, POTA and the UAPA, having been extraordinarily successful in defending the accused under these laws. As his junior Nihalsingh Rathod notes, 'Almost all cases filed under these laws have been handled by him over last two decades. In them, barring only three cases, he managed to get acquittal in all others.'[124]

As a student, Sudha Bharadwaj worked with the inspirational trade union leader Shankar Guha Niyogi in Chhattisgarh. She went on to become a lawyer 'at the ripe old age of 40' and has devoted her life to working as a trade unionist and lawyer among the Adivasi communities of the state.[125] As a lawyer, she is associated with PUCL and also formed her own legal-aid organisation, Janhit, to provide legal support to various kinds of people's movements. The range of cases she has taken up testifies to the challenges of practising law in the relatively recently formed state of Chhattisgarh, which is both 'militarised' and 'beholden to corporate power'. The cases she fought included cases related to the unlawful acquisition of Adivasi land for industries, arbitrary arrests, disappearances of Adivasi activists, rape and violations of labour law. Janhit, led by her, has worked to 'bring the constitution to life' for the oppressed people of Chhattisgarh.[126]

Ferreira, though a trained lawyer, is best known in the public eye for his memoir on his life in prison—*Colours of the Cage*, published in 2014. It describes the horrors of prison life; the lack of nutritious food, a clean place to sleep in, protection from the cold draughts that come in from broken windows, among numerous other privations. However, the narrative is not only about the difficulties of prison life but also the solidarities among prisoners as well as the attempts to improve life inside through the one weapon prisoners have—the hunger strike. A successful hunger strike, according to Ferreira, is contingent on prisoners succeeding in getting the media to cover it, thereby putting pressure on the State. In prison, he utilised his knowledge of the jurisprudence of prisoners' rights as developed by the Supreme Court, as well as the procedures encoded in the Prison Manuals, to demand that the prison authorities comply with the law. So, for instance, he demanded conformity with the law that prisoners have the right not to be handcuffed when produced before the courts. Though the rights of prisoners are more often observed in the breach, Ferreira notes that their success was apparent to him when prison officers 'spoke nostalgically of the good old days before the spread of awareness about human rights and prisoners rights'.[127]

Gonsalves's son Sagar sees his father as his 'role model' for having fought for the ideals that he believed in—'to stand up for what is right and help those whose rights are denied'. Despite his father's incarceration, Sagar knows that 'He has always done that and will continue to do so. This did not deter him the last time and will not do it now as well. He has an unbreakable spirit and will always stay true to what he believes in.'[128] True to Sagar's description, in *Colours of the Cage*, Ferreira describes how the inmates of Nagpur Central Jail called Gonsalves 'Vakeel Uncle', as he provided legal help to them.[129]

The third strand that unites the BK-16 is the fight for tribal rights. Swamy in Jharkhand, Bharadwaj in Chhattisgarh and Raut in Maharashtra defended Adivasi land and lives from both corporate and

State excesses. The excesses of the State against the Adivasi population have left activists with no choice but to fight State violence against Adivasi people.[130] Though activism in this area largely begins as a fight to protect Adivasi land against corporate takeover in violation of constitutional protections, those who work for the rights of Adivasis end up becoming civil liberties activists working on issues as diverse as encounter deaths, prisoners' rights and habeas corpus petitions.

One of the youngest of the BK-16, Raut turned thirty-three in July 2020.[131] A tribal rights activist from Gadchiroli, Maharasthra and a part of the Bharat Jan Andolan, he graduated from the Tata Institute of Social Sciences in Mumbai and worked as a Prime Minister's Rural Development Fellow in Gadchiroli. He is also a co-convenor of the anti-displacement platform Visthapan Virodhi Jan Vikas Andolan (VVJVA). Under the VVJVA, he campaigned along with the Adivasi communities of the region for the implementation of the Provisions of the Panchayats (Extension to Scheduled Areas) Act (PESA), 1996, which 'the villagers consider as their essential legislature to ensure Adivasi autonomy'. He was also involved in a successful campaign against middlemen in tendu patta collection in several blocks in Gadchiroli, which ensured that the Adivasi farmers were paid their due.[132]

Raut was arrested a day before he was to file a petition in the Nagpur bench of the Bombay High Court along with other activists, to challenge the 'mining corporate giants', Adivasi leader Sainu Gota told *The Polis Project*. This was after the 'state ... granted permission to mine iron ore on over three hundred and forty-eight hectares of land in the Surjagad region alone'.[133] Gota's statement to *The Polis Project* indicates the challenge that the work of Adivasi rights activists poses to the corporate takeover of land used by Adivasi communities.

Father Stan Swamy, at eighty-three years of age, was the oldest of the BK-16. He established Bagaicha, a Jesuit social research and training centre near Ranchi, with which he was active for fifteen years till he was arrested. At Bagaicha, he worked in 'collaboration with people's movements that were working against unjust displacement, human rights violations, illegal land acquisitions, and policies that were designed or amended to acquire more land, making the indigenous people landless'.[134]

He tirelessly advocated for the implementation of PESA 1996, which empowers gram sabhas in Adivasi areas to safeguard their cultural identity and exercise control over 'community resources'. He also advocated for the implementation of the judgement of the Supreme Court in *Samatha v State of Andhra Pradesh*[135] which aimed to 'protect the tribals from exploitation' and to 'preserve the tribal culture and their holdings'. His life's work was to bring the Constitution to life for the Adivasi people of Jharkhand. Concerned about the number of 'innocent Adivasis languishing in jails on trumped-up charges', Swamy helped conduct a study on left-wing undertrials in Jharkhand. The study found that there was a serious miscarriage of justice, and that 'prolonged detention and exceedingly slow pace of progress of cases, especially retarded due to the serial foisting of multiple cases, jail transfers on administrative grounds, non-production from jails to all the courts on the respective dates of hearing, production through video-conferencing also hindered for months and years on end due to technical failures of the machinery, communication failures and administrative lacunae—all these together result in accused persons being punished for offences which they may not have committed'.[136]

The plight of Adivasi people in prisons led to Swamy forming the Persecuted Prisoners Solidarity Committee (PPSC) along with Sudha Bharadwaj, which took up the cases of such prisoners. In a letter published in the *EPW*, both Bharadwaj and Swamy, as members of the PPSC, condemned 'the arbitrary and illegal manner in which the Giridih Central Jail administration has imposed solitary confinement on undertrials arrested following the crack-down on the Mazdoor Sangathan Samiti (MSS), which was a registered trade union which was illegally banned by the Jharkhand State'.[137] He also filed a case in 2017 in the Jharkhand High Court, highlighting the plight of around 3,000 Adivasi detenus. All these activities to make the State accountable and ensure that it worked within the four corners of the Constitution, ironically, but not unsurprisingly, put Stan in the cross hairs of the State.

The fourth strand is activism which challenges State repression. Navlakha and Wilson have questioned the State for years, be it on the policy of encounter killings, militarisation in Jammu and Kashmir or the rights of political prisoners. Their work challenged the hard power of the State and its repressive apparatus—the military, police and intelligence agencies. What the duo challenged is what E.P. Thompson, in *Writing by Candlelight*, calls the 'secret state', the 'unrepresentative and unaccountable state within the state'.[138] Josy Joseph in his book *The Silent Coup* calls it the 'deep state' made up of the security establishment comprising of the police forces, intelligence agencies, federal investigative agencies and their like.[139] For Thompson, the challenge in a democracy is to 'bring the police under much stricter democratic controls' and 'strip the security services of their invisibility'.[140] It is this task of bringing the 'secret state' or the 'deep state' within democratic and constitutional control which the State feels threatened by.

A journalist and activist with the human rights organisation Peoples Union for Democratic Rights (PUDR), Navlakha is a public intellectual who has advocated for unpopular causes like human rights violations in Kashmir and Chhattisgarh and written and spoken about draconian laws such as POTA and AFSPA. An editor of *EPW* and managing editor of the Hindi literary magazine *Hans*, he has written extensively in the *EPW* on State repression, especially in Jharkhand, Chhattisgarh, Jammu and Kashmir and the Northeast. Writing on Chhattisgarh's security establishment, he observes how 'crimes committed by government forces—rape, murder, fake encounter, custodial torture, and loot—are seldom recorded or investigated'.[141] He is among the few in the Indian mainland to write consistently on the situation in Kashmir, demanding accountability for human rights violations and speaking to the concerns of the Kashmiri people.[142] He is also one of the few to write about national security policy from the viewpoint of human rights, including issues such as the role of the private sector in defence production,[143] exposing the 'Make in India' mantra as nothing more than 'bluster' behind which lie 'strategic confusion and ill-thought-out decisions'.[144] His activism and writing expose the hypocrisies of the State, especially when it comes to the hard power of the military and police issues on which public discourse is muted.

Wilson's work includes speaking and writing extensively on the history of anti-terror laws and their misuse against 'those critical of the government and Muslims and Kashmiris in particular'. Till his arrest, he served as the public relations secretary of the Committee for the Release of Political Prisoners (CRPP), which was founded by S.A.R. Geelani, who too was arrested under anti-terrorism laws and sentenced to death for his alleged involvement in the 2001 Parliament attack, but was later acquitted of all charges. The mandate of the CRPP, in Wilson's words, is to 'release all political prisoners unconditionally', to press for 'repeal of all draconian laws', to remove armed forces from areas of people's struggles. He is also committed to exposing the violations committed by the National Counter Terrorism Centre and the NIA.[145]

Wilson, in his public speeches, sought to expose the repressive nature of anti-terror laws and argued that the only way forward was to coalesce public opinion into a mass movement against them. He was aware that this was not an easy task as one would have to go against 'state owned media' and 'private owned media' to build 'counter profiles' which question the narrative that the 'Muslim is always the terrorist'.[146] Wilson was also tireless in his advocacy for the release of G.N. Saibaba, a teacher at Delhi University who was sentenced to life imprisment for being a member of the CPI (M)[147]

The fifth strand uniting the BK-16 is a broad vision of progressive politics in the university, as seen in the work of Rao, Sen and Babu. As teachers, the three went outside the ivory tower and were involved in a range of issues, seeding an activist culture in educational institutions and speaking to the future by impacting young minds. This idea of the organic intellectual is repugnant to anti-intellectualism, something the prime minister himself has embodied. In the context of Amartya Sen's critique of the demonetisation policy, Modi commented in 2017, '... hard work is more powerful than Harvard'.[148]

A poet and retired college lecturer based in Hyderabad, Rao was an editor of the literary magazine *Srujana* and one of the founders of

Virasam, or Revolutionary Writers' Association. He has been jailed many times but has been discharged or acquitted each time. When he was subjected to 1,000 days of solitary confinement between 1985 and 1989 in Secunderabad Jail, journalist Arun Shourie invited him to write about his experiences in the *Indian Express*. These pieces were later published in the remarkable collection *Captive Imagination*, the best possible introduction to Rao's life and thoughts for an English-speaking audience.

In the introduction to the book, the famous Kenyan writer Ngũgĩ wa Thiong'o writes that the reason the State imprisons artists and writers is because they have the 'power of imagination' and are able to 'intimate possibilities even within apparently impossible situations'. The artist publicly challenges the narrative of the State, exposes the State's truth as a lie and shows that the emperor has no clothes. That is why the State 'tries to imprison the artist to hold the imagination captive'. But the 'imagination cannot be limited by temporal and spatial confinement. It breaks free from captivity and roams in time and space'.[149]

Ever since his first arrest under MISA in 1973, and subsequent arrests during the Emergency and in the 1980s under conspiracy laws, Varavara Rao has embodied the idea of the writer as an engaged intellectual who is committed to social justice struggles. His poems and speeches supporting the revolutionary cause attracted numerous conspiracy cases for which he spent almost a decade in jail. He was also a strong critic of State policy, be it neo-liberalism or the violence of encounters and custodial deaths.

In 2014, Varavara Rao was one of the speakers in a panel on the release of Arun Ferreira's book *The Colours of the Cage* and in his speech, he again made the point about the responsibilities of an intellectual. In his opinion, the high-handedness of the police in Maharashtra and the torture they practised owed much to the silence of the intellectuals in the state. Varavara Rao's life is a testament to this vision of who an intellectual must be. He speaks truth to power and is willing to suffer the consequences of the same. Throughout his years of imprisonment, the poet never gave in to despair.

The arrest of Varavara Rao in the evening of his life only testifies to the State's perception of the power of ideas. Poets, writers and intellectuals, when they move out of the ivory tower and espouse people's concerns, pose an ideological challenge to the narrative of the State. The poetic imagination of Varavara Rao, which embodies the struggles of the Adivasis, Dalits and working people, is one such dissenting voice.

Sen was a professor and head of the English department at the Rashtrasant Tukadoji Maharaj Nagpur University when she was arrested. As an active member of the national collective Women Against Sexual Violence and State Repression (WSS) and as a feminist scholar, she has contributed to scholarly publications such as the *EPW* and the *Journal of Commonwealth Literature* on the intersections of gender and caste as well as revolutionary ideologies.

She is also one of the most important voices in understanding the role of patriarchy in Maoist movements. In her writings in the *EPW*, she charts the thinking of organisations such as the Krantikari Adivasi Mahila Sangathan (KAMS), a banned Maoist women's organisation, and the way they deal with the gender question. In Sen's analysis, the Maoist movement sees the 'link between patriarchy and class' and 'without working class struggle' ... 'patriarchy cannot be challenged because every type of class society perpetuates patriarchy in different forms'.[150] However, she acknowledges that patriarchy continues to prevail in many forms within the Maoist movement. She also highlights other issues within the movement, such as the 'denial of issues pertaining to queer issues, like same sex relations, transgender or intersex people'.[151]

Her writings indicate that she has formed her worldviews based on both wide reading and being a part of on-the-ground movements. In fact, when she was arrested, her daughter told the campaign platform India Civil Watch International that the literary evidence the Pune police collected from her mother's house included 'basic Communist literature, like books by Marx and Lenin'.[152]

As WSS rightly notes, 'After a lifetime of working for others, people like Shoma Sen are branded "anti-national" by the Indian State. Humane and perceptive people who have spent their lives working to recognise, transform and build a more democratic society, are being treated as criminals waging war against "national interests".'[153]

An associate professor in the English department of Delhi University, Babu is a linguist, a scholar of caste and has been active in the pro-reservation movement, the Committee for the Defence and Release of G.N. Saibaba[154] and other social justice movements within the university. He was accused of being a co-conspirator in the propagation of 'Naxalite and Maoist ideology' and arrested by the NIA in July 2020.

In an interview to *Caravan* after the first raid in his house, in 2019, when books as well as electronic equipment were seized, Babu reflected that he was being targeted because the State wanted to send a warning signal to academics. To him, this was a blow to academia, as 'there can be no academic work without free thinking'.[155]

From his reading of the charge sheets in the Bhima Koregaon case, Babu feels that it is clear that the State is fearful of the coming together of Left and Dalit groups to challenge the hegemonic thinking of the Sangh Parivar. Babu sees his own work as the result of collaboration with different groups—from the Dalit community to political prisoners. When movements come together, they garner strength in challenging the State apparatus, which is something the State not only seems to want to discourage but also criminalise.[156]

While these arbitrary and wrongful arrests of those who defend constitutional values should have angered citizens across the country, the conscience of most Indians has remained unmoved. Those incarcerated remain a name at best and a statistic at worst, with the larger citizenry having no knowledge of how their work embodies the constitutional imagination of a plural, democratic and inclusive India. In fact, rather than talk about the invaluable work the sixteen activists have done, sections of the mainstream media have legitimised the State narrative of the BK-16 as 'urban naxals' deserving of no sympathy whatsoever. In this climate, when the truth is a casualty at the altar of far-fetched conspiracy theories that have no basis in fact, there is an urgent need for patient work amongst people to bring attention to the lives of the BK-16.

Remembering individual lives with both the quirks of personality as well as how they were impacted by history is an important task. Hannah Arendt, in her book *Men in Dark Times*, writes about the lives of figures such as Rosa Luxemburg, Walter Benjamin and Bertolt Brecht, in the hope that a telling of these lives will provide some illumination in dark times:

> That even in the darkest of times we have the right to expect some illumination, and that such illumination may well come less from theories and concepts than from the uncertain, flickering, and often weak light that some men and women, in their lives and their works, will kindle under almost all circumstances and shed over the time span that was given them on earth—this conviction is the inarticulate background against which these profiles were drawn. Eyes so used to darkness as ours will hardly be able to tell whether their light was the light of a candle or that of a blazing sun.[157]

To remember and recount the lives of the BK-16 is to continue to build resistance to the policies of the State, as it places before the public the existence of an alternative viewpoint, countering the loud noise of TV anchors and resisting all efforts to silence it. The stories of these sixteen activists and innumerable others, based as they are on the defence of constitutional values, have a small but committed audience nurtured by alternative news media like the *Wire*[158], *Scroll.in*[159] and *The Polis Project*[160], among others. The courage of people like these, who fight the State against all odds, has the power to inspire others to come forward in opposition, keeping dissent alive in the public imagination. The inestimable value of the life's work of each of these sixteen can be captured in Milan Kundera's aphorism, 'The struggle of man against power is the struggle of memory against forgetting.'[161]

The Anti-CAA Arrests

The second wave of arrests in which human rights activists were particularly targeted during the Modi regime was during the anti-CAA protests. The CAA, 2019, proposed to confer citizenship on 'illegal migrants' using religion as a marker, expressly excluding those of the Islamic faith. The CAA, when read with the preparation of the National Population Register (NPR) and the National Register of Citizens (NRC), will render precarious the citizenship rights of all those who do not have the requisite documentation, which could be a huge range of people in this country—those who have lost their documents to natural disasters like floods, migrant workers, women, trans people and others who have moved away from their birth families and so on. The NRC gives the local registrar enormous power to declare a person a 'doubtful citizen', awakening legitimate fears as to whether this power will be used to de facto render the citizenship of Muslims 'doubtful'.

The passing of the CAA witnessed protests around the country. Rapidly, the Constitution became the iconography of these protests—with the Preamble being read at the beginning or the end of a demonstration—along with images of Gandhi, Ambedkar and other freedom fighters. Muslims, in particular Muslim women, participated in large numbers alongside students, Dalit groups and those concerned with the defence of the Constitution.[162]

These demonstrations aimed to reclaim an idea of inclusive nationalism as refracted through the Constitution, thereby posing a significant ideological challenge to the Hindutva groups that claim a monopoly over nationalism. The BJP government could not let this go unanswered.

The police were instrumentalised to stifle and muzzle the movement through the filing of a series of cases against anti-CAA protestors around the country.[163] The Uttar Pradesh police, Delhi police, Karnataka police, all under BJP-ruled states, as well as the Mumbai police, targeted protestors, often booking them for speeches which fell well within the ambit of the right to freedom of speech and expression under Article 19(1)(a) as interpreted by the Supreme Court.

In Uttar Pradesh, well-known activists such as humanist and doctor Kafeel Khan, former IPS officer S.R. Darapuri, president of the rights advocacy group Rihai Manch and senior advocate Mohammad Shoaib, advocate Mohammad Faisal, Congress worker Sadaf Zafar, Dalit rights activists Pawan Rao Ambedkar and Anoop Shramik, journalist Omar Rashid, social activists Robin Verma and Deepak Kabir, and members of the Blue Panthers, such as Sushil Gautam, were arrested. Kafeel Khan was preventively detained under the National Security Act, 1980.[164]

The Karnataka police arrested twenty-four-year-old Ardra Narayan, who held a sign at a protest saying, 'Muslim, Dalit, Kashmir, Trans, Adivasi, liberation now', under Section 153A of the IPC, which penalises the 'promotion of enmity between different groups'.[165] They also arrested nineteen-year-old Amulya Leona for sedition under Section 124A of the IPC for shouting 'Pakistan Zindabad', while the second half of her slogan 'Hindustan Zindabad' was muffled out without allowing her to complete her humanist message of love for all, irrespective of nationality.[166] In Mumbai, twenty-two-year-old trans activist Kris Chudawala was arrested under Section 124A for raising slogans in support of those arrested while protesting the CAA. The slogan deemed objectionable was the one which said, 'Sharjeel, we will realise your dreams,' referencing Sharjeel Imam, who himself was arrested earlier under charges of sedition for a speech he gave. Imam's arrest was condemned by many public intellectuals and civil society activists. Although the police arrested Chudawala on grounds of sedition, i.e. exciting disaffection against the government, the gathering that they addressed concluded with a declaration of Constitutional faith with the reading of the Preamble.[167]

Delhi saw vibrant anti-CAA protests, symbolised by the Muslim women of Shaheen Bagh as well as the students of Jamia Millia Islamia (JMI) and Jawaharlal Nehru University. In response to the vigour of the student-led movement, on 15 December 2019, the police raided the campus of JMI, 'forcing their way into the libraries, thrashing students, hurling tear gas shells into reading rooms and beating those who were praying'.[168] Similar scenes unfolded in the campus of Aligarh Muslim University in Uttar Pradesh.

But the students could not be cowed. The police brutality, instead of shutting down the protests, galvanised their energy, and soon, many sit-in protests popped up across Muslim neighbourhoods in Delhi as well as across the country. This seemed to further enrage Hindutva groups, who posted open threats on social media.[169]

The unchecked hate propagated by various Hindutva groups and leaders led to a pogrom in Delhi in 2020. Perusal of the report of the DMC fact-finding committee on the riots in north-east Delhi in February 2020 appears to suggest that for four days, beginning 23 February 2020, mobs were allowed to target and destroy Muslims shops and houses and desecrate mosques in the north-east of the city. The violence resulted in the death of fifty-three persons, thirty-five of them Muslim and fifteen Hindu.[170] Sexual violence was perpetrated against a few Muslim women. Twenty-two Muslim dargahs, kabristans and mosques were desecrated.[171]

This targeted violence against the protestors and the Muslim community was described in a report by the Delhi Minority Commission (DMC) as 'seemingly planned and directed to teach a lesson to a certain community which dared to protest against a discriminatory law'. The report documents the complicity of the police in the violence and how one of the slogans of the anti-CAA protests, 'Azadi', a chant for freedom, was used to taunt members of the Muslim community. A cruel video that went viral shows the Delhi police surrounding five young Muslim men lying bleeding on the street and beating them with sticks and boots. 'The police told them to sing "Jana Gana Mana" and directed one Kausar to say "Bharat Mata Ki Jai". While beating them, the police were saying, "You want Azadi? Take this Azadi!"' reported the DMC's fact-finding team.[172]

The anti-CAA protests challenged the nationalist narrative of the Right, which appears to have provoked a violent response through the pogrom, with the police acting in complicity with the mob to teach the Muslim community 'a lesson'.[173] The question, of course, is what is the constitutional responsibility of the Central government which exercises control over the Delhi police? To answer this question, one would need to institute an independent commission of inquiry that has the power to summon officials and unearth the documentary trail. In short, what is required is the work of a commission of inquiry that can document and analyse the chain of responsibility, like the Shah Commission did during the Emergency.

The pogrom was followed by the declaration of an unplanned countrywide lockdown as a response to the COVID-19 pandemic, towards the end of February 2020. The lockdown, along with the promulgation of Section 144 of the CrPC, banning a gathering of more than five people in public places, meant that the anti-CAA protests perforce came to an end. However, the State, heedless of the dangers posed by incarceration during a pandemic, utilised the lockdown period, when crowds couldn't gather to protest and question State action, to continue arresting anti-CAA protestors under the UAPA. The police also instrumentalised the investigation into the Delhi pogrom to concoct a narrative that the violence was the result of a conspiracy by anti-CAA activists to disrupt the then US president Donald Trump's visit to India.[174] Peaceful student protestors like Natasha Narwal and Devangana Kalita, and young Muslim activists like Safoora Zargar, Gulfisha Fatima and Umar Khalid, only some of the more visible among the many arrested, were charged with conspiracy to commit violence under both ordinary criminal law as well as draconian laws like the UAPA. With the police refusing to publish details of the 1,300 arrested, as mandated by law, it is difficult to know if there is a correlation between those arrested and the violence in Delhi.[175] However, what is clear is that those who gave inflammatory communal speeches, like BJP's Kapil Mishra, have not even been brought in for questioning and roam scot-free.[176]

The international attention on Zargar's arrest, with her being pregnant at the time of incarceration and it being in the middle of a pandemic, seems to have forced the Modi government not to oppose the bail application in the Delhi High Court on 'humanitarian grounds'. However, the Central government was careful to ensure that the release of Zargar would not become a precedent which could be used by others who were arrested—till today, they languish in jail.[177]

What is also significant about these arrests is that, like in the Emergency, the Central government went after articulate young people who understood State violence and excesses and criticised it in public forums. On 7 July 2020, Sharjeel Usmani, a young student activist from Aligarh Muslim University, was detained by the ATS of the Uttar Pradesh police. Before the arrest, Usmani had written a powerful analysis of police violence against Muslims in an article titled 'Charting History of Indian Muslims and the Police: From British Era to AMU Violence, a Story of Injustice'. Citing scholar Irfan Ahmad in the article, Usmani distinguished a riot from a pogrom and suggested that the use of the word 'riot' turned 'invisible the role of the State in orchestrating the pogrom, and left no space to challenge the complicity of the police'. He emphasised that we need to move beyond seeing the police in terms of good and bad individuals, and recognise that 'the police is an institution', especially one that is 'communally biased in its behaviour and anti-Muslim in its conduct'. Only then could 'possible reform measures ... be conceptualised'.[178]

Usmani's arrest is an illustration of the State targeting those who emerged in the crucible of the anti-CAA protests and in time would begin to play the role that people like Teltumbde or Navlakha play, namely that of a public intellectual. Similarly, the arrest of Kalita, Narwal and Tanha, all student protestors and leaders, illustrates the kind of person the State perceives as a threat.

In both the Bhima Koregaon arrests and those following the anti-CAA protests, the State stuck to a similar methodology. It produced a false narrative, the complicit media turned 'victims' into perpetrators and those affected were ironically and cruelly subjected to persecution under arbitrary laws.[179]

As per Arendt's thesis of 'men in dark times', the lives of all those who are arrested serve as points of illumination in the darkness into which we are plunged. They face the ire of the State because they refuse to 'stand aside and look' in the midst of human suffering. Their work is a counter to the politics of indifference—the logical end position of a market ideology in which looking out for one's self-interest is the dominant value.

The arrested embody the idea of a 'public conscience' as articulated by Ambedkar: 'Public conscience means conscience which becomes agitated at every wrong; no matter who is the sufferer and it means that everybody whether he suffers that particular wrong or not, is prepared to join him in order to get him relieved.'[180]

Arrests Following the Abrogation of Article 370 in Kashmir

Between 5 and 6 August 2019, two presidential orders, C.O. 272 and C.O. 273, were issued that had the effect of abrogating Articles 370 and 35A of the Constitution and effectively dismantled the limited protection afforded to Jammu and Kashmir in self-governance, territorial integrity and the collective rights to land and livelihood. The repeal of Article 370 was a part of the BJP's poll promise. The party's 2019 manifesto reiterated the promise to abrogate Article 370, and also pledged the 'annulment of Article 35-A'. The BJP contended that 35-A was 'discriminatory against non-permanent residents and women of Jammu and Kashmir'.[181]

It was only in 2019 that the BJP felt confident enough to move ahead and repeal Article 370 without any public consultation with any stakeholder in the valley. The BJP also took the unprecedented step of splitting Jammu and Kashmir into two parts, namely Jammu and Kashmir and Ladakh, and demoting both parts to union territories.

The declaration was followed by a wave of preventive arrests of the top leadership of all major political parties in the state, including former chief ministers Omar Abdullah and Mehbooba Mufti, alongside prominent lawyers, businessmen, civil society members and activists. Former president of the Jammu and Kashmir Bar Association Mian Abdul Qayoom was also preventively detained. The police dossier in his case read, 'We apprehend that you [Qayoom] will motivate people to agitate against abrogation of Article 370.'[182]

A fact-finding report by representatives of human rights groups like PUCL, People's Democratic Forum and All India People's Forum as well as trade unionists and independent researchers on Kashmir concluded:

> From August 5, 2019 more than 330 Habeas Corpus petitions had been filed till September 30, 2019. There are countless detentions that are unlawful, hence, no one except the State knows how many persons are illegally detained. The people said there are reports that more than 13,000 people have been unlawfully detained. In many instances the draconian PSA [Public Safety Act, 1978] is slapped arbitrarily on people. Many detenues are being transferred outside the State of J&K, which, the lawyers said, was intentionally done in order to prevent family members and lawyers appearing for those detained from having access to them.[183]

As per a statement made by Union Minister G. Kishan Reddy in the Rajya Sabha, over 5,000 preventive arrests have been made in Jammu and Kashmir since 5 August 2019, when the Centre announced the abrogation of Article 370. As of 27 November 2019, 609 of them were still in custody.[184]

A petition to the chief justice of India by the state's bar association noted that by 5 August, nearly 13,000 people from the Kashmir valley had been arrested, and 'after few days or weeks hundreds were booked under the PSA and are lodged in various jails of India'.[185] In what can only be termed an egregious instance of turning a blind eye to constitutional obligations, of the more than 600 habeas corpus petitions filed before the Jammu and Kashmir High Court, not even 1 per cent of the cases had been decided as of June 2020.

However, for the people of Jammu and Kashmir, the suspension of habeas corpus was not new. Article 35C, which was inserted into the Indian Constitution through the Constitutional Order of 1954, states, '... no law with respect to preventive detention made by the Legislature of the State of Jammu and Kashmir, shall be void on the ground that it is inconsistent with any of the provisions of the Fundamental Rights

Chapter [Part III] of the Indian Constitution'. This provision, concludes a PUCL report, allows for 'virtually unregulated preventive detentions without even the minimal procedural safeguards of Article 22 of the Indian Constitution'. Thus, in Jammu and Kashmir, the fundamental right to life and liberty was suspended by a constitutional order. This was, unfortunately, upheld by a constitutional bench decision of the Supreme Court in the 1968 decision of *Sampath Prakash v State of Jammu and Kashmir*.[186]

Since 2019, the Jammu and Kashmir administration has booked over 2,300 people in more than 1,200 cases under the UAPA and 954 people under PSA. Of these, 46 per cent of those booked under the UAPA and about 30 per cent of those detained under PSA are still in jail, both inside and outside Jammu and Kashmir.[187]

According to a 'legal expert', the number of PSA cases showed a marked decline in 2020 and the number of UAPA cases increased. This is because there was a 'shift on the part of the police to book individuals under the more stringent law instead of PSA, which required regular extensions of custody'.[188]

The arrests that followed the abrogation of Article 370 bear perhaps the closest parallel to Indira Gandhi's Emergency, when the State targeted both civil society and political leaders. Kashmir challenges the notion of an undeclared emergency being a temporary phenomenon. Its people have suffered unjust and arbitrary incarceration as the rule rather than the exception. Kashmiri journalist Anuradha Bhasin, who delivered the fortieth JP Memorial Lecture organised by the PUCL, put forth the proposition that the undeclared emergency in mainland India is merely the extension of techniques which have long been the norm in Kashmir.[189]

Role of Media: Complicity in the Undeclared Emergency

One of the significant checks on any authoritarian tendencies of a government is the media, which can, by casting a searching spotlight on governmental actions, ensure accountability. One such media moment of holding the State responsible was its reportage of the corruption scams under the UPA-2 government of 2009–14, which put the administration on the defensive and under constant scrutiny by amplifying the narrative of a corrupt government.

What has happened to the same media during the Modi years? It is important to understand that India's media landscape is perhaps one of the largest in the world with more 'than 17,000 newspapers, 100,000 magazines, 178 television news channels'[190], as reported by the *New York Times,* as well as an expanding social media sphere.

The rise of social media provides one big part of the puzzle. Media critic Sevanti Ninan took stock of all the changes in the media under the Modi rule in an article for *Scroll.in.* She notes that the media has exploded in the Modi era with the 'Indian public sphere' being 'increasingly mediated not just by conventional media' but 'technology in the hands of millions of users seeking information, pushing disinformation and instant gratification'. With 500 million Indians on the internet, 200 million WhatsApp users, 30 million Twitter accounts and close to 294 million on Facebook, social media today feeds the news cycle.[191] The emergence of social media platforms such as Twitter means that the government can engage in communication with the public on its terms, marginalising that media which serves an entirely different function—not being the communication vessel of the State, but its critic. The relationship between the media and the State has undergone a transformation, with conventional media having lesser bargaining power with the State. In effect, the Modi government can do without the media and has not hesitated to limit its role.

This has paved the way for the State to sideline and arm-twist conventional media. Right from when the Modi government came to power for the first time in 2014, media accountability has taken a hit. To begin with, the prime minister has not held a press conference in seven years. The role of the media as an institution which makes the government accountable, in full display during the UPA years, has been quietly forgotten. There are 'no press conferences', no 'interviews to journalists other than hand-picked ones' and only 'pre-screened questions and [often] only written answers' are allowed. Ninan also recalls an observation by the Editors Guild of India in 2014: 'By delaying the establishment of a media interface in the Prime Minister's Office, in restricting access to ministers and bureaucrats in offices and in reducing the flow of information at home and abroad, the government in its early days seems to be on a path that runs counter to the norms of democratic discourse and accountability.'

To ensure media compliance, the Central government carried advertisements only in those newspapers which toed the State line. It also withdrew appearances from sponsored events, a major source of revenue for media houses, writes Ninan. In 2019, the government pulled advertising from three major English newspapers, including the *Times of India*, in what appeared to be 'retaliation for critical stories', notes Rest of World, an international non-profit journalism organisation. The *Times of India* lost nearly 15 per cent of its ad revenue as a result.[192]

It is the fear of not only losing advertisements but also of tax raids that hangs heavy over India's media houses. As recently as July 2021, the offices of the Hindi daily *Dainik Bhaskar* and the Hindi news channel Bharat Samachar were raided. Both media houses were critical of the Central government's handling of the second wave of the pandemic. The online news portal NewsClick was raided by the Enforcement Directorate in February 2021, believed to be in retaliation for its pioneering coverage of the farmers' protests.[193] NDTV, which has been constantly critical of the BJP government, was raided by the CBI in 2017.[194]

As Nirjhari Sinha, the director of Pravda Media Foundation which supports the fact-checking news site Alt News, put it in Hindi, the BJP government's relationships with the media can be summed up by the phrase '*sham dham dand bhed*'—persuade, purchase, punish and exploit every weakness.[195]

The government also leans on newspapers in different ways to moderate their content. One telling example is the resignation of the editor of the *Hindustan Times*, Bobby Ghosh, just fourteen months into his job, after which the newspaper took down a 'hate-tracker' which was 'a national database on crimes in the name of religion, caste, race', writes Ninan. The resignation happened after a 'personal meeting between Prime Minister Narendra Modi and HT proprietor Shobhana Bhartia and sustained objections raised by top-level government officials to editorial decisions taken during Ghosh's tenure'. Post the meeting, the *Hindustan Times* began to 'distance itself from the hate-tracker'.

While there is undoubted State pressure on the media, there is also the response of the media houses themselves, which have quietly adapted to the new status quo, with a 'host of channels—Zee News, India TV, Republic TV, Times Now, among others—turning openly partisan', according to Ninan. BJP politician L.K. Advani's comment on the pliant, uncritical media during the Emergency of 1975—'You were asked only to bend, but you crawled'[196]—is as appropriate today. Ninan goes on to note, '... media houses in India (TV, print and online) discovered the virtues of self-censorship. Published news items disappeared from websites. TV channels dropped interviews or stories done by their correspondents. The entertainment channel Star Plus decided not to air a comedy act that mimicked Prime Minister Modi.'

Ninan also records how news seen to be critical of the government has been systematically taken down during Modi's rule, including a report by global media watchdog Reporters Without Borders that found 'journalists were less free under the Modi government due to threats from Hindutva nationalists'. Both the *Times of India* and the *Economic Times* took down the report. When Amit Shah was elected BJP president in 2014, there were 'voluntary takedowns' of articles which were critical of him. The Mumbai daily *DNA* first published a piece on his past record, titled 'A New Low in Indian Politics', and then removed it. *Quartz* reported that after Shah's election, CNN-IBN's bulletin at night as well as the graphics on air were edited to remove references to the criminal charges faced by Shah. Since May 2014, when the Modi government came to power, the 404 error page on media websites is showing up rather more frequently than before.

A satirical piece by Jug Suraiya, a columnist with the *Times of India*, criticising the government for mismanaging COVID, was dropped from the print edition. The piece was subsequently published in the *Wire*.[197]

The trend of 'over-compliance' has spilled over into online entertainment media and self-censorship in the realm of culture. An empirical study by the Centre for Internet Society found that intermediaries tended to 'over-comply with such takedown requests to limit their liability and this has a chilling effect on free speech and expression of all users'.[198] Self-regulation has already given way to self-censorship on OTT platforms, with on-demand video streaming media platforms exercising caution and discretion. Several TV shows and movies, already at the post-production stage, have been cancelled for fear of government reprimand, notes the Internet Freedom Foundation.[199]

Tandav, a web series released on the OTT platform Amazon Prime Video in 2021, was criticised for hurting the religious sentiments of Hindus. In spite of the makers of the series issuing an unconditional apology and offering to remove the parts considered objectionable, multiple FIRs were filed in different states against the series' actors, producers and directors as well as the India head of Amazon Prime Video, Aparna Purohit.[200] Though the Supreme Court finally granted protection from arrest to Purohit, undoubtedly, the persecution faced by her and *Tandav*'s cast and crew will have a chilling effect on internet freedom.

The 2021 World Press Freedom Index produced by Reporters Without Borders has again placed India at 142 out of 180 countries. In 2016, two years after Modi came to power, India's rank was 133.[201] The Reporters Without Borders study says that since 2019, when Modi's BJP came back to power with an overwhelming mandate, 'pressure has increased on the media to toe the Hindu nationalist government's line' with 'coordinated hate campaigns waged on social media networks against journalists who dare to speak or write about subjects that annoy Hindutva supporters including calls for journalists to be murdered'.[202]

Individual journalists who do not toe the line are also subject to consequences, if not by the State then by the larger right-wing ecosystem, as seen in the vicious online trolling of NDTV's Ravish Kumar and Mojo Story's Barkha Dutt.[203] Young women journalists questioning the State have been subjected to not only trolling but also threats of murder and rape.[204] These troll armies have been linked to the ruling party. Journalist Swati Chaturvedi illustrates in her book *I Am a Troll* that the BJP orchestrates online campaigns through its social media cell to intimidate perceived government critics.[205]

Such threats have not been limited to words on digital media. The most chilling example is the assassination of Gauri Lankesh, a vociferous critic of Hindutva politics and the current administration.[206] She was shot dead outside her house in Bengaluru by unidentified assailants in 2017. Since then, eighteen people have been arrested in connection with her killing. An NDTV report indicates that she was killed following a 'conspiracy hatched by the gang linked to the Sanatan Sanstha and its offshoot Hindu Janjagruti Samiti. The gang is also allegedly linked with the killing of rationalists MM Kalburgi, Narendra Dabholkar and Govind Pansare'.[207]

According to a study by Free Speech Collective, 198 serious attacks on journalists have been documented in the period between 2014 and 2019, including thirty-six in 2019 alone. The study also states that there has not been a single conviction in attacks on journalists in India, who have been consistently targeted for their investigative work during this time period.[208]

That being said, there is also a 'significant rise in independent media, most of it online, several offering specialised content'. Ninan writes:

> Region-specific news sites have blossomed. *The News Minute*, a digital news platform which has a specific focus on the five southern states, began publishing in 2014, and *Dool News*, headquartered in Kozhikode in Kerala, is a Malayalam digital news site that covers politics and societal issues. *Azhimukham* is another Malayalam news portal. Then there is *Samachara.com* in Karnataka, which classifies itself as an independent digital news media. There is also *The Wire.in*, *The Print*

and the *East Mojo*, headquartered in Guwahati. Along with several others begun earlier, such as *Newsclick*, *Scroll.in*, *Huffpost India*, and *Newslaundry* as well as *The Caravan*, which does long-form narrative journalism, they constitute a dogged counter to co-option, self-censorship, fake news and much else. But the new online independent media publications remain small ventures that enrich the public sphere but lack the share of voice of the mainstream.

Though independent news media now largely exist in online avatars and their reach is limited, even that limited expression of an alternative viewpoint is being targeted by the Central government. Recently, the Centre notified the Information Technology (Intermediary Guidelines and Digital Media Ethics Code) Rules, 2021, which attempts to specifically bring digital news media under tighter State control. Online media is supposed to comply with a 'code of ethics' and complaints on violation of this code will be first decided within the digital media establishment, then by a self-regulatory body—which the government has a say in deciding the composition of—and finally a government-constituted oversight mechanism. The regulatory framework over digital news media is stronger than the regulation of print and broadcast media: print media is only subject to a self-regulatory mechanism under the Press Council of India Act, 1978, while broadcast media is only subject to a self-regulatory mechanism called the News Broadcasting Standards Authority, which only governs the members of the National Broadcasting Association. However, digital media has to answer for its content to the State, which exercises total control over the third stage of the regulatory process and partial control over the second stage.

All these modes of control over the media recall the Emergency era. While there is no declaration of emergency today, the State censors the media, directly and indirectly, through both overt and covert acts, producing a largely conformist media, no less pliant than its counterpart during the declared Emergency of 1975.

Role of the Constitutional Court: Failing the Constitution?

Some of the strongest critiques of the Supreme Court's role in recent times have come from consummate insiders, namely former judges. They have given voice to the increasing sense of disquiet felt by legal scholars and lawyers as well as ordinary citizens. A.P. Shah, a former chief justice of the Delhi High Court,[209] and Madan Lokur, a former justice of the Supreme Court,[210] have been particularly vocal in their criticism. In an unprecedented move, four sitting judges of the Supreme Court, Kurian Joseph, Jasti Chelameswar, Ranjan Gogoi and Lokur, addressed a press conference in 2018 highlighting their sense of unease at the then chief justice Dipak Misra's style of functioning, with important cases being assigned to junior judges.[211] At various other points, former Supreme Court judges Deepak Gupta and Gopal Gowda have also criticised the court. The criticisms of the court detailed below span the tenures of chief justices Misra, Gogoi and Bobde.

The Failure to Hear

One of the key roles of the Supreme Court is to ensure that executive and legislative actions are undertaken within the ambit of the Constitution. In this sense, the Supreme Court is the guardian of the Constitution, ensuring that this foundational document is not limited to being just words on paper but rather becomes the normative basis on which the constitutionality of State action is tested. It is for abdicating this grave responsibility of being the guardian of the Constitution that the court has been criticised.

The passing of the CAA by the Central government triggered one of the most widespread protest movements in contemporary times, indicating that for many citizens, jurists, public intellectuals and academics, the law fundamentally challenged the basic values of the Constitution—non-discrimination on the grounds of religion and the ideal of secularism. The deep concern over the law was also apparent in the fact that over 140 petitions were filed in the Supreme Court challenging the CAA.[212] The court should have heard and decided the matter with a degree of urgency. However, the matter has been kept pending by the court as of November 2021, twenty-two months since the first petition was filed.

Similarly, the unilateral abrogation of Article 370 and Article 35A and the reduction of a state of the Indian Union to two union territories by the Parliament on 5 August 2019 raised a number of issues of deep constitutional concern around the questions of federalism, the constitutional sanctity of treaties and the power of the Centre to unilaterally terminate the existence of a state. Twenty-three petitions were filed challenging this, but the matter has not been heard by the Supreme Court as yet, almost two years since the first petition was filed. The failure of the court to hear the matter expeditiously raises legitimate fears, for the longer the court delays the more the status quo would be altered, rendering the challenges infructuous.[213]

This failure of the court to hear matters of undeniable constitutional importance also extends to its handling of the challenge to the electoral bonds scheme, which facilitates anonymous corporate funding to political parties. The programme is designed such that neither the buyer of the bond nor the seller is mandated to disclose their identity, rendering the funding of political parties completely opaque.[214] In fact, the Election Commission, in an affidavit in the Supreme Court, contended that the 'scheme is contrary to the goal of transparency in political finance'. The commission also noted that the 'amendment to the Companies Act could lead to the infusion of black money through shell companies and make political parties vulnerable to influence by foreign companies'. However, the court is yet to decide on the matter, over three and a half years on.[215]

When it came to migrant workers who were stranded during the hasty and unplanned lockdown to counter COVID-19, the initial response of the court was to ignore the magnitude of the suffering of the poor. In spite of widespread reporting on the migrant crisis, with images of thousands of workers walking many miles back home flooding mainstream and social media, and many analogising the situation to the mass migration during Partition, the court chose to accept the State's false contention that 'there is no person walking on the roads in an attempt to reach his/her home towns/villages'. Astonishingly, the court went on to dismiss the reports of the mass exodus of the migrant workers and their plight as 'isolated incidents' or 'fake news', and abdicated its constitutional responsibility. This response triggered a public outcry, with former Supreme Court judge Gopala Gowda calling it an instance of 'supreme failure' and comparing it to the negligence of the constitutional court during the Emergency in an article for the *Deccan Herald*. As he put it, '*ADM Jabalpur* will no longer be remembered as the darkest moment of the Supreme Court. That infamy now belongs to the Court's response to the preventable migrant crisis during the COVID-19 pandemic.'[216]

It is only post this furious response from its own brethren as well as the media and wider civil society that the court finally responded to the migrant crisis by passing a series of orders to ensure that the workers had a safe passage home. However, as Justice Madan Lokur scathingly observes in an article for the *Wire*, if one were to grade the Supreme Court's performance, 'it deserves an F'. The late intervention by the court, Justice Lokur says, is but a 'tepid order'—it merely stated that 'appropriate action' would be taken by the government. This formed the basis to dispose of the petition. Justice Lokur poignantly concludes, 'On that day, humanitarian law died a million deaths.'[217]

There is an unmistakable trend of the apex court shirking its responsibility to ensure that executive actions do not trample the Constitution. As a result, the executive has repeatedly besmirched the Constitution, emboldened by the knowledge that its actions will go unchallenged.

The Abuse of the Power of the 'Master of the Roster'

Another criticism of the court has been about the choice of judges to adjudicate over those important matters that it does end up hearing. This decision, made by the chief justice, is in exercise of his administrative power to be the 'master of the roster'. This power exercised by the chief justice, though meant to facilitate court administration, has over a period of time transformed into a more substantive power. With the increase in the number of judges from the original eight to thirty-four, it has transformed into the authority to potentially determine the outcome of a case by deciding who will hear it.

It was the arbitrary exercise of this power by the then chief justice Dipak Misra in constituting benches that the four sitting judges of the Supreme Court complained of at the unprecedented press conference in 2018. As the judges put it in their letter, 'There have been instances where case (sic) having far-reaching consequences for the Nation and the institution had been assigned by the Chief Justices of this court selectively to the benches "of their preference" without any rationale for such assignment.' On being repeatedly asked at the press conference about the reason for the judges' criticism, Justice Gogoi said that it was prompted by 'issues surrounding the case on the death of special CBI judge B.H. Loya'.[218] Justice Loya was hearing the matter on the encounter death of Sohrabuddin, in which Amit Shah was the accused, in a special court when he died. Justice Loya's family alleged that his death was suspicious. Chief Justice Misra assigned the request for an inquiry into Justice Loya's death to Justice Arun Mishra, who, though a relatively junior judge, was assigned many politically sensitive cases.

Justice Joseph later gave an interview in which he was quoted as saying, 'Someone from outside was controlling the CJI, that is what we felt', and that there were 'signs of influence with regard to allocation of cases to different benches selectively, to select judges who were perceived to be politically biased'.[219]

The possible abuse of the role of the master of roster is also made rather sharply by Justice Shah in a piece in the *EPW*. The untrammelled power of the chief justice to allocate judicial work, he notes, has meant that an executive who wants to control the judiciary need not 'expend energy' in 'packing the Supreme Court' with judges favourable to the administration. This would anyway be difficult as one cannot easily find '30 judges who think alike'. All that is required is a 'certain kind' of chief justice and a 'handful of "reliable" judges' combined with the 'opaque master of the roster' system. This, Justice Shah notes, 'is far from being a hypothetical scenario' and 'is, in fact, playing out in India right now'.[220]

This power of the chief justice to determine the roster, which has had such far-reaching consequences, was challenged in a PIL by eminent senior advocate Shanti Bhushan in 2018, wherein he argued that 'concentration of unbridled powers on a single person was an anathema to democracy' and argued that the power to determine the roster must vest in the 'collegium instead of the CJI alone'.[221] The Supreme Court in its judgement negatived the plea and instead chose to 'accept the submission of Attorney General K.K. Venugopal that allocation of business by collegium will affect the day to day functioning of the Court'.[222]

Unfortunately, the judges in *Shanti Bhushan v Supreme Court of India* saw the master of the roster as a purely administrative device, failing to recognise the genuine dangers the concentration of power in the chief justice pose for the independence of the constitutional court, leaving it vulnerable to the influence of an overweening executive.

Failure to Perform the Role of a Counter-majoritarian Institution

In the span of a single month in September 2018, the Supreme Court delivered three judgements which explicitly privileged an understanding of constitutional morality over the dictates of popular morality. The three issues adjudicated upon were all sensitive matters concerning the criminalisation of homosexuality, adultery and the prohibition of women of a menstruating age from worshipping at the Sabarimala temple in Kerala. In all three cases, the Supreme Court stood up for 'discrete and insular minorities' often at the receiving end of a majoritarian morality.[223]

In *Navtej Singh Johar v Union of India*,[224] the court read down Section 377 of the IPC, which criminalised same-sex conduct, recognising that the Constitution mandated that the 'subject of liberty and dignity of the individual' was 'beyond the reach of majoritarian governments' and the courts had a responsibility to ensure that 'constitutional morality always trumps any imposition of a particular view of social morality by shifting and different majoritarian regimes'. In *Joseph Shine v Union of India*,[225] the court struck down Section 497 of the IPC, which criminalised the act of adultery by a man. The court held that the law on adultery embodied a patriarchal understanding of sexuality that was antithetical to a constitutional morality based on a commitment to the 'free, equal, and dignified existence of all members of society'. In *Indian Young Lawyers Association v State of Kerala*,[226] the Supreme Court, by a majority of four is to one, struck down the regulations prohibiting women from the age of ten to fifty from worshipping at Sabarimala temple, arguing that 'the menstrual status of a woman is deeply personal and an intrinsic part of her privacy' and cannot be the basis on which 'exclusion can be practised' and 'denial perpetrated'. The court explicitly held that in the 'constitutional order of priorities', the 'individual right to freedom of religion' was subject to the 'overriding constitutional postulates of equality, liberty and personal freedoms'.

However, this brief efflorescence of what the court called 'constitutional morality' and 'transformative constitutionalism' was quickly reversed. What signposted the retreat of the court from espousing constitutional morality was the unprecedented decision by the bench constituted to review the Sabarimala judgement. As per the Supreme Court's interpretation of Article 137, the review jurisdiction of the court is legally and constitutionally a narrow one, where the court examines if there is an 'error apparent on the face of the record', and if there is no such error, a review petition is dismissed.[227] However, when the Sabarimala judgement was petitioned for review by the head priest at Sabarimala, Kantaru Rajeevaru,[228] the majority disregarded the technical limits of the review jurisdiction and raised substantive questions and concerns such as 'the need to delineate' the 'contours' of 'constitutional morality', 'lest it become subjective' in their judgement. The court also ignored the fact that the contours of constitutional morality had already been laid down in a plethora of constitutional bench decisions of the Supreme Court, and decided to 'keep the review pending' till the questions they raised were decided by a larger bench of the Supreme Court. Though the review was kept pending and the Sabarimala verdict of 2018 was still the law, the de facto result of the review decision was a return to the status quo with menstruating women again not being allowed to enter the Sabarimala temple.

It is hard to understand this judgement without being familiar with the political exigencies the court was responding to. The period following the Sabarimala verdict witnessed violent protests against the judgement. The charge against the court's ruling was led by the ruling BJP and the RSS, with the then BJP president Amit Shah openly calling for the disobedience of the Supreme Court verdict. He was quoted as saying that a number of court verdicts 'had not been implemented', including the ban on Jallikattu, the traditional bullock-cart race celebrated in Tamil Nadu, the use of loudspeakers in mosques, a Shia-Sunni dispute over a graveyard in Varanasi and the height of the dahi handi—a pot of yoghurt suspended in the air, which men try to break with a stick—during Janmashtami in Maharashtra. 'Why are you after one judgement when there are so many that are not implemented? The governments in this country haven't dared to implement these orders. So, why is the [Kerala] government enthusiastic about implementing the court order on Sabarimala?'[229] He went on to 'advise' the court to 'desist from pronouncing verdicts which cannot be implemented'.[230] It was unprecedented to have a president of a ruling party publicly advocate that the judgement of the Supreme Court not be followed.

In response to this veiled threat to the court to not privilege constitutional morality over majoritarian religious sentiment, the court, instead of standing its ground, buckled. Out of the five judges of the review bench, justices Gogoi, A.M. Khanwilkar and Indu Malhotra signed on to the majority opinion, going beyond the ambit of the review and allowing for the matter to be relitigated.

The minority opinion by justices Chandrachud and Rohinton Fali Nariman gave a sense of the pressures which may have led to reopening the Sabarimala verdict. As the judges noted, '... extreme arguments were made by some learned counsel stating that belief and faith are not judicially reviewable by courts'. The judges reiterated that 'such arguments need to be rejected out of hand' as they flew in 'the face of Article 25'. These arguments did not constitute 'errors apparent on the face of the record', which is the constitutional requirement under Article 137 of the Constitution, and hence did not 'fall within the parameters of a review petition' and deserved to be rejected.

To any observer of contemporary Indian politics, the kinship between the arguments in the court and the arguments on the street, more specifically by high constitutional functionaries, would be apparent. The minority judgement's meaning was quite clear: the political executive was expressing an opinion clearly at odds with the Constitution and it deserved to be rejected.

Justices Nariman and Chandrachud seemed to be troubled by the majority opinion, which had held that 'mass protests against implementation of this judgment' necessitated a 're-look at the entire problem'. The minority rejected this line of argument and held that 'it is no longer open to any person or authority to openly flout a Supreme Court judgment or order'. It went on to say, 'It is necessary for us to restate these constitutional fundamentals in the light of the sad spectacle of unarmed women between the ages of 10 and 50 being thwarted in the exercise of their fundamental right of worship at the Sabarimala temple. Let it be said that whoever does not act in aid of our judgment, does so at his peril—so far as Ministers, both Central and State, and MPs and MLAs are concerned, they would violate their constitutional oath to uphold, preserve, and defend the Constitution of India.' However, the minority opinion was at best the 'intelligence of a future day'.[231]

The majority ignored the fact that members of the ruling party wilfully subverted the rule of law by openly stating that they would not follow the verdict delivered by a constitutional bench of the Supreme Court. By specifically reopening the contents of 'constitutional morality', the Supreme Court, instead of deepening the idea of counter-majoritarianism embedded in *Joseph Shine*, *Navtej* and *Sabarimala*, turned its back on it. It embraced the majoritarian logic articulated by members of the executive and turned a blind eye to the fact that the president of the ruling party was calling for defiance of the court's judgement.

The other critical judgement that highlights a majoritarian shift is the Supreme Court verdict in 2019 in the decades-long Ayodhya controversy.[232] The Babri masjid located in Ayodhya was a disputed site between Hindu and Muslim litigants, both of whom have claimed the right to worship at the spot ever since the nineteenth century. Hindus consider the Babri masjid as the site of Lord Ram's birth, while for Muslims, it had been a place of worship ever since the mosque was constructed in 1528 CE. In the colonial period, the courts granted both parties the right to worship adjacent to each other, and maintained this status quo. This decision, delivered in 1886 by W. Young, the judicial commissioner of Oudh, was a judicious one. It was made in the face of pressure from Hindu litigants 'trying to persistently increase those rights and to erect buildings on two spots in the enclosure, namely the Sita ki Raso and the Ram Chandar ki Janam Bhumi'.[233]

However, since Independence, the status quo was repeatedly and illegally violated, with each violation resulting in a further sanctification of the rights of the Hindu litigants. A Ram idol was installed illegally under the central dome of the Babri masjid in 1949, the locks to the masjid compound were opened and Hindu prayers were allowed to be offered by an order of the district judge, Faizabad, in 1986, and eventually, the Babri masjid building was brought down by a Hindutva mob in 1992. Each of these acts established new 'facts' on the ground, and the law invariably legitimised a new status quo, to the further detriment of the Muslim litigants.

In 2010, the Allahabad High Court delivered a verdict dividing the property where the Babri masjid stood, giving one-third to the Nirmohi Akhara, one-third to 'Ram Lalla'—the deity placed illegally in the mosque in 1949—and one-third to the Sunni Wakf Board.[234] This judgement was overruled in 2019 by a five-judge bench of the Supreme Court, which awarded the whole disputed area to Ram Lalla.

While idols have long been recognised as legal persons in Indian law, it is important to note who represented the deity in this case. Ram Lalla was represented by his 'next friend' Deoki Nandan Agarwal, a former judge of the Allahabad High Court and also once the vice president of the Vishva Hindu Parishad (VHP), a Hindu nationalist organisation which is a part of the Sangh Parivar. In effect, granting Ram Lalla the ownership of the disputed structure was to recognise the VHP as the one who would protect the interest of Ram Lalla as the 'next friend'.[235]

It was this 'next friend', along with ideological cohorts, who were responsible for the demolition of the Babri masjid. As the Justice Liberhan Commission noted, '... the leadership provided by the RSS, BJP, VHP' resulted in the 'victorious battle' of the 'destruction of the disputed structure'.[236] As Justice Shah notes in his critique of the Supreme Court judgement, the court bypassed the principle of equity, that 'one must approach the court with clean hands' and 'effectively rewarded the wrong doer'.[237]

The judges attempted to hold on to the constitutional high ground by defending the Places of Worship Act, 1991, which seeks to 'prohibit conversion of any place of worship from the status it was on 15th August, 1947, excepting the Babri Masjid'. Crucially, the court held that the Places of Worship Act imposes a 'non-derogable obligation towards enforcing our constitutional commitment to secularism'. One can read the upholding of the rationale of the Places of Worship Act as the judges' attempt to compensate for the abysmal failure to ensure that those forces which destroyed the mosque were not rewarded for the destruction. The court held that the law which was enacted post the demolition 'speaks to our history and to the future of the nation. ... Historical wrongs cannot be remedied by the people taking law in their own hands. In preserving the character of places of worship, parliament has mandated in no uncertain terms that history and wrongs shall not be used as instruments to oppress the present and the future'.[238]

In plain words, the court did not do justice to the Muslims who suffered the takeover of the mosque by the Hindus, but held out a promise that a similar injustice would not occur again. The court agreed that there could be no 'retrogression into the past' post Independence. It held this principle of 'non retrogression' as foundational to 'secularism'. In effect, the soothing balm applied to those who were wronged by the judgement was an edict to tolerate this on the assurance that the same fate would not befall any other place of worship.

However, it remains to be seen if the court will stand firm and continue to affirm this part of the judgment. The first salvo against the preservation of the status quo of existing places of worship has been fired with the court admitting a petition by BJP leader and advocate Ashwini Kumar Upadhyay challenging the constitutionality of the Places of Worship Act on the ground that the cut-off date of 15 August 1947 is arbitrary.[239] This petition will only increase the sense of unease among minorities and concerns about whether the court will renege on its commitment to not open for debate the status quo at existing places of worship.

Justice Shah simply reads the Sabarimala and Ayodhya judgements as the 'Court turning away from decades of its own history' and 'instead, aligning with the majoritarian view unhesitatingly and without question'.[240]

Use of Contempt Jurisdiction to Limit the Freedom of Speech and Expression

The failure of the Supreme Court to protect the freedom of speech and expression appears to be evident in the way it has dealt with the arrests of the BK-16 and the anti-CAA protestors as well as in the arrests in Kashmir post the abrogation of Article 370. Some of those arrested, in spite of flimsy evidence linking them to the alleged crime, continue to be behind bars. In Kashmir, the writ of habeas corpus has not functioned as the guardian of individual liberty. The Supreme Court has abdicated its constitutional responsibility of being a 'sentinel on the qui vive', a watchful guardian, writes Justice Shah.

The frustration with the passive role taken by the court was expressed by many. However, when citizens sought to bring its failures home, as it were, the Supreme Court took objection to the exercise of freedom of speech and expression. The court took umbrage against well-known social activist and lawyer Prashant Bhushan for two tweets he put out during the first nationwide COVID-19 lockdown in 2020.

In what has popularly come to be called the 'Two Tweets Case', the Supreme Court, in a bench headed by Justice Arun Mishra, decided to proceed suo motu against Bhushan in the exercise of its contempt jurisdiction. The two tweets which were the subject matter of the contempt notice were:

> The CJI rides a Rs 50-lakh motorcycle belonging to a BJP leader at Raj Bhavan, Nagpur, without wearing a mask or helmet, at a time when he keeps the SC on lockdown mode denying citizens their fundamental right to access justice!

> When historians in the future look back at the last six years to see how democracy has been destroyed in India even without a formal emergency, they will particularly mark the role of the SC in this destruction, and more particularly the role of the last four CJIs. [241]

In his reply affidavit to the contempt notice, Bhushan went into great detail to establish the bona fides of his opinion that the last four chief justices of India had a role to play in the destruction of democracy in the country by not performing their constitutional duty of 'being a check and balance on the power of the executive' and by not 'ensuring that the Supreme Court functions in a transparent and accountable manner'. [242] Bhushan, a long-term legal and social activist, substantiated his opinion through a detailed list of failings of the court, which included charges of corruption, sexual harassment, an unhealthy closeness to the executive as well as allegations of quid pro quo.

With respect to the first tweet, the court held that it was 'undoubtedly false, malicious and scandalous' and had the 'tendency to shake the confidence of the public at large in the institution of judiciary'. The second tweet, said the court, had 'the effect of destabilising the very foundation of this very important pillar of democracy'. Based on this finding, the court held Bhushan guilty of contempt. [243] However, it is not immediately apparent from the judgement how the tweets by themselves undermine the dignity of the court, as the court provides no further rationale, other than to assert that the majesty of the law was affronted.

The judgement did not engage with Prashant Bhushan's 142-page affidavit justifying the two tweets as an 'expression of opinion, however outspoken, disagreeable or unpalatable to some' which 'cannot constitute contempt of court'.[244] The judgement by the Supreme Court was criticised in an open letter signed by 3,000 people, including twelve former judges, lawyers, retired bureaucrats and retired police officers. It read:

> To hold that such criticism shakes the foundations of the judiciary and needs to be dealt with an iron hand, appears to be a disproportionate response which could, in fact, diminish the reputation of the Court. ... Every institution in a democracy has to earn the public's affection and respect, and the hallmark of a strong institution is its openness to public scrutiny and commentary. ... Stifling of criticism by stakeholders does not bode well for any institution, especially the highest court in the country.[245]

Bhushan, in a statement post his conviction, noted that the 'two tweets represented my bonafide beliefs, the expression of which must be permissible in any democracy', that 'public scrutiny is desirable for healthy functioning of judiciary itself' and that 'open criticism of any institution is necessary in a democracy, to safeguard the constitutional order'.[246]

He went on to vigorously defend the tweets, saying, 'My tweets were nothing but a small attempt to discharge what I considered to be my highest duty at this juncture in the history of our republic.' His justification for them was of someone unwilling to surrender his freedom. He quoted Mahatma Gandhi's words after being convicted of sedition: 'I do not ask for mercy. I do not appeal to magnanimity. I am here, therefore, to cheerfully submit to any penalty that can lawfully be inflicted upon me for what the Court has determined to be an offence, and what appears to me to be the highest duty of a citizen.'

Bhushan's clear-sighted and morally compelling defence of his tweets as well as the support within the legal and judicial fraternity boosted the perception of him not as a contemnor but as a defender of freedom of speech and expression.[247]

A week later, pronouncing the sentence for an offence which it had characterised as 'destabilising the very foundation of democracy', the court sentenced Bhushan to 'a fine of Rs 1' and on failing to pay the fine, he was to undergo imprisonment for three months and be debarred from practice for three years.[248] There was a mismatch between the court's understanding of the 'gravity' of the offence and the punishment it awarded. The nominal punishment awarded to Bhushan by the bench headed by Justice Arun Mishra leads one to speculate that it could be the result of the pushback from the academia, media and judiciary against the judgement.[249]

Anuradha Bhasin: The Sanctification of Executive Supremacy

Alongside the preventive detention of almost the entire political leadership of Kashmir, the abrogation of Article 370 was followed by internet access being cut to the entire Kashmir valley, plunging the state into an information and communication black hole.

As noted earlier, the Supreme Court was yet to even hear the challenge to the abrogation of Article 370 as of October 2021, and had not shown any sense of urgency in speedy hearing and disposal of the habeas corpus petitions before it. It did, however, hear and decide on the petition against the blanket shutdown of all 'modes of communication including internet, mobile and fixed line communication' filed by *Kashmir Times* editor Anuradha Bhasin and Congress leader Ghulam Nabi Azad in *Anuradha Bhasin v Union of India*.[250]

The main petitioner, Bhasin, was impelled to approach the Supreme Court under Article 32 because the total communication blackout had 'silenced almost the entire local media'. She was unable to get 'in touch with her reporters' and get a grasp of the 'situation on the ground'. She was deprived of information when her profession needed her to be in the know. In Bhasin's experience as a journalist from Kashmir, even during the worst unrest, such as in '2008, 2010 and 2016', a 'complete blackout' had 'never happened before'.[251]

The petitioners argued that the total shutdown of the internet for the entire state did not meet the constitutional standard of proportionality. Kapil Sibal, representing the petitioners, argued that 'the least restrictive option should have been put in place, and the State should have taken preventive or protective measures. Ultimately, the State needs to balance the safety of the people with their lawful exercise of their fundamental rights'. He submitted that 'a less restrictive measure, such as restricting only social media websites like Facebook and Whatsapp, should and could have been passed'.

The government, defending the total shutdown, based its argument on the State being the best judge of whether to permit the internet or not as it was a question of 'national security'. The opacity of State action extended to not providing access to the orders under which the internet was shut down. It was only after the court's insistence that the Central government even produced some of the orders under which the internet shutdown in Jammu and Kashmir was given legal status.

The court, which took exception to this standard of opacity, reasoned that 'Article 19 has been interpreted to mandate right to information' and that 'a democracy, which is sworn to transparency and accountability, necessarily mandates the production of orders as it is the right of an individual to know'. The court also delivered a rare rebuke, observing that the 'state has to act in a responsible manner to uphold Part III of the Constitution and not to take away these rights in an implied fashion or in casual and cavalier manner'.

The court came to the conclusion that the argument of 'national security' did not obviate the scrutiny of the court. It held, 'As emergency does not shield the actions of Government completely; disagreement does not justify destabilisation; the beacon of rule of law shines always.' The court conceded that it does not sit in appeal on State decisions with respect to national security as the 'State is best placed to make an assessment of threat to public peace and tranquillity or law and order'. But, the court noted, the 'law requires' the government to 'state the material facts for invoking this power' as 'this will enable judicial scrutiny and a verification of whether there are sufficient facts to justify the invocation of this power'. The court thus held that 'the existence of the power of judicial review is undeniable'.

In the court's view, the State's actions were not of the nature of prerogative power requiring no explanation but rather were to be guided by the principle of proportionality. As the court put it, '... the principle of proportionality could be easily summarized by Lord Diplock's aphorism, you must not use a steam hammer to crack a nut, if a nutcracker would do'. A key dimension of the proportionality analysis was for the court to consider if the measure was 'disproportionate in its interference with the fundamental right' and whether 'a less intrusive measure could have been adopted consistent with the object of the law'.

The court gestured towards the 'disproportionate impact' of the total communication ban when it stated, 'the importance of internet cannot be underestimated', and that 'our most basic activities are enabled by the use of internet'. The 'disproportionate' nature of the shutdown is also recognised in the judgement in which the court directed the State to 'consider forthwith allowing government websites, localized/limited e-banking facilities, hospitals services and other essential services, in those regions, wherein the internet services are not likely to be restored immediately'.

However, the court fell shy of acting as an independent third pillar of the State and finding that the executive had indeed violated the rights of the petitioner through disproportionate State action. Instead, it delivered what could only be described as an advisory opinion when it 'direct[ed] the respondent State/competent authorities to review all orders suspending internet services forthwith' and enjoined the State that 'orders not in accordance with the law laid down above, must be revoked'.

Although the court admirably articulated the standards which should govern State action, it did not adjudicate on whether these standards had been followed in the facts before the court. This grave constitutional responsibility was outsourced back to the government. Thus, in its operative part, the court did not follow up on its own judicial findings and deliver any meaningful relief to the millions of Kashmiris who were affected by this disproportionate State action nor did it penalise the government for having comprehensively violated the constitutional principles, laid down by the court itself, within which it must function.

The fact that the court did not seriously test the State's claims was further buttressed in its decision in *Foundation for Media v Union Territory of Jammu and Kashmir,*[252] which was delivered four months after *Anuradha Bhasin* in May 2020. After the partial restoration of the communication network following the *Anuradha Bhasin* judgement, the court was asked to adjudicate on whether the continued ban on 3G and 4G was constitutionally valid. The petitioners argued that the restriction of internet speed to 2G had an adverse impact on the rights of the Jammu and Kashmir residents to health, education and business, as well as freedom of speech and expression. The court noted that while it may be 'desirable to have better internet', it could not ignore the fact that 'outside forces' were 'trying to infiltrate the borders and destabilize the integrity of the nation'.

In *Foundation for Media*, the court did not even articulate the standards it had in *Anuradha Bhasin* but instead simply referred the matter to a committee of bureaucrats 'to look into the prevailing circumstances and immediately determine the necessity of the continuation of the restrictions' in the region.

There was no reference to the 'doctrine of proportionality', and so the committee was not explicitly mandated to decide with reference to any constitutional standards. Even if it were mandated to do so, the committee was a creature of the executive and could not be expected to go against the will of the government even if it violated constitutional principles. In effect, the court outsourced its core function of ensuring the executive acts within the constraints of the Constitution to the executive itself, doing great damage to the theory of separation of powers.

Easy Complicity Between the Executive and the Judiciary

The closeness between the executive and the judiciary through the chief justiceship of Misra, Gogoi and Bobde during 2017–21 is perhaps best symbolised by Gogoi taking oath as a nominated member of the Rajya Sabha four months after retiring from the Supreme Court. Gogoi said that he accepted the nomination because of his 'strong conviction that the legislative and the judiciary must at some point of time work together for nation-building'. He asserted that his 'presence in Parliament will be an opportunity to project the views of the judiciary before the legislature and vice versa'.[253]

The only other precedent for this was the election of former chief justice of India Ranganath Mishra to the Rajya Sabha on a Congress ticket in 1998, seven years after his retirement.[254] However, compared to the impropriety of Ranganath Mishra, Gogoi's acceptance of a nomination to the Rajya Sabha a mere four months after retirement raises more fundamental questions about the independence of his judgements pertaining to 'important constitutional lodestars: Habeas corpus, non-discriminatory citizenship, the evidence act, federalism, free speech', as Pratap Bhanu Mehta points out in an article for the *Indian Express*. 'The very fact that a judge accepts such an appointment', writes Mehta, 'could cast doubt on his judgements. It would signal that the judiciary is not independent, but lives for crumbs thrown by the executive'.[255] As Justice Shah told NDTV, '… the message it sends to the judiciary as a whole is that if you give judgments that are favourable to the executive, you will be rewarded. If you don't do so, you will be treated adversely or you might be transferred or not considered for elevation.' He called it a 'death knell for the separation of powers and the independence of the judiciary'.[256]

In his blog, legal scholar Gautam Bhatia argues that Gogoi's tenure saw the drift of the Supreme Court from 'an institution that—for all its patchy history—was at least *formally* committed to the protection of individual rights as its primary task, to an institution that speaks the language of the executive, and has become indistinguishable from the executive'.[257] Bhatia sees this drift to an executive-minded court in Gogoi's use of 'sealed cover jurisprudence' while he was the chief justice.[258] The executive was asked to submit replies in sealed covers on the basis of which the judiciary would pass orders. The contents of the 'sealed cover' were not known to the other parties to the litigation. This fundamentally impinges on the right to a fair trial. Justice Gogoi used this mode in litigations on Rafale, electoral bonds and Assam NRC, as well as in many other matters, rendering justice opaque.[259]

Former Supreme Court judge Lokur writes in the *Wire* how, in 2019, under the chief justiceship of Gogoi, a bench headed by Justice N.V. Ramana denied the petitioners a copy of the final Juvenile Justice Committee report on the detention of children in Kashmir with the report being submitted in a sealed cover to the court. The court dismissed the petition filed by child rights activists Enakshi Ganguly and others asking for a copy of the report.[260] As Justice Lokur puts it, 'The right to know and the right to information are now passé—secrecy is the name of the game in which the state has been given the upper hand by the courts.' The sealed cover, writes Lokur, also became the way the court chose 'to cloak the response to the sexual harassment allegation against the former CJI Gogoi' with 'even the complainant not being entitled to a copy of the same'.[261]

This sealed cover jurisprudence shields executive action. By allowing for secrecy where there should be transparency, the court allows the writ of the executive to run unchallenged, abdicating its constitutional responsibility.

Legitimising the Prerogative State

The judiciary in the Modi era has shown an unconstitutional faith in the executive. The judgements in cases like *Anuradha Bhasin* and *Foundation for Media* seem to be legitimising the lawless actions of the executive—much like the judgement in *ADM Jabalpur* did.

This dynamic of the increasing power of the executive vis-à-vis the judiciary is best conceptualised by Ernst Fraenkel, a German Jewish labour lawyer writing in the middle of Nazi rule. His book *The Dual State* was conceived in 'an atmosphere of lawlessness and terror' based on 'impressions that were forced upon [him] day in, day out' and 'out of the need to make sense of these experiences theoretically in order to be able to cope with them'.[262]

Fraenkel's thesis is that Nazi Germany was an uneasy coexistence of two States, one of which he calls the 'normative state' that generally respects its own laws, and the other a 'prerogative state' that violates the very same laws.[263] For Fraenkel, '... the essence of the prerogative state is its refusal to accept legal restraint, i.e. any "formal" bonds".'[264] He characterises the prerogative State as 'institutionalized lawlessness', with the 'absence of boundaries being its very nature'.[265] The prerogative State, in his analysis, seeks to constantly expand its jurisdiction as it 'advances into the province of the normative state'. [266]

Was there a role for the German judiciary in this dynamic set-up of the expanding of the prerogative State and the shrinking of the normative State? Was the judiciary the defender of the normative State from the executive, which sought to dismantle it, or did it instead entrench and expand the prerogative State?

In Fraenkel's analysis, the judiciary did not resist the entrenchment of the prerogative State. Thus, when the executive authorised imprisonment without trial, the judiciary silently acquiesced in the new status quo. Germany was a country in which thousands could be 'incarcerated for years without being convicted in a court of law', possessions could be 'seized without judicial authorization', and lives could be 'destroyed without recourse to law'.[267] Implicit in this statement is the fact that the judiciary did nothing to defend the rights of an accused to be tried in accordance with law.

Apart from not resisting the expanded jurisdiction of the executive, the judiciary also moulded its decisions to suit the new political dispensation. Fraenkel cites examples of 'ordinary courts' aligning their conduct in line with the prerogative State by 'voluntary abdication of their powers of judicial review'. He cites a judgement regarding the Reichstag Fire Decree, which had 'permitted the regime to arrest and incarcerate political opponents without specific charge, dissolve political organizations, and to suppress publications'.[268] The judgement regarding the legality of the decree ruled it legitimate and removed 'all federal and state restraints on the power of the police to whatever extent is required for the execution of the aims promulgated in the decree. ... In addition to issuing a blank check to the powers at the helm of the prerogative state, the judges placed an arbitrary and immovable limitation on judicial review: "The question of appropriateness and necessity is not subject to appeal."'[269]

Going one step further, the judiciary, apart from acquiescing in executive actions, even shaped new principles of law to suit the regime. International relations scholar Jens Meierhenrich, who wrote an introduction to Fraenkel's *The Dual State*, observes that judges who were 'nominal representatives of the normative state' used their 'discretion ... to continue the general dismantling of the normative state, even introducing "novel" principles of law'. He draws attention to Fraenkel's citation of a judgement which held that 'in serious cases of high treason ... an adequate sentence has to be imposed in all circumstances regardless of all legal principles. The protection of state and people is more important than the adherence to formalistic rules of procedure which are senseless if applied without exception'. This judgement, in effect, set aside the well established legal principle that no person can be tried for the same offence twice, when it came to trying offences such as treason. The court internalised the ethos of the executive and, according to Fraenkel, 'degraded its status to that of an instrument of the prerogative state'.[270]

India is today at the heart of the expanding jurisdiction of the prerogative State, especially in the context of preventive detention laws and its latest and most deadly avatar, the UAPA. Under the regime of the UAPA, executive authority is dramatically increased in relation to the prisoner, with longer periods of pre-trial detention under the statute and the difficulty, if not impossibility, of release on bail. The detention of some of the Bhima Koregaon accused for over three years without bail or trial as well as the detention of the anti-CAA protestors without bail or trial points to the expanding contours of the prerogative State. The Supreme Court has legitimised this exercise of State power by allowing the status quo of continued detention without trial. The BK-16 are only emblematic of the arrest of thousands of civil society activists under the UAPA without adequate review by the courts. The unchecked and arbitrary invocation of the UAPA against peaceful protestors and civil society activists is reminiscent of the instrumental use of the law against dissenters in apartheid South Africa, Nazi Germany and during the Emergency of 1975 in India.

This dynamic of the 'dual State' is captured in the continued expansion of the powers of the executive in India. For instance, the Uttar Pradesh Special Security Force Ordinance, 2020, passed by the BJP-ruled Yogi Adityanath government, gives any 'member of the force' the power to preventively detain a person without warrant and without authorisation from the magistrate if there is a 'reasonable suspicion' against the person that they are going to commit an offence related to property as defined in the Act.[271] According to senior advocate Farman Naqvi, there is no provision for production of the arrested before a magistrate and for knowing the whereabouts of the arrested person, as the police will not disclose where they have detained the person.[272] The conduct of the officer concerned cannot be challenged in the courts, as they are barred from taking cognisance without sanction of the state government.[273] The Special Security Force has been ostensibly set up to protect courts, airports, administrative buildings, metros and banks among other government offices, but its real aim seems to be to grant unchecked powers of arrest to members of the force.

This is an expansion of the prerogative State without any check by the judiciary. Interestingly, Farman Naqvi writes in his blog that it is not 'far fetched' to compare this to the Nazi secret police, as the 'Gestapo was also created with the sole purpose to quell dissent'.[274] The Indian judiciary is yet to examine whether this statute, which increases the power of arrest without the authorisation of the magistrate or production before the magistrate, is constitutional.

In *Anuradha Bhasin* and more particularly in *Foundation for Media*, the

Supreme Court conceded executive supremacy in the absence of any law authorising the same. The judiciary brought itself into alignment with the viewpoint of the executive on the mere argument of 'national security' put forward by the State. What makes the judiciary concede its own jurisdiction to the executive? Although, at the level of legal justification, national security was put forward as the reason, at a deeper level, it is possibly due to a culture of fear generated by executive action. The unexplained death of Justice Loya, for instance, when he was overseeing a politically charged trial in which the accused was the current home minister and the inability of the higher judiciary to ensure that there was a transparent investigation into the death of one of their own is compelling evidence that the judiciary is not immune to the State's cruel excesses.[275]

Finally, the higher judiciary has also rewritten established rules of law, thereby establishing a new jurisprudence. Criminal lawyer and academic Abhinav Sekhri points to some of these forms of rewriting in a post on the blog of Gautam Bhatia,[276] when he references the order by a division bench of the Jammu and Kashmir High Court regarding the detention in 2019 of Mian Abdool Qayoom, the seventy-six-year-old president of the state's High Court Bar Association. The high court held that the preventive detention of Qayoom was on the basis of his 'ideology':

> Having considered the matter, we may say that an ideology of the nature reflected in the FIRs and alleged against the detenue herein is like a live volcano. The ideology has always an inclination, a natural tendency to behave in a particular way; It is often associated with an intense, natural inclination and preference of the person to behave in the way his ideology drives him to achieve his latent and expressed objectives and when he happens to head or leading a group, as the allegations contained in the FIRs suggest, his single point agenda remains that his ideology is imbued in all those whom he leads. ... So far as the ideology attributed in the FIRs is concerned, public disorder is its primary object and surviving factor.[277]

The high court, points out Sekhri, after laying out the doctrine of 'ideology' as a ground for preventive detention, went on to further insulate the executive from any form of judicial oversight by holding that 'subjective satisfaction of the detaining authority to detain a person or not is not open to objective assessment by a court. A court is not a proper forum to scrutinize the merits of administrative decision to detain a person'.

The court's reasoning ignored the fact that *ADM Jabalpur*, which held that the order of detention could not be subject to judicial scrutiny, stood annulled after the decision of the Supreme Court in *Puttaswamy v Union of India*, which expressly overruled *ADM Jabalpur*, holding that it had to be buried 'ten fathoms deep' with 'no chance of resurrection'.[278]

As Sekhri argues, 'The J&K High Court has, seemingly unwittingly, shown us a system that runs on punishing thoughts and beliefs. Only, here, we have no punishment with a trial and courts, but prevention, with the executive serving as judge, jury, and executioner.' If the high court was manifestly in error in ignoring *Puttaswamy* and in evolving a new rule of jurisprudence based on punishing thought, then it was up to the Supreme Court to correct the error.

Bhatia, in his blog, excoriates the judgement of the Supreme Court when the matter went up on appeal. He notes that the court seemed to express relief at the fact that both parties had agreed to the release of Qayoom on certain conditions and hence 'we are not called upon to examine the legality and validity of the impugned judgments and we leave it at that'. According to Bhatia, 'the Supreme Court had the opportunity to correct the High Court in its failure to appreciate the constitutional contours of freedom of thought and conscience as well as the failure to appreciate the dictum in *Puttaswamy*, but the Court let the opportunity pass.'[279]

This allows for the growing salience of new ideas which have no basis in the text of the Constitution and calls to mind Fraenkel's description of how Nazi courts convicted on the basis of ideology:

The Supreme Administrative Court of Saxony (Oberver-waltungsgericht) refused to be outdone by this decision and denied a permit to a midwife because she was suspected of being a member of the Jehovah's Witnesses with the following argument: It is indeed true that until now Mrs. K. has not participated in any activities hostile to the people or the state. Nonetheless, her remarks leave no doubt that if a situation were to arise in which the orders of the state clashed with her interpretation of the Bible and with the commandments of 'Jehovah,' she would not hesitate to decide against the people and its leadership. ... Although persons of the type of Mrs. K. individually can scarcely be said to constitute a danger to the state, their attitudes and opinions encourage those who actually are enemies of the state and promote their destructive activities.[280]

In India today, the prerogative State has made significant inroads into the normative State, aided in no small part by such acts of omission and commission by the judiciary. A range of legislations and executive actions which should have been subjected to a searching constitutional scrutiny have not yet been heard. Where the judiciary should have adjudicated on constitutionality of executive actions, it has outsourced the job right back to the executive and, dangerously, it has articulated principles which mirror the unconstitutional thinking of the executive.

4

Slouching Towards a
Totalitarian Future

And what rough beast, its hour come round at last,
Slouches towards Bethlehem to be born?[1]

— W.B. Yeats

WHILE THE CURRENT MODI REGIME MIRRORS THE AUTHORITARIAN
one of the Emergency, it also has features which make it inaugural.
These features call to mind Juan Linz's description of totalitarianism
as a 'regime form for completely organizing political life and society'.[2]
In Linz's analysis, the ambitions of a totalitarian government are far
wider and its abilities far deeper than those of an authoritarian one. A
totalitarian rule goes beyond retaining total control over the State to
trying to 'politicise the masses' and shaping individuals in accordance
with its ideology. It draws its strength and support not just from its
control over the levers of the State but also from organisational fronts
which work at the societal level, aiming to transform society in terms
of its ideology. A combination of these factors—of having an ideology
as well as many organisational fronts—results in totalitarianism having
an 'appeal', compared with the 'generally passive acceptance of
authoritarian regimes'.[3]

One of the significant differences between the Emergency period and the contemporary era is that the former did not have a popular base. Once the Emergency was declared, there was a desperate attempt to shore it up with people's support, but in vain. The State used propaganda to 'promote the twenty point program' and 'Sanjay's notorious family planning campaigns', as Gyan Prakash notes. The propaganda was only indicative of the State's desperation to reach people. But, as Gyan Prakash perceptively notes, the people were not enthused, with the popular mood being 'sullen, not enthusiastic'. The lack of popular support during the Emergency is in striking contrast to 1930s Italy and Germany, when 'the coercive state operated' with 'the mobilization and militarization of mass society'. In the Emergency era, there were 'no paramilitary squads like those in Fascist Italy and Nazi Germany, no populist mobilization around nationalism'. [4]

The current government, in contrast, has been able to garner popular support based on its ideological moorings in Hindutva. The most visible campaigns of this government—around anti-conversion laws, cow slaughter laws, anti–'love jihad' laws or the building of the Ram temple in Ayodhya—are all rooted in Hindutva ideology and are popular with a significant section of the people. Even the brazen language of hate deployed against the Muslim as not belonging to India and the constant reiteration of the superiority of Hindu culture over others, especially Islam, contributes to the regime's popularity.

The Modi rule has shored up popular support and legitimised it in many ways. For one thing, unlike an authoritarian regime which is dependent on the coercive power of the State alone, the current regime draws support from the vast civil society networks of the RSS, members of which actively work to transform society along the lines of Hindutva ideology. Two, as with most totalitarian regimes, the two-term BJP government has supplemented the power of the State with that of a mob which enforces its will regardless of the constitutional requirements of rule of law. Lynching has increased manifold since the BJP came to power. Three, the project of societal transformation is also carried out through fake news and hate speech aimed at altering the societal common sense. And finally, the law, till now largely secular, is being used to systematise a Hindutva framework. The beginnings of this project are visible in the laws which set in place unequal citizenship, like the CAA, laws which interfere with freedom to eat the food of one's choice, like the ban on beef, laws which impede the freedom of profession and trade, such as cow slaughter laws, and laws which dictate which faith one can follow and who one can marry, such as the anti-conversion laws.

While all these seem to be based on a majoritarian understanding of the subcontinent's history and culture, these are not the only changes being implemented by the current government. As much as the stress is on the social and cultural dimensions of the programme, far-reaching economic changes are also being implemented which further marginalise the concerns of labour, environment and public health. Though these may be less visible, they are an integral part of the agenda of the current regime.

The shifts analysed below point to the birth of a 'rough beast' slouching its way towards a totalitarian future.

The People Become a Mob

Ever since the Modi government came to power, there has been an intensification of mob lynching. As much as 90 per cent of religious hate crimes since 2009 have occurred after Modi led the BJP to power at the Centre in 2014, as the data compiled by the India Spend media group shows.[5]

From the murder of Mohammed Akhlaq for supposedly having beef in his house in 2015 to the lynching of Pehlu Khan on the 'suspicion of smuggling cattle' and the knifing of Junaid Khan over an argument on seat-sharing in a train in 2017,[6] India has witnessed the rise of the lawless mob, which has with impunity attacked Muslims, Dalits and Adivasis. This lynching culture has extended to just about anyone perceived as different and hence construed to be a threat, including migrants, women suspected to be 'witches' and men suspected to be child abusers, sometimes mistakenly. There are 'many different kinds of mobs' in India today, notes journalist Ravish Kumar in *The Free Voice*. 'One mob might set out on the issue of cow slaughter; another on the equally spurious issue of love jihad; yet another because a certain film was made. The social structures of different mobs are distinct in themselves, but they all have one thing in common: the cloak of religious fervor.'[7]

While the mob inflicts mindless, brutal violence on persons who have committed no crime, the crimes of the mob are often documented by the perpetrators themselves and forwarded as WhatsApp videos. They often take place in broad daylight, indicating that the mob does not fear the law enforcement authorities. Lynchings are also characterised by a sexualised form of brutal violence in which the public seems not only to participate but revel.

A sense of the brutality of lynchings emerges from some of the narratives documented by one of India's best-known civil society activists Harsh Mander, and his team, chronicled in *Scroll.in*. Mander went on a 'Karwan e Mohabbat', or caravan of love, crisscrossing the country to meet with and console the families of those lynched.[8]

On one stop, the Karwan team met the family of an Oraon man in Jharkhand who was lynched on the suspicion of killing a cow. When the family washed the body of Prakash Lakra, 'they wept as they saw the way many bones of his body were smashed. But what agonised them most was when they found that his penis had been mutilated. It was a cruelty they could not fathom. Villagers said later that the word went around that this was done as a message to all future "cow-killers". "It is Muslims who eat the meat of cows," they taunted. "If you want to be a Muslim, be one properly—therefore, we circumcised him."'[9]

Elsewhere, the team met the family of Zainul Ansari. Ansari had got caught on his way home in the middle of a mob which was incensed by the rumour that stones had been thrown at a Durga statue from a mosque as a Durga Puja procession passed by it. In fury, the crowd turned into a lynch mob and fell upon Ansari, raining blows on him with their sticks and iron pipes.

In a now-commonplace pattern, members of the mob also took videos and photographs of the lynching. ... The photographs show that the crowd had many young men, teenagers, even children, and at least one woman and a young child are clearly visible wielding large iron pipes as weapons. It appears from the photographs that the crowd bludgeoned the old man with sticks and the iron pipes, and hit him on the head and other parts of his body. [...] The police station is barely a five-minute drive from where Ansari was slaughtered, in the middle of a busy market square, and it was mid-morning. Yet the police did not come on time to save the man's life. By the time they did come, the man's body was charred beyond recognition, his face unrecognisable, his limbs entirely burned. [10]

What is troubling about these lynchings is the combination of brutal violence, the indifference of the police and the turning of the moral order on its head with the perpetrators feeling neither shame nor guilt but rather pride in their deed, often taking pictures of the lynchings and putting them on social media.

The phenomenon of lynching was taken cognisance of by the Supreme Court in 2018 in the case of *Tehseen S. Poonavala v Union of India*.[11] The court decried lynching as an 'affront to the rule of law and to the exalted values of the Constitution itself'. The court asserted that 'lynching by unruly mobs and barbaric violence arising out of incitement and instigation cannot be allowed to become the order of the day'. It cited affidavits filed by the Gujarat and Uttar Pradesh governments, both of which designated nodal officers to 'curb such illegal activities'. The court issued guidelines for taking preventive, remedial and punitive measures to tackle the 'tumultuous dark clouds of vigilantism'. These guidelines focus on the creation of an enforcement structure within the police force consisting of a nodal officer to deal specifically with lynching. The secretary of the home department of the concerned state governments was enjoined to issue directives to these nodal officers to be 'extra cautious' if any such instances of mob violence came to their notice. The Central and state governments were urged to 'broadcast on radio and television' and 'other media platforms' that 'lynching and mob violence of any kind shall invite serious consequences under the law'. Among the remedial measures, the state government was to 'prepare a lynching/mob violence victim compensation scheme' in the light of Section 357A of the CrPC, which mandates state governments to prepare a more general victim compensation scheme.

However, the judgement of the Supreme Court has been more honoured in its breach. This is illustrated most poignantly in the lynching of the police officer Subodh Kumar Singh in Bulandshahr of Uttar Pradesh in December 2018, a mere five months after the *Tehseen S. Poonavala* judgement was delivered. Media reports indicate that Singh 'was attacked by a mob of around 400 people when he went to restore calm in the area where violence had erupted with the [alleged] finding of carcasses of 25 cows. The police said a man armed with an axe chopped off two of his fingers and hit him on the head. Others shot him. His body was found inside his official police vehicle, abandoned in a field'.[12]

The reasons behind Singh's lynching may lie in the fact that he was a committed and efficient police officer who was not afraid to perform his duty. He was the first officer appointed to investigate the killing of Mohammad Akhlaq over rumours of cow slaughter in 2015. His 'prompt action in bringing evidence samples to the lab in time aided the arrest of the accused.'[13] He was transferred to Varanasi within three months.

The investigation of Singh's murder was handed over to a SIT, which chargesheeted and arrested thirty-eight persons, including Bajrang Dal local convenor Yogesh Raj and BJP youth-wing leader Shikhar Agarwal.[14] Almost nine months after the arrest, seven who were alleged to be the conspirators behind the killing were released on bail, including Raj and Agarwal. The released were welcomed by their supporters with garlands and cries of 'Jai Shri Ram'.[15] Tellingly, as of July 2021, the Uttar Pradesh government is yet to file an appeal against the order.[16]

Singh's wife described her husband's death to the *Hindu* as a 'planned lynching of an officer on duty'. 'I waited for a year,' she said, 'for it was for society and his department that he laid down his life. I thought society and the system will get him justice but he was let down.' Mrs Singh suspected a link between his killing and him being the first investigating officer in the Akhlaq lynching case.[17] Singh's son Abhishek told *Firstpost*, 'My father wanted me to be a good citizen who doesn't incite violence in society in the name of religion. Today my father lost his life in this Hindu-Muslim dispute, tomorrow whose father will lose his life?'[18] For seeking to implement the constitutional values of non-discrimination on grounds of religion and the guarantee of the security of life to all, the police officer had to pay with his life.

The impunity vigilantes enjoy owes much to biased investigations that make conviction a distant possibility. Human Rights Watch, in their study titled 'Violent Cow Protection in India',[19] found that the police action was biased, with delays in filing FIRs in cases of vigilante violence. In almost a 'third of the cow-related vigilante killings since 2015', the police filed 'cases against victims or witnesses. In some cases, witnesses turned hostile because of threats from the police or from the accused and their supporters'.

The police end up toeing the line of the political executive of the day. Human Rights Watch quotes Meeran Borwankar, a former police commissioner of Pune, who said, '... the unprofessional conduct of the police in such cases may come from their personal beliefs and bias, as well as what they perceive to be the message from the political leadership'. She added, 'The general atmosphere in the country is that it is our holy duty to save the cow.'

The biased police action has a cascading effect, with judges being presented with insufficient evidence linking the accused to the crime, making an acquittal more likely and cementing the impunity enjoyed by vigilantes.

This troubling sense of impunity for crimes which the Supreme Court has itself described as an 'affront to the rule of law', makes one question whether this is unique to India or other societies have dealt with this problem as well. One example of a society where activism has both helped to make sense of, and gradually bring lynching to an end, is the United States. In fact, the idea of mob justice outside the law originated in the actions of Charles Lynch, whose espousal of informal citizen juries dispensing justice during the years of the American revolution was what gave rise to the term 'lynch law'. [20]

The lynching of Black people disfigured the deep South in the US from the end of the American civil war to the mid-twentieth century. The fight against lynching was initially taken up by activist-journalist Ida Wells and well-known Black scholar W.E.B. Dubois and finally, by organisations such as the National Alliance for the Advancement of Coloured People. Wells was moved by the horrific instances of lynching and she writes that 'thinking of the list of unfortunates ... my eyes filled with tears'. They 'had no requiem, save the night wind, no memorial service to bemoan their sad and horrible fate ... and no record of the time and place of [their] death ... like many a brave Union soldier their bodies lie in many an unknown and unhonoured spot'. [21]

There are at least 5,000 cases of lynchings documented in the history of the US from 1859 to 1861—which historians believe is only a partial figure. [22] Wells, in particular, visited the places where lynchings took place, documented what happened and then publicised the findings of her reports through meetings and editorials in papers. As she put it, the 'lynching record should be allowed to plead, trumpet-tongued, in defence of the slandered dead'. [23] The point of ceaselessly documenting cases of lynching, according to Wells, was to 'give the public the facts, in the belief that there is still a sense of justice in the American people and that it will yet assert itself in the condemnation of outlawry and a defence of oppressed and persecuted humanity'. [24]

This sustained activism brought the issue to the attention of the national media and even the US political leadership was forced to pay attention to it. Wells, in a meeting with the then president William Mckinley, said that 'nowhere in the civilized world save the United States of America do men, possessing all civil and political power, go out in bands of 50 to 50000 to hunt down, shoot, hang or burn to death a single individual unarmed and absolutely powerless'. [25] However, the president chose not to publicly condemn lynchings and Wells notes that the silence of the nation's first citizen had its costs—there was 'a startling spike in the breadth and viciousness of lynchings from 1896 and 1900'.[26] A parallel between the silence of the political leadership in the US in the nineteenth century on the lynching of Blacks and the failure of the Modi regime to unequivocally condemn the lynching of Muslims and Dalits can be instructively drawn. US history teaches that the silence of the political leadership has its costs: the mob perceives an implicit support for the act of lynching, the police perceive that the political leadership wants the accused to be let off, and both factors result in more widespread lynchings.

Nonetheless, determined and relentless campaigning against lynchings in the US, which began in 1892, resulted in fewer lynchings over a period of time. Sustained activism debunked the myths about race and gender underlying lynchings and 'forced many to see how lynching threatened the deepest values of a modern democracy'.[27] However, it still took over eighty years of sustained activism for lynchings to finally end by the 1960s. Since 1918, 200 anti-lynching bills were introduced in the US Congress, none of them passed. Lynching was recognised as a federal crime only on 26 February 2020, when the Emmett Till Antilynching Act became law.[28] That year, apart from the legislative changes, advocacy and activism persuaded ninety members of the US Senate to apologise for failing to enact an anti-lynching law for over 140 years. In India today, although bills have been introduced to tackle lynching in Opposition-ruled states like Rajasthan[29] and West Bengal,[30] they are yet to become law in any part of India.

Apart from taking legislative action against lynching, the struggle to remember and account for the past continues in the US. Important, though long-overdue, steps have been taken. The National Memorial for Peace and Justice in Montgomery, Alabama, was opened in April 2018. This was 'the Nation's first memorial dedicated to the legacy of enslaved Black people, people terrorized by lynching, African Americans humiliated by racial segregation and Jim Crow, and people of color burdened with contemporary presumptions of guilt and police violence'.[31] Despite all these efforts, racism-induced violence against Black people is very much a reality in the US today.

In India, apart from civil society activism and media reporting, the horrors of lynching find few avenues for recording and remembering. With the State failing in its duty to bring the perpetrators to justice, the battle against lynching is at an incipient stage and any effort to remember those lynched is met with determined resistance. For instance, when the Karwan team led by Mander reached Alwar in Rajasthan—to mark the spot where Pehlu Khan, a dairy farmer, was brutally killed on his way back from buying cows—they were stopped by the police. After Mander stood his ground, the Karwan team was finally 'allowed' to publicly mourn the death of Khan by placing 'two fistfuls of marigold flowers' on the nondescript spot where the 'ageing Khan had been cruelly lynched'.[32] Mander's Gandhian mode of wanting to 'wipe every tear from every eye' was significantly different from that of the State, which was at best indifferent and at worst complicit in the lynching.

For now, the victims of lynching only live in the individual memories of those who lose a loved one to this brutalism and any attempt to weld individual injustices into a collective memory is fiercely resisted. This hostility hints at the importance of collective memory. Remembering those who lost their lives to hate crimes is to remember that the Constitution mandates a society based on rule of law. It is to remember that the basis of Indian democracy is not the sentiment of the majority but the protection of the rights of all its citizens.

One of the differences between the lynchings in the US and in India is the justification offered by the mob. In the US, lynching was done to protect a Southern way of life that White society perceived to be threatened. The most elemental threat was seen to be the almost always made-up threat of rape of a White woman by a Black man. As Wells persuasively demonstrated, in the majority of cases of lynching, the accusation of rape was not even made and even where it was, the allegations invariably turned out to be false, with 'the South ... shielding itself behind the plausible screen of defending the honor of its women'.[33] A Black man accused of this crime was believed to be 'deserving of the harshest imaginable punishment. ... The instant verdict of death for this black "crime" was accepted as a kind of elemental truth, an immutable natural reaction. Lynch mobs were compelled to act', notes US historian Philip Dray in *At the Hands of Persons Unknown*.[34]

In India, the mob is driven to act by what Ravish Kumar describes as 'the cloak of religious fervour'. For the mob, the cow is the symbol of a Hindu nation and it justifies its brutal acts as defending the Hindu nation. As Arendt puts it, 'the mob' becomes a 'direct agent' of 'nationalism'.[35] In Kumar's analysis, the perverse logic of 'inciting mobs' to fulfil so-called nationalist agendas is that 'if democracy is the will of the majority, is not a mob the majority?'[36] The mob represents the ethnic nation and is based on a rejection of diversity. For example, in Hitler's Germany, the mob claimed to represent the Aryan nation and targeted those who did not conform to that model of nationhood, be it Jews, homosexuals or other ethnic minorities. In India, those outside the ('upper'-caste) nation are caste and religious minorities.

The mob, as representative of the majoritarian nation, challenges the norms of a liberal democracy. It is defined by 'lawlessness' and attacks liberal democracy as an effete and outmoded form of governance which does not recognise the rightful place of the majority. When liberal democracy is challenged as being non-representative of the majority, the emerging parallel to Hitler's Germany and Mussolini's Italy becomes chillingly evident. As Kumar presciently notes, '... to become a mob, at any place, at any time, is to become Hitler's Germany'.[37]

So, who comprises the mob? According to Arendt, 'The mob is primarily a group in which the residue of all classes are represented. This makes it so easy to mistake the mob for the people, which also comprises all strata of society. While the people in all great revolutions fight for true representation, the mob always will shout for the "strong man," the "great leader". For the mob hates society from which it is excluded, as well as Parliament where it is not represented.'[38]

It is those who stood excluded from society and the benefits of the economy who were the recruits to the mob in Hitler's Germany. Leon Trotsky put forward a similar analysis on who comprised the mob in Tsarist Russia:

Now this man without shoes has become king. An hour ago he was a trembling slave hounded by the police and by hunger. Now he feels like an absolute despot, he can do anything he likes, everything will pass, he is master of life and death. If he feels the urge to do so, he throws an old woman from the window of the third floor to the pavements below, he smashes the skull of a baby with a chair, he rapes a small girl in front of a crowd of people. He shrinks from none of the tortures which only a brain driven mad with liquor and frenzy could contrive. For he can do anything he likes, everything will pass. God bless the Tsar.[39]

One account of who comprises the mob in India today is provided by the Karnataka unit of the PUCL, in a report on the infamous vigilante attack on girls in a Mangalore pub in 2009. The report excavates the background of the members of the right-wing Hindutva group Sri Ram Sene, who carried out the attack:

Those who are part of the Sri Ram Sene and attacked the pub are poor; they have no visible future, no pocket money—they can't go to Coffee Day, for example. They also cannot go out with or even talk to the girls whom they attacked. The fact that these girls don't even look at them but only talk to certain boys increases their anger. They have a lot of anger that they cannot enjoy holidays, that they cannot go to hotels and that they have to carry lunch boxes from home. While on the outside, the attacks seem to be motivated by the ideals of Hindutva, on the inside, it is anger.[40]

The PUCL report points to the ecosystem in which Hindutva establishes a hold on the minds of many. Those who become footsoldiers are often in marginal positions and without social or cultural capital. They are despised by the elites and though they aspire to the lifestyle of the elites, they don't have the means. All of this generates anger at society for being excluded, and is channelled through the mob, which provides the means to vent frustration.

Nobody has analysed what it means for an individual to belong to a mob better than Arendt.

In Arendt's analysis, the mob is an essential aspect of 'totalitarian movements [which] are mass organizations of atomized, isolated individuals'.[41] Being a part of a totalitarian movement in Nazi Germany 'gave the masses of atomized, undefinable, unstable and futile individuals a means of self-definition and identification' which 'restored some of the self-respect they had formerly derived from their function in society' and 'created a kind of spurious stability'. The totalitarian movement's propaganda was able to 'rationalize the essentially futile feelings of self-importance and hysterical security that it offered to the isolated individuals of an atomized society'.[42]

The mob arises out of conditions of socio-economic deprivation, and being part of a mob provides otherwise 'atomized' individuals a sense of 'spurious stability'. This accounts for the fact that the mob in contemporary India is a significant actor, as it was in Nazi Germany and fascist Italy. There is no better indicator of India's slide towards totalitarianism than the threatening presence of the mob as an integral part of its polity.

Hindutva: Ideology and Organisational Forms

While a mob may be able to attract lumpen elements and grow in size seemingly organically, it is undeniable that there is a level of organisation underlying it, alongside an ideology which motivates it and legitimises its actions. In fact, participants in mob violence who believe in Hindutva see themselves as noble warriors protecting the national interest, and it is this ideology of nationalism which allows them to transmute crimes into 'seva' for the nation.

Clues to the ideology that animates this mob can be found in the work of V.D. Savarkar and M.S. Golwalkar, key ideologues of Hindutva. At its core, the doctrine strives to unite and strengthen the Hindu community and assert the superior claim of the Hindus on the territory of India.

Savarkar believed Hindus to be the 'bedrock on which an Indian independent state could be built', as political philosopher Jyotirmaya Sharma writes in *Hindutva*. He believed India's freedom from colonial rule was inextricably linked to 'the independence of our [Hindus] people, our race, our nation'. Hindus had to be 'masters in our own house'.[43] In his essay 'What Is Hindutva?', Savarkar lays down the condition for minority communities to be considered part of the nation:

> Ye who by race, by blood, by culture, by nationality possess almost all the essentials of Hindutva, and has been forcibly snatched out of our ancestral home by the hand of violence—ye, have only to render whole hearted love to our common Mother and recognize her not only as Fatherland (pitribhu) but even as Holyland (Punyabhu); and ye would be most welcome to the Hindu fold.[44]

Savarkar considered India to be a land for only Hindus. If minority communities wanted to belong to the country, they would have to give up their religious faith and 'return' to the Hindu fold.

For Golwalkar, the essence of Hindutva lay in the dissolution of the individual within the collective, be it an organisation, society or the nation. As Sharma writes in *Terrifying Vision*, 'Addressing the Sangh in 1954, he [Golwalkar] likened the annihilation of individuality in favour of the nation to a piece of salt falling in water and losing its existence. What remains of the salt is just the taste ... but the physical form withers away completely.' For Golwalkar, the 'dissolution of individuality was the true indicator of a nation's welfare and progress' and, ultimately, 'the individual becomes the nation itself'.[45]

The most frightening part of the 'terrifying vision' which Sharma highlights is the intolerance of diversity and the effort to shape human beings in one mould. What this production of conformity attacks, in essence, is human individuality, which is the very basis of freedom. This is the imperative of totalitarianism, according to Arendt.

At heart, totalitarian regimes are at war with human individuality. Political philosopher Bhikhu Parekh notes in *Hannah Arendt and the*

Search for a New Political Philosophy that 'a student asking a question in a class room, a man contradicting another in a discussion, a worker organizing a strike' are acts that announce 'the presence of an independent and unpredictable centre of self-consciousness, to which the world must now adjust'.[46] As Parekh observes, it is this quality of being 'unique, creative', and of being able to 'think differently' and be 'capable of unpredictable actions' which totalitarianism wants to subsume under a uniform ideology.[47]

What is this collective in which the individual is to be subsumed? Golwalkar, like Savarkar, believed that the essence of India was 'the Hindu race with its Hindu Religion, Hindu Culture and Hindu Language (the natural family of Sanskrit and her offsprings)', as he writes in *Bunch of Thoughts*. He goes on to say, 'In Hindustan exists and must needs exist the ancient Hindu nation and nought else but the Hindu Nation. All those not belonging to the national i.e. Hindu Race, Religion, Culture and Language, naturally fall out of the pale of real "National" life.'[48]

In his view, the Hindu nation was based on the caste order. As journalist Aakar Patel writes in *Our Hindu Rashtra*, Golwalkar was 'openly enthusiastic about the benefits of caste'—in *Bunch of Thoughts*, the Hindutva leader argues that 'caste kept Hinduism intact' and 'tyranny at bay'. Patel caustically notes that Golwalkar's argument that 'caste kept Hinduism intact while Buddhism surrendered to Islam in Afghanistan is also original'.[49]

This defence of caste has disturbed Dalit activists like Bhanwar Meghwanshi in particular. In *I Could Not Be Hindu*, he notes, '*Bunch of Thoughts* had characterised caste as a unique feature of the Indian social system and had firmly supported it' and that 'what was for Dalits a painful foundation of our lives was for the Sangh thinkers unique, special, something to be proud of'.[50]

But this ideal of the dissolution of the individual in the larger collective of the Hindu nation faces many challenges in India. The Hindu nation in Golwalkar's rendering is reliant on language, preferably Sanskrit or its offspring. This, of course, creates a vast divide as the southern Indian languages do not have a Sanskrit origin. Also, Hindutva leaders, like Golwalkar, believe in perpetuating the caste system and the 'Hindu Rashtra' has, of course, shown no inclination to tackle the problem of caste head on. As Meghwanshi poignantly asks:

> ... in its ninety plus years of existence has the RSS launched a single struggle against caste and untouchability? Dalits wage daily struggles for dignity, from the right to enter temples and perform yagnas, to ride a ceremonial horse to their wedding, or simply to sit quietly on a charpoy outside their own home—where is the Sangh during these struggles, in what little chicken coop does it hide itself?[51]

Unable to address the questions of caste and language that stood in the way of building a Hindu Rashtra, Golwalkar instead focused on his other obsession, the three 'internal threats' to the Hindu nation—Muslims, Christians and Communists.[52] On what was to be done with those designated as 'threats', he was unambiguous in his book *We, or Our Nationhood Defined*:

> To keep up the purity of the race and its culture, Germany shocked the world by her purging the country of the Semitic races—the Jews. Race pride at its highest has been manifested here. Germany has also shown how well nigh impossible it is for races and cultures, having differences going to the root, to be assimilated into one united whole, a good lesson for us in Hindustan to learn and profit by.[53]

It is clear that the thinking of Golwalkar and Savarkar provides the foundational ideology that justifies Hindutva mob action in the country today, based as it is on the elimination of internal differences as well as the purging of those seen to be outsiders in the Hindu nation. Hindutva is not only based on the notion of the collective's supremacy over the individual but is also a fundamental challenge to the idea of territorial nationalism. Not all inhabitants of a nation, according to Hindutva, get equal rights, going against the very basis of the Indian

SLOUCHING TOWARDS A TOTALITARIAN FUTURE

Constitution. Those who are not Hindu, the doctrine propagates, should either be assimilated into Hinduism or live as second-class citizens or be eliminated.

The ideology of leaders has to permeate the consciousness of the people for a movement to coalesce at the ground level. Investigative journalist Ashish Khetan infiltrated the ranks of grassroots-level Hindutva workers, pretending to be a votary of Hindutva. His book *Undercover* shows, among other things, how these workers have absorbed the ideology of Hindutva. During his sting operation, he captured on video Hindutva workers speaking openly of committing murder and rape during the Gujarat pogrom of 2002 and others proudly proclaiming their role in covering up the pogrom at the behest of the state administration. He writes that 'it did not take much to impersonate Hindutvavadis'. Their ideology was not based on any 'real knowledge of the Hindu scriptures', nor were they 'well versed in Hindu religious practice'. Khetan underlines what the ideology meant to them:

Hindutva for the right-wing extremists I interacted with, was a political, rather than religious, commitment; the only devotion necessary was to hate and violence. Spew some abuse in the direction of Muslims and you were most of the way to being welcomed into the fold.[54]

The dissolution of the individual self into a collective self, based on an exclusionary Hindutva nationalism, sets the base for the operation of violent mobs. The sense of belonging to the Hindu nation is buttressed through violent attacks on minorities. The mob claims both nationalism and lawlessness as its birthright.

The work of disseminating Hindutva ideology so it becomes the common sense of the people is carried out by the RSS and the numerous organisations it has spawned. This is done through indoctrination of students, mobilising support among professionals, rewriting Indian history and instigating street-level violence. The RSS and its network of organisations work at every level. Apart from the well-known political wing of the RSS, namely the BJP, there is the VHP and Bajrang Dal, Hindutva's storm troopers, and the Bharatiya Mazdoor Sangh, a trade union, as well as others that are working across different areas in India and even abroad.

Andersen and Damle in their book *Messengers of Hindu Nationalism* document the extent of the RSS's spread. There are platforms and organisations for different spheres of social, cultural, political and professional life. They note that there is the Akhil Bharatiya Vidyarthi Parishad for students, Akhil Bharatiya Adhivakta Parishad for advocates and the judiciary, Arogya Bharati for public health, Bharatiya Mazdoor Sangh for labour, Bharatiya Kisan Sangh for farmers, Bharat Vikas Parishad for social service, Bharatiya Itihas Sankalan Yojana for history, Balagokulam, the children's cultural organisation, Gau Samvardhan for cow protection, etc.[55]

In education, there is the Vidya Bharati network of schools, which, according to its leaders, is RSS 'inspired' but not RSS 'managed', notes scholar Padmaja Nair in a research paper.[56] However, observers such as Meghwanshi are clear that they are 'Sangh led schools'.[57] The focus in the Vidya Bharati school network is on 'developing generations of young men who will have complete faith in Hindu values and ideals' and 'will be nationalists to the core'.[58] Established in 1967, this organisation has spread rapidly throughout the country with '13,067 schools, 1,50,190 teachers and 34,75,757 students', as Meghwanshi details in his book. 'It is difficult to find a taluka today without a Sangh led school.'[59]

The Sangh also runs several publishing houses, which enable it to reach more people, as well as social organisations with different names at the local level. This vast network leads to the indisputable conclusion that 'without being formally registered, the Sangh is the world's largest NGO'.[60] Apart from organisations which spring from the Sangh, RSS followers are present in a diverse range of fields, including 'media, education, politics and administration'.[61]

Most troubling of all, the Sangh is a 'quasi military organisation' which 'promotes the arming and militarization of the Hindu community'.[62] The bomb blasts carried out in Malegoan in 2008 in which six people were killed, on the Samjhauta Express in 2007 in which sixty-eight people were killed, and the assassination of public intellectuals like Gauri Lankesh, Narendra Dabholkar, Govind Pansare and M.M. Kalburgi point to the emergence of an even more extremist strand of Hindutva. While legal responsibility has not been pinned on the masterminds behind the blasts, there is evidence of the role played by extremist organisations like Sanathan Sanstha and Abhinav Bharat.[63] For example, based on excerpts of a report on the Malegoan blast prepared by police officer Hemant Karkare, Jaffrelot shows in an article for the *EPW* the inter-relationships between the members of Abhinav Bharat, the VHP, the RSS and the student group affiliated to the RSS, the Akhil Bharatiya Vidyarthi Parishad (ABVP). While Abhinav Bharat is clearly an extremist organisation, it is not isolated. Instead, there is affinity between the 'Savarkarites and the RSS'. 'Bajrang Dal, an RSS affiliate' tends to 'operate like Abhinav Bharat'.[64] Jaffrelot's proposition that these organisations are entwined is quite accurate if one sees the career trajectory of Pragya Thakur. She was a member of the ABVP, then she was a part of the Abhinav Bharat. Accused in the Malegaon and Samjauta Express blasts, today, she is a BJP MP representing Bhopal, having won her seat with a massive margin in 2019.

The way this vast network of organisations comes together to achieve the Sangh's goals is best described by Justice Manmohan Singh Liberhan in his 2009 commission report on the destruction of the Babri Masjid, for which he pinned the responsibility on the leaders of this family of organisations:

> These organizations are collectively an immense and awesome entity with a shrewd brain, a wide encompassing sweep and the crushing strength of the mob. The leadership provided by the RSS, BJP, VHP and the other mutating and constantly transforming organisations like the Hindu Mahasabha and the Jan Sangh, in furtherance of the suspect theories of the founders of these organisations was consistent and unabashed. The ends are all that matter to the core group of thinkers and the destruction of the disputed structure was only one

victorious battle in their ongoing campaign against secularism and the multicultural society, clothed in the garb of religion.[65]

'Mutating and constantly transforming organisations' gestures to the various organisational forms, from local-level cow protection committees and state-level so-called 'voluntary' organisations to 'the leadership provided by the RSS, BJP, VHP'. Although their forms may vary, all these groups take forward the claim that Hindus have a superior if not exclusive stake to the Indian nation. It is this idea of ethnic superiority that is the motivating ideology behind this loose multiplicity of organisations, which work at changing societal consciousness on the one hand and enforcing a form of vigilante justice on the other.

Popular Support for Hindutva

One of the most troubling parts of the rise of Hindutva is its undoubtedly popular character. Socialist Arthur Rosenberg alludes to this characteristic of fascism in his perceptive essay 'Fascism as Mass Movement'. Writing during the Nazi era, Rosenberg went against the line of the Communist International—an association of national communist parties—that fascism embodied the power of finance capital. He argued that it was instead a mass movement. According to the academic Jairus Banaji, Rosenberg's insight is vindicated by later thinkers. German Marxist theorist Clara Zetkin, in 1923, warned that it would be an error to 'see fascism only as a military terrorist movement, not as a mass movement with deep social roots'.[66]

The actions of the mob in a society usually has wider support. The reason the lynching of Dalits and Muslims goes on with impunity in India is not only due to State complicity, but also due to the vocal support from the media and from what Ravish Kumar calls the 'WhatsApp university', and the more tacit complicity of those who do not speak up against lynching, either because they are scared to, or worse, because they agree with it.

In Hitler's Germany, Nazi rule enjoyed the legitimacy of popular support, which was demonstrated through repeated electoral victories.

The people of Germany backed Hitler's policies, as seen in the referendums organised after the occupation of the Rhineland and the union with Austria, both of which were deemed foreign policy successes by a large majority of Germans. After 90.8 per cent of the people voted for the reunification of the Saar region with Germany, German-born US writer Klaus Mann, who had hoped for another result, noted, 'this is our worst political defeat since January 1933. It proves that the slogans of the left have no appeal. ... For the foreseeable future, all hope is dead.'[67] Hitler's popular appeal was succinctly captured by an observer for the Social Democratic leadership in exile, who noted that 'you can force a people to sing, but you cannot force a people to sing with such enthusiasm'.[68] Rosenberg, writing in the 1930s, saw the mass appeal of fascism and concluded, 'The depressing process of absorption of ever-larger masses of people by the nationalist right can be tracked from one election to the next.'[69]

Even the genocide of the Jews was perpetrated in the name of the German people and found support among them. As contemporary US writer Daniel Goldhagen argues in his book *Hitler's Willing Executioners*, 'A survey of the political and social life of Weimar reveals that virtually every major institution and group in Germany—including schools and universities, the military, bureaucracy, and judiciary, professional associations, churches and political parties—was permeated by anti-Semitism.'[70] In the 1930s, towns throughout Germany issued official prohibitions on Jews entering them, and such signs were a near-ubiquitous feature of the German landscape.[71] Goldhagen documents that even prior to the Nuremberg Laws mandating the exclusion of Jews from the institutions of German life, municipalities as well as ordinary Germans had begun to exclude them from universities, swimming pools, public baths and other facilities.[72] Based on this extensive anti-Semitism, Goldhagen makes the chilling case that the Holocaust had its roots in the widespread prejudices of the German people, who were, in fact, Hitler's 'willing executioners'.

In India as well, the two decisive electoral victories by the current regime clearly indicate that the programmes of the BJP government have a level of popular support. Shiv Sunder, a journalist and activist from Karnataka, notes that the vote share of the BJP has been on a steady upswing ever since 1984. In 2014, they got 31 per cent of the vote share and in 2019 they got 37.94 per cent:

> The groundswell had an all India character, with the 2019 mandate being not only comprehensive but also far more dangerous than the mandate in 2014. This is because in 2014 there were many factors responsible for the victory of the BJP including anti-incumbency/corruption/aspirational voters as well as the Modi factor. In 2019, the government had failed with respect to the economy and on the social front, yet people voted for the BJP overwhelmingly.
>
> The BJP had a credible message with the electorate and a credible messenger in the form of Modi. If we try and decipher the message, what is clear is that the most extreme voices within the BJP have won overwhelmingly. The highest margins of victory in Karnataka was by those who were the most extreme. Anant Kumar Hegde won by a margin of 4,79,000 votes (higher than even Modi at 4,50,000 lakh), Naveen Kumar Kateel by 2,63,000 lakh votes and Tejasvi Surya by 2,20,000. At a national level, Pragya Thakur who defended Godse, and was part of Sanatan Sanstha which is behind the killing of Gauri Lankesh won by 3,64,822 votes. It was a massive endorsement of a masculinist and militarist agenda.[73]

The bias against the Muslim minority is not just the project of a majoritarian State but has its roots in the endeavours of the RSS and its affiliates, which have worked to create a Hindu majoritarian society. Today, across the country, people are participants in a kind of communal consensus in which a whole series of assumptions and myths about the Muslim community have turned into common sense. According to historian Sumit Sarkar, this project of altering the common sense of the ordinary Indian has been a long 'Gramscian process of building up hegemony through molecular permeation'. The time scale within which Hindutva has developed has given it far greater opportunities to change society than even fascism in Italy and national socialism in Germany. Sarkar notes:

> Unlike fascism, then, which came to power in Italy and Germany within a decade or less of its emergence as a political movement, Hindutva has had a long gestation period. This, no doubt has given it added strength and stability, time to get internalized into common sense. But there is an element of hope here too, for despite the tremendous efforts spread across decades, the conquest of hearts and minds remains far from complete.[74]

Much of what was observed in Nazi Germany can be seen in India today. Educational institutions, workspaces, cultural spaces as well as media reproduce the communal consensus which sees Muslims as 'outsiders'. The communal consensus functions to deny Muslims access to institutions of social and economic life, even as the State remains complicit in this violation of the constitutional promise of equal citizenship.

To take just one example, during the first wave of the COVID-19 pandemic, the mainstream media relentlessly manufactured the image of Muslims as 'corona criminals' who were apparently propagating a 'corona jihad'. The media laid the blame for the spread of the pandemic on Muslims by using fake news, misrepresentation and half-truths. The Campaign Against Hate Speech, a collective comprising lawyers, researchers and activists, documented how the vilification of Muslims by the mainstream media was followed by calls for social and economic boycott of the community on social media. This included calls for the boycott of 'Muslim shops, Muslim street vendors and other Muslim establishments'. 'Miscreants' took the law into their own hands and forced 'the general public not to buy fruits/vegetables from Muslim street vendors', while resident welfare associations boycotted Muslims in their apartments and colonies and prevented volunteers from providing 'relief measures to the poor, because they are Muslims'.[75] The newspaper the *Star of Mysore*, in a direct reference to Muslims, called for getting 'rid of the bad apples in society, which are proving to be more harmful than the dreaded virus itself'. These statements calling for elimination of an entire religious community come within the understanding of what is the '"crime of crimes", genocide'.[76]

This permeation of an anti-Muslim sentiment has been difficult to challenge because Hindutva ideology has deep roots in the psyche of individuals, giving otherwise marginal individuals a sense of belonging and power. In Arendt's analysis, the success of the totalitarian movement in Nazi Germany was premised on the fact that it did not cater to a narrowly economic vision of the welfare of the working class, as did the socialist and communist parties. Rather, the totalitarian movement was about giving an individual a sense of identity, belonging and power. This sense of belonging was based on *weltanschauung*, a worldview that could take 'possession of man as a whole', something difficult to challenge.[77]

According to philosopher Martha Nussbaum, the 'power of the Hindu right' draws upon feelings of 'fear, shame and humiliation' engendered in the majority, as she writes in *The Clash Within*. It is based on the 'fantasy that one has been humiliated' and draws on the 'fear and hatred of the other'. This form of wounded nationalism 'plays to the psychology of people who seek a nationhood that is masculine and aggressive to compensate for the deep wounds [inflicted by the British] empire'.[78]

For an otherwise ordinary human being without an obviously larger vision of who they are, Hindutva bolsters their self-esteem and provides a deep meaning to life. The alienated, socially disconnected, atomised individual feels a sense of belonging to the powerful Hindu community and exults in the power to exercise dominance over hapless minorities.

Khetan illustrates the immense popularity of this ideology, even if it was responsible for the murders and rapes committed during the Gujarat 2002 pogrom:

> While Indian liberals may have thought of Modi as a wannabe fascist … for a majority of Gujarati Hindus, their chief minister was a hero,

especially after the riots. … Modi's legions of supporters stood firmly behind him, sweeping him to power in election after election. For them, the Gujarat riots of 2002 were to be numbered among his accomplishments, a source of pride, not shame. For them, this was no blot on India's copybook, it was a Hindu awakening.[79]

Regardless of the power and popularity of Hindutva, it can and should be challenged. The political basis of the challenge can be derived from Arendt. She quotes Clemenceau, a key opponent of anti-Semitism during the Dreyfus affair, to make the point that 'the people' are not "God"' and that 'a collective tyrant spread over the length and breadth of the land is no more acceptable than a single tyrant ensconced upon his throne'.[80]

Entrenching Hindutva in Indian Law

The enactment of CAA, 2019 marked a new phase in the attempt by the Modi regime to remake India. While the power of the mob is one way through which conformity is manufactured, the CAA marked a moment when legislative change emerged as a viable route to take forward the ideological vision of the Sangh. Apart from the CAA, anti–cow slaughter, anti-conversion and anti-'love jihad' laws indicate an emerging legal framework which puts in place second-class citizenship for both religious and caste minorities.

This is a well-trodden path—other totalitarian regimes have moved from inciting violence on the streets to 'official, orderly and properly state sponsored persecution', as US advocate and scholar James Whitman writes in *Hitler's American Model*. Nazi Germany followed this path as did the American South. Whitman cites Swedish economist and sociologist Gunnar Myrdal, who, referring to the American South, wrote that persecution was the task for 'the centralized organization of a fascist state'.[81] In the deep South in the US, persecution by law was carried out through voter-identification laws and anti-miscegenation laws. Nazi Germany too went from street violence by Nazi goons to the enactment of the Citizenship Law and the Blood Law at Nuremberg, which deprived those who did not have 'German blood' of citizenship rights. By doing so, the Nazi regime 'put the business of persecution safely in the hands of the state'.[82]

In India, this emerging framework of persecution has centred on three key legislative interventions—the CAA/NPR/NRC, the anti-conversion laws and the anti–cow slaughter laws.

The CAA, 2019

The contradiction between the patently discriminatory intent of the CAA and the values of the Constitution triggered the first mass protests against the Modi regime throughout the country, with people pegging their resistance to the defence of the Constitution.

The problematic heart of the Act was that it allowed for a certain category of persons to not be treated as an 'illegal migrant'. This grouping as per the CAA was 'any person belonging to Hindu, Sikh, Buddhist, Jain, Parsi or Christian community from Afghanistan, Bangladesh or Pakistan, who entered into India on or before the 31st day of December, 2014...' The CAA makes it easier for this category of persons to be conferred citizenship. This classification of persons not to be treated as 'illegal migrants' expressly excluded Muslims from its purview. Further, the benefit of not being treated as 'illegal migrants' and then being provided an easier path to citizenship accrued to those who by virtue of religious background were perceived to have been 'persecuted on grounds of religion' in Afghanistan, Pakistan and Bangladesh. Muslims too are persecuted in these countries and there is persecution on grounds other than religion, both of which were not taken into consideration by the Act.

This law presages a new development because it frontally challenges the constitutional guarantee of equality and non-discrimination on the grounds of religion. Though there were 140 petitions filed challenging the CAA, the Supreme Court is yet to hear the matter. This is in spite of the fact that the CAA has deeply agitated public opinion in India, has produced a sense of insecurity in the Muslim community and is undeniably a matter of constitutional importance.[83]

As the home minister Amit Shah indicated, the CAA cannot be seen in isolation but as part of a chronology, with it being followed by the NRC.[84] What he omitted to mention is that the NRC itself is based on the preparation of the NPR, which is a register of all persons residing in a place.[85] The purpose of the NPR is solely to prepare the NRC. The information to be collected during the NPR process is to do with the birth details of persons and their parents, and documentation of the same, with a view to establishing their claim to citizenship.[86]

For preparing the NRC, the local registrar would first verify and scrutinise 'the particulars collected of every family and individual in the Population Register'.[87] During the verification process, the registrar is given the power to mark the 'particulars of such individuals, whose Citizenship is doubtful' in the register for 'further enquiry'. In an empowerment of third-party vigilantism, the rules give power to anyone to 'object to the inclusion or exclusion of certain names' from the first list.[88]

Depending on the kind of proof of citizenship required, a threat of detention will hang over the heads of many millions who do not have the documentation required to prove citizenship. While the NPR and NRC processes do not prima facie discriminate against religious minorities, the rules give the local registrar unprecedented power to behave in a discriminatory fashion. Based on the animus the State has shown towards Muslims, there is a legitimate fear that this power vested in the registrar will be exercised with a discriminatory intent and will adversely affect Muslims who do not have documentation of their place of birth or their parents' place of birth as well as categories of people who often do not have proper documentation such as single women, LGBT+ persons estranged from their families, divorced women, homeless people, tribal people and the economically poor.

The NPR/NRC at a national level will entrench the discrimination embedded in the CAA by creating two categories of citizens in India, 'citizens' and 'doubtful citizens'. The second category of people will face lingering doubts around whether they will be permitted to exercise their right to vote, have access to welfare schemes, etc., though the Election Commission has clarified that 'the exclusion of a person's name from NRC does not amount to her declaration as a foreigner. By implication, such persons remain on the voters' list and shall be eligible to vote until a decision is taken by concerned tribunals'.[89]

The fears which a nationwide NRC invokes draw their sustenance from the experience of Assam updating its 1951 NRC. The draft of the NRC, released on 30 June 2018, excluded forty lakh persons. This number has now come down to nineteen lakh in the final list, which was released in August 2019.[90] As per a study by cultural antropologist Angana P. Chatterji, the 2019 Assam NRC list reportedly excluded 486,000 Bangla Muslims (25.5 per cent of those excluded from the August 2019 NRC list) of a total of 700,000 excluded Muslims (36.7 per cent of the excluded); 500,000–690,000 Bangla Hindus (26.2–36.2 per cent of the excluded); and 60,000 Assamese Hindus (3.1 per cent of the excluded).[91] Clearly, both Bangla Muslims and Hindus are affected by the NRC process, but for the Hindus there is the possibility of being granted citizenship under the CAA (once the rules are notified and the CAA comes into force), which is not an option for the Muslims.

Leaving aside this possibility of citizenship, once a person is excluded from the list, they have to undertake the onerous task of submitting documentation before a Foreigners Tribunal, tracing their origin to India before 1971. An investigation carried out by award-winning journalist and writer Rohini Mohan into Assam's Foreigners Tribunals showed 'an ominous glimpse of what awaits the masses left off the citizens register who will soon be summoned to trial'. The tribunals, according to Mohan, followed 'a biased process barely resembling India's traditional legal system'. This was apparent in the fact that the tribunal members were incentivised to declare persons who appeared before them as foreigners. Mohan noted that the tribunals were heavily biased: 'nine out of 10 cases were against Muslims' with 'almost 90% of those Muslims being declared illegal immigrants—as compared with 40% of Hindus tried'.[92] Chatterji's study notes that 'As of October 2019, it appears that the cases of 4,68,905 persons have been brought before the Foreigners Tribunals. Of these cases, reportedly 1,36,149 people were declared to be "foreigners" as of July 31, 2020. Community leaders, lawyers and journalists state that of those declared "foreigners," 70 to 80 percent are reportedly Muslims'.[93]

'In November 2019, 1043 persons were reportedly being held in detention ... By March 2020, it was reported that 3331 persons had been held in the six detention centers in Assam ... In May 2019, the Supreme Court ordered that those regarded "non citizens," and detained for more than three years, be conditionally released. Despite the apex court's directive, people continued to be detained ... In June 2021, local communities and lawyers noted the number of incarcerated detainees to be approximately 500.'[94]

The detention is supposed to be till the process of deportation begins. However, as it is improbable that any neighbouring country will accept these detainees, they are likely to be indefinitely detained in camps. The Central government has denied any planning for the contingency of detention on its part, merely stating that the responsibility vests with the states. The current minister of state for home affairs, Nityanand Rai, in response to a question in the Rajya Sabha, said, 'Detention centres are set up by state governments and Union Territory [UT] administrations as per their local requirements to detain illegal immigrants and foreigners.'[95] However, there are also news reports which indicate that 'In 2014, the Centre had told all the states to set up at least one detention centre for illegal immigrants so as not to mix them up with jail inmates.' Since then, there have been reports of construction of detention centres in Assam, Goa and Karnataka.[96]

The target of the CAA/NPR/NRC process is the Muslim community, as made clear by the exclusion of Muslims from the CAA. The potentially dangerous end point of the process can be grasped through two comparative examples.

In 2019, the Gambia filed a case in the International Court of Justice (ICJ) against Myanmar's violation of the Genocide Convention. The violation alleged by the Gambia occurred when 744,000 Rohingyas were expelled from the state of Rakhine in Myanmar in 2016. The court in its preliminary order noted that since 'October 2016, the Rohingya in Myanmar have been subjected to acts which are capable of affecting their right of existence as a protected group under the Genocide Convention, such as mass killings, widespread rape and other forms of sexual violence, as well as beatings, the destruction of villages and homes, denial of access to food, shelter and other essentials of life'.[97]

The ICJ noted the worrying implications of exclusionary citizenship laws in its preliminary order in the case filed by the Gambia against Myanmar. The court traced this development to Myanmar's Citizenship Law of 1982, which defines Burmese citizens as 'Nationals such as the Kachin, Kayah, Karen, Chin, Burman, Mon, Rakhine or Shan and ethnic groups as have settled in any of the territories included within the State as their permanent home from a period anterior to 1185 B.E.,[98] 1823 A.D.'[99] This exclusionary law specifically leaves out Rohingyas, though they may have been residing in Myanmar before the cut-off date.

While the ICJ has still not decided on the matter, it has indicated that horrific crimes like genocide and crimes against humanity originate in exclusionary citizenship laws. In what should serve as a warning to other countries around the world, the ICJ cited the General Assembly Resolution which had noted its 'grave concern that, in spite of the fact that Rohingya Muslims lived in Myanmar for generations prior to the independence of Myanmar, they were made stateless by the enactment of the 1982 Citizenship Law and were eventually disenfranchised, in 2015, from the electoral process.'[100]

This redefinition of citizenship in India is also reminiscent of Nazi Germany. The first law affecting citizenship enacted by the Nazis was the Revocation of Naturalisation and the Withdrawal of German Citizenship, 1933, to 'facilitate the denaturalisation and expulsion of Eastern European Jews who had arrived after the first World War' from Germany.[101] This was followed by the infamous Nuremberg Laws which defined who a Reich citizen was. According to Section 2 of the Reich Citizenship Law:

(1) A Reich Citizen is exclusively a national of German blood or racially related blood who demonstrates through his conduct that he is willing and suited to faithfully serve the German Volk and Reich.

(2) The right of Reich citizenship is acquired through the conferral of the brevet of Reich citizenship.

(3) The Reich citizen is the sole bearer of full political rights, to be exercised according to the measure of the laws.[102]

Citizenship in Nazi Germany was not a matter of birth and was limited to those of 'German' or 'related blood'. Further, citizenship was conditional on 'willingness to serve the German Volk' and only the citizen was entitled to 'full political rights'.

The Nuremberg Laws revoked Reich citizenship for Jews and rendered them stateless or without what Hannah Arendt referred to as the 'right to have rights'.[103] The situation of rightlessness into which the Jews were thrown effectively expelled them from the civic community and set the stage for the final assault on the very existence of the Jewish people.[104]

The comparative examples of Nazi Germany and Myanmar show that graded citizenship through law, such as the CAA, is often the first step in a regime of State-sanctioned persecution. The next step in India, which is the beginning of the NPR/NRC process, has been stayed for the moment both due to the protests as well as the onset of COVID-19. Going forward, the ability of the Indian State to implement the next step in excluding Muslims from citizenship will depend on the level of acquiescence of the ordinary Indian in this project.

Criminalising Love: The Uttar Pradesh Prohibition of Unlawful Conversion of Religion Act, 2021

While the CAA/NPR/NRC set in place a new legal template for institutionalising second-class citizenship at the level of the Central government, there are also state-level legislative efforts to do the same. Uttar Pradesh under Adityanath has emerged as a leader in legislating unequal status for minorities, with the state becoming a Hindutva laboratory where new laws and administrative practices are first field-tested.

Nothing embodies the success of this laboratory more than the once fringe idea of 'love jihad' peddled by Hindutva forces, which has not only moved to the centre of the political and popular discourse but has also become a part of the legal framework. The right-wing has for a long time been obsessed with how the 'purity' of the Hindu woman is being defiled by Muslim blood. They coined the term 'love jihad' to refer to the alleged conspiracy by Muslim men to entice and marry Hindu women and convert them to Islam. This fringe idea was even investigated by the NIA in 2017 as directed by the Supreme Court in *Shafin Jahan v K.M. Asokan*.[105] After investigation, the NIA closed the matter as it did not find 'any evidence to suggest that in any of these cases either the man or the woman was coerced to convert'.[106]

Nonetheless, love jihad has become a part of the Hindutva ecosystem with each and every case of a couple choosing to marry across lines of religion being targeted in its name. Perhaps the most infamous 'protector' of Hindu women from the alleged ravages of the Muslim man was Babu Bajrangi, a leader of the Bajrang Dal in Gujarat, who openly spoke about forcibly 'rescuing' Hindu women from relationships or marriages, regardless of the fact that this 'rescue' was nothing other than criminal intimidation and an intrusion into their intimate lives.[107] Bajrangi symbolises the vigilantism of Hindutva groups who feel emboldened to intimidate and threaten those who choose to love outside their caste and religion. The so-called love jihad is used as a pretext by the mob to attack inter-religious couples in many parts of India.

This language of the mob has today become a part of the law with the passing of the Uttar Pradesh Prohibition of Unlawful Conversion of Religion Act, 2021, under which unconstitutional interference in personal decisions such as the choice of marriage partner as well as the choice of faith has been legitimised.[108] With this, followed by the enactment of similar laws in Madhya Pradesh, Uttarakhand, Gujarat and Goa, and with Karnataka and Haryana contemplating such laws as well, India has taken the next dangerous step towards institutionalising and legalising unconstitutional measures.

The parent Act in Uttar Pradesh is a short enactment of thirteen sections but rife with unconstitutional implications.

Section 3 of the Act penalises anyone who 'converts' or 'attempts to convert' by use of 'misrepresentation, force, undue influence, coercion, allurement, fraudulent means or by marriage'. As early as 1977, a Madhya Pradesh statute which criminalised conversion by 'force, fraud or allurement' as well as an Orissa statute which criminalised conversion by 'force, fraud and inducement' were deemed constitutional by the Supreme Court in *Rev Stanislaus v State of Madhya Pradesh*.[109] This remains a problematic decision as 'allurement' and 'inducement' are not the same as 'force' and 'fraud'. The Supreme Court failed to recognise that the criminalisation of 'allurement' and 'inducement' impinges upon a person's constitutional right under Article 25 to practise, profess and propagate one's religion.

However, even setting this aside, what surely has no place in a country in which the right to privacy is constitutionally recognised is the criminalisation of 'marriages for the sake of conversion' along with the criminalisation of forceful and fraudulent conversions. If a person decides to convert for the sake of marriage, that conversion is a matter of personal and intimate choice and it should not come within the realm of criminal sanctions in a constitutional democracy based on a rule of law framework.

The Uttar Pradesh Act also shreds the constitutional protection for the rights of the individual against the dictates of society. Under Section 4, 'any aggrieved person … his/her parents, brother, sister or any other person who is related to him/her by blood marriage or adoption' is given the power to 'lodge a First Information Report of such conversion'. Love marriages are, at their heart, the assertion of an individual's choices against the wishes of family and society. By empowering society to prosecute the individual, this provision sacrifices individual choice at the altar of societal conformity.

The 'choice of faith', which is a 'substratum of individuality' according to the Supreme Court in *Shafin Jahan*, is sought to be strangulated by bureaucratic regulation, police investigation and the empowerment of vigilante action.

Bureaucratic regulation is legitimised by Sections 8 and 9. A person who wants to convert is required under Section 8 to give a 'declaration … sixty days in advance' to the district magistrate that such conversion is 'with his or her free consent' and without any 'force, coercion, undue influence or allurement'. The priest who performs the conversion is also to give one month's advance notice of the proposed conversion to the district magistrate.

To this is added a layer of police intrusion as the district magistrate, on receipt of the two declarations, is required to 'get an inquiry conducted by the police with regard to the real intention, purpose and cause of the proposed religious conversion'. A police investigation into the 'real intention' of conversion, again, shreds the Supreme Court protection granted to intimate choice in the privacy decision of the court in *Puttaswamy*.[110]

To bureaucratic regulation and police intervention is added the final deadly layer of empowering vigilante action. Schedule III read with Section 9 of the Act requires the person converting to give various details such as their permanent address, present place of residence, occupation, monthly income and marital status. The district magistrate will then 'exhibit a copy of the declaration on the notice board of the office'. This mandatory disclosure of personal details to the public is a violation of the right to privacy. By ordering that these be put up on a public notice board, the ordinance empowers self-styled defenders of faith to take vigilante action against those who choose to exercise their constitutional right to 'profess and propagate the religion of their choice'. This violates the Supreme Court dictum laid out in *Shafin Jahan*, 'Our choices are respected because they are ours' and that the 'Constitution protects personal liberty from disapproving audiences'.

If one is charged with performing a conversion through 'misrepresentation, force, undue influence, coercion, allurement, fraudulent means, or marriage', then the burden of proving that such was not the case lies on 'the person who caused the conversion'.[111] This reversal of the burden of proof goes against one of the fundamental tenets of criminal law, that a person is presumed innocent until proven guilty.

The Act is also discriminatory as it only penalises those who convert from Hinduism to another religion and not those who choose to convert to Hinduism. Thus, Adivasis or Muslims or Christians who convert to Hinduism do not come within this law, as the proviso to Section 3 lays down that if 'any person reconverts to his/her immediate previous religion, the same shall not be deemed to be a conversion under this ordinance'. While 'immediate previous religion' is not defined, within the Hindutva worldview, 'Hinduism is the only original religion of the Indian subcontinent; all others are foreign and corrupt,' as sociologist Amita Baviskar writes in the *EPW*.[112] The rhetoric of 'ghar vapasi' points to the ideological framework which views Adivasis who convert to Hinduism as merely returning 'home' and not really changing their religion. Adivasis are seen as 'lapsed Hindus' and Muslims and Christians are seen as formerly Hindu and hence, if they choose to return to their 'mother religion', it is not an offence.

Criminalising intimate choice, such as the choice of religion and the choice of spouse, violates the Supreme Court judgement in *Puttaswamy* in which Justice Chandrachud held:

> The family, marriage, procreation and sexual orientation are all integral to the dignity of the individual. … Read in conjunction with Article 21, liberty enables the individual to have a choice of preferences on various facets of life including what and how one will eat, the way one will dress, the faith one will espouse and a myriad other matters on which autonomy and self-determination require a choice to be made within the privacy of the mind.

The ratio of *Puttaswamy* was applied in *Shafin Jahan*, in 2018. A young woman from the Ezhava community in Kerala was in love with a Muslim man and chose to convert to Islam. This was not to the liking of the father, who filed a habeas corpus petition before the Kerala High Court, seeking her custody. The court granted the same. The young woman, when under the custody of her father, sought the court's permission to go to Salem to do a course and, as per the Kerala High Court, under the 'pretext' of doing a 'course', Hadiya married Shafin Jahan. The marriage was annulled by the court and the matter came up in appeal.

The Supreme Court reversed the Kerala High Court judgement and a bench of Chief Justice Dipak Misra and Justice A.M. Khanwilkar laid down that while 'social values and morals have their space', they are not 'above the constitutionally guaranteed freedom'. They defended the 'freedom of faith' as being 'essential' to 'autonomy' and held that 'choosing a faith is the substratum of individuality and sans it, the right of choice becomes a shadow'.

Justice Chandrachud, in his concurring opinion, also asserted the freedom of individual choice over 'social approval'. He said, 'Neither the state nor the law can dictate a choice of partners' as this forms 'the essence of personal liberty under the Constitution'. He went on to chastise the high court for deciding 'whether Shafin Jahan is a fit person for Hadiya to marry' as by doing so the high court had 'entered into prohibited terrain'. In a ringing assertion of individual rights, Justice Chandrachud held, 'Our choices are respected because they are ours. Social approval for intimate personal decisions is not the basis for recognising them. Indeed, the Constitution protects personal liberty from disapproving audiences.'

The Uttar Pradesh Act runs counter to the established constitutional position in India and has been challenged in the Supreme Court.[113] However, till such time as the Supreme Court declares it unconstitutional, the freedom of faith as well as the freedom to marry stand diminished by this legislation, and the Supreme Court pronouncements on the fundamental right to privacy remain as mere words on paper.

There are global resonances to this law that seeks to regulate marriage, with similar laws enacted by other regimes with totalitarian ambitions. The anti-conversion law is a variant of the Nuremberg Laws in Nazi Germany, which forbade 'marriages between Jews and nationals of German blood or racially related blood'. Such marriages if entered into were declared null and void. The law also prohibited 'extramarital intercourse between Jews and nationals of German blood'.[114] The other analogy which the Uttar Pradesh law invites is to the anti-miscegenation statutes of the US deep South, which also prohibited marriages between Black and White people.

Laws on Prohibition of Cow Slaughter

While the CAA and the laws against conversion for marriage are relatively new legal instruments, the laws on prohibition of cow slaughter have a more hoary history. One of the earliest vehicles through which Hindu sentiment was consolidated was the cow protection movements all over north India. Historians have attested to the impact this movement, which began towards the end of the nineteenth century, had on creating a communal consciousness. They were led by 'Gaurakshini Sabhas active all over north India and supported by landlords, government officials and Sadhus' and had a 'powerful revivalist appeal', as historian K.N. Panikkar details in an article for the *Social Scientist*.[115] Historian Rohit De argues that the cow came to represent 'the greater Hindu community' which was 'being threatened by a demon', with the demon being either the government or the Muslim.[116]

This consolidation of Hindu sentiment behind the cow came head to head with the more secular, inclusive vision of the nation foregrounded by Nehru and Ambedkar during the drafting of the Indian Constitution, when the conservative Hindu elements pushed for constitutional recognition of the prohibition of cow slaughter either in the Fundamental Rights or the Directive Principles. The compromise formula was Article 48 of the Constitution located in the Directive Principles, which reads as follows:

The State shall endeavour to organise agriculture and animal husbandry on modern and scientific lines and shall, in particular, take steps for preserving and improving the breeds, and prohibiting the slaughter, of cows and calves and other milch and draught cattle.

There are three prongs to Article 48 with the state being enjoined to 'organise agriculture and animal husbandry on scientific lines', 'take steps for preserving and improving breeds' and also prohibit the 'slaughter of cows and calves, and other milch and draught cattle.' By placing prohibition of cow slaughter in the Directive Principles, the Constituent Assembly deferred the issue to the future government. In any future legislative endeavour, the State was meant to be guided by Article 48's mandate, in which the prohibition of slaughter of cows was to be understood as serving the larger purpose of organising agriculture on scientific lines and preserving breeds. Notably, there was no mention of the real reason behind this provision, namely the Hindu sentiment which underlay the demand.

The speeches in support of the prohibition of cow slaughter in the Constituent Assembly referenced economic as well as religious arguments. A passionate case was made for the 'prohibition of cow slaughter' on grounds of 'agriculture and food' by Pandit Thakur Das Bhargava. Seth Govind Das said that it was a 'matter of religion' but 'also a cultural and economic question'. Dr Raghu Vira argued that in the Indian civilisational ethos, 'Brahma Hatya and go-hatya', the 'killing of the learned man' and the 'killing of the cow are on par'. R.V. Dhulekar declaimed that 'Hindu society or our Indian society ... has included the cow in [the] fold' of the family and 'it is just like our mother'.[117]

The fact that those in support of prohibiting cow slaughter vacillated between the language of science and the language of Hindu sentiment was not lost on the minority members of the Constituent Assembly. Z.H. Lari said, '...if the house is of the opinion that slaughter of cows should be prohibited, let it be prohibited in clear, definite and unambiguous words'. To him, 'modern and scientific agriculture' could mean 'mechanisation' and did not 'fit' with 'the banning of the slaughter of cattle'. Syed Muhammad Saiadulla was even more forthright in stating, '... [let the] framers of our Constitution ... come out in the open and say directly: "This is part of our religion. The cow should be protected from slaughter and therefore we want its provision either in the Fundamental Rights or in the Directive Principles."' He took apart the scientific argument against cow slaughter with impeccable logic: if the purpose was to 'improve the economic condition of the people', then 'useless cattle should be done away with' and 'better breeds introduced'. The introduction of the economic argument, according to him, 'created a suspicion in the minds of many that the ingrained Hindu feeling against cow slaughter is being satisfied by the backdoor'.[118]

In the years since Article 48 was passed and the Constitution was adopted, twenty-four out of twenty-nine states proceeded to enact anti–cow slaughter laws.[119] When these laws were challenged in the Supreme Court, the issue most fiercely adjudicated was whether the prohibition of the slaughter of cows could also cover the slaughter of bulls, bullocks and buffaloes.

In the first case, *M.H. Qureshi v State of Bihar*,[120] over '3,000 members of the Qureshi community who were engaged in butchering and its subsidiary undertakings like supplying, tanning and curing hides, glue making, gut merchants, and blood dehydrating' from 'more than a hundred villages in the states of Bombay, Madhya Pradesh, Uttar Pradesh and Bihar', jointly challenged the cow slaughter laws in Bihar, Uttar Pradesh and Madhya Pradesh. The main argument they pressed flowed from the fact that the absolute ban on cow slaughter interfered with their right to practise their trade and profession. They also made the subsidiary argument that the laws violated their right to freedom of religion.[121]

The Supreme Court in its decision in 1958 held that a total ban on the slaughter of 'cows and calves' was valid and did not violate the fundamental right of Indian Muslims under Article 25(1) of sacrificing cows on the Bakr Id day as 'there is no religious compulsion on the Mussalmans to sacrifice a cow on Bakr Id day'. However, the court also held that the total prohibition of the slaughter of 'breeding bulls and working bullocks without prescribing any test or requirement as to their age or usefulness', offended against Article 19(1)(g), which guaranteed the right to 'practice any profession, or to carry on any occupation, trade or business' and was 'void to that extent'. Rohit De argues in *A People's Constitution* that the uniqueness of the 3,000-strong petition by butchers spread across four states was that it shifted the focus from the religious right to sacrifice cows to how the absolute prohibition of slaughter violated their right to 'trade and profession'. Though the media reported it as if the Qureshis had lost the case, the court, by striking down the absolute prohibition of slaughter, had, in fact, given the Qureshis limited success.[122]

This balancing approach between Hindu sentiment, disguised as concern for 'useful cattle' or 'compassion for living creatures', and the freedom of trade and profession under Article 19(1)(g) got skewed in favour of Hindu sentiment by the beginning of the twenty-first century. In 2005, in *State of Gujarat v Mirzapur Moti Kureshi Kassab Jamat and Others*,[123] the Supreme Court upheld a complete ban on the slaughter of cows, bulls, bullocks, heifers and calves in Gujarat, reasoning that bulls and bullocks continued to be useful in terms of the urine, manure and biogas that they produced. The court also held that 'usefulness' was not the sole criterion as the Constitution also mandated 'compassion for living creatures' as a fundamental duty,[124] and hence it 'would be an act of reprehensible ingratitude to condemn a cattle in its old age as useless and send it to the slaughter house'.

With the ascendency of the BJP, new laws have been enacted, which have widened the sphere of prohibition. The Maharashtra Animal Preservation (Amendment) Act, 2015, applied the ratio of the *Mirzapur* judgement to widen the prohibition of slaughter of cows to bulls and bullocks.[125] It also criminalised the transport of cattle within the state for the purpose of slaughter[126] as well as the 'sale, purchase or disposal' of any 'cow, bull or bullock', knowing that such 'cow, bull or bullock shall be slaughtered'.[127] It went on to criminalise the possession of the 'flesh of cow, bull or bullock slaughtered in contravention of the provisions of the Act'[128] as well as the 'possession' of the 'flesh of any cow, bull or bullock slaughtered outside the State of Maharashtra'.[129] For these offences, the burden of proof was reversed, with the 'accused' having to prove that the 'slaughter, transport, possession of flesh of cow' was not in 'contravention of the provisions of the Act'.[130]

This was challenged before the Bombay High Court[131] but, other than two provisions, the constitutionality of the statute was upheld in 2016. The parts of the law which the court struck down were the criminalisation of the possession of the flesh of any cow, bull or bullock slaughtered outside Maharashtra and the reverse onus clause, which put the burden of proving their innocence on the accused. In its reasoning for striking down the clause criminalising the possession of beef, the court held, 'If the State starts making intrusion into the personal life of an individual by preventing him from eating food of his choice, such act may well affect his personal liberty.' The reverse onus clause was struck down as the court reasoned that it was impossible for a consumer to know if the flesh she was consuming was of a cow or a buffalo and hence to presume that the 'accused had knowledge of the nature of the flesh' as well as that the animal was 'slaughtered in contravention of the Act' was 'clearly impermissible'.

However, the Bombay High Court upheld the provisions criminalising the transport as well as purchase and sale of cattle for the 'purpose of slaughter', holding that there was a nexus between the objective of 'preventing slaughter' and 'preventing transport, purchase and sale'. This legal reasoning was oblivious to the ground reality where vigilante elements were policing the movement of cattle and punishing all those who moved cattle regardless of the purpose for which cattle was being moved. The Act gave further legal strength to such vigilante elements. Their illegal actions were given the colour of law, with the police now empowered to stop, search and seize any cattle which was being moved, on mere suspicion that it was meant for slaughter.

The Karnataka Prevention of Slaughter and Preservation of Cattle Act, 2020, builds upon these prohibitions to add yet another layer. While *Mirzapur* upheld the ban on slaughter of cow, bull and bullock, the Karnataka law added 'he or she buffalo below the age of thirteen years to the prohibited category'.[132] It also reproduced the criminalisation of purchase, sale and transport of cattle for the purpose of slaughter from the Maharashtra law. Karnataka too has been plagued by cow vigilantism. The Karnataka unit of PUCL and the Forum Against Atrocities on Women, in a study of communal policing between 1998 and 2012, document forty-four instances of vigilante attacks on the transportation of cattle and the sale of beef. The report concludes that the attacks showed an upward trajectory because 'the inaction of the state has emboldened vigilante elements in the state to continue to enforce their version of morality on the larger public'.[133] With the transport, sale and purchase of cattle for the purpose of slaughter being made an offence, vigilantism has become the law.

The Karnataka law added another dimension by setting in place a new procedure for search and seizure of not only cattle but also vehicles which transport cattle and premises where cattle are alleged to be slaughtered. The procedure for search and seizure does away with the protections of the CrPC and allows for confiscation of the property as well as the 'sale of confiscated premises in a public auction'.[134]

If one surveys the development of the law under Article 48, it has moved from the 'protection of Hindu sentiment', which Muslim members of the Constituent Assembly, Lari and Saiadulla, saw as the hidden rationale of the law, to a proactive targeting of those who by caste or religion make their living from the cattle trade, mainly the Muslim and Dalit communities. The law, by moving beyond the cow to prohibit the slaughter of bulls, bullocks and buffaloes, targets the right to food of millions for whom beef is a cheaper source of protein. Bulls, bullocks and buffaloes are protected from slaughter using the economic rationale of the usefulness of the animal, but the hidden subtext remains the intent to target entire communities.

The Karnataka and Maharashtra laws would destroy the backbone of the cattle industry by criminalising the transport of cattle for the purpose of slaughter. The adjudication of whether the reason for transportation is indeed for the purpose of slaughter remains in the hands of state authorities and allows for an arbitrary targeting of persons. The Karnataka law goes one step further in this direction by providing for the confiscation of premises and vehicles and making it extraordinarily difficult to retrieve one's property regardless of whether an offence has been committed or not.[135]

The laws around cow slaughter reinforce the second-class citizenship of communities who make their living from cattle products and those who eat beef. They are evidence of a much longer historical project which has now gone way beyond the objective of 'protecting Hindu sentiment'. Today, these laws have become another means to target the Muslim and Dalit communities' food habits, livelihood and basic dignity. In the case of the cow slaughter laws, the Supreme Court has been complicit in the coded project of targeting minority communities using the language of Article 48. Challenging these laws in court has only offered limited relief as the courts now see cattle slaughter within the lens of Article 48 and without taking forward the early precedent of *M.H. Qureshi*, which also saw the issue within the lens of the fundamental right to freely practise one's occupation, trade or profession.

Continuing Resistance to a Majoritarian Project

A survey of these three families of laws targeting citizenship, food and love shows that the majoritarian legal project has partially succeeded. When it comes to the criminalisation of the freedom to convert and the right of butchers to practise their trade, the Supreme Court has set its seal of approval on the restriction of these rights.

The battle against institutionalising laws of second-class citizenship as well as those prohibiting 'marriages for the sake of conversion' is still on. If the Supreme Court were to examine both these laws using the framework of the constitutional protection against discrimination on grounds of religion as well as the protection of the right to autonomy, it would have to hold these laws unconstitutional.

There are some hopeful signs in the decision of the Gujarat High Court, which has stayed the operation of provisions of the Gujarat

Freedom of Religion (Amendment) Act, 2021, which like the Uttar Pradesh statute conflated conversion for the sake of marriage with force, fraud or allurement. The court held that '... pending further hearing the rigors of Sections 3, 4, 4A to 4C, 5, 6 and 6A shall not operate merely because a marriage is solemnised by a person of one religion with a person of another religion without force or by allurement or by fraudulent means and such marriages cannot be termed as marriages for the purposes of unlawful conversion'. The court was clear that this interim relief was being granted to 'protect the parties solemnizing marriage from being unnecessarily harassed'.[136] The decision of the Gujarat High Court shows that the challenge laws that seek to constrain the freedom to marry will have to face is the constitutional guarantee of dignity, autonomy and privacy. With all its imperfections, there is no doubt that the Constitution continues to be a roadblock for legislation that seeks to discriminate on grounds of religion as well as legislation that seeks to constrain individual choice. Regardless of a win or a loss in a specific case, the Constitution, which enjoys popular legitimacy, will continue to be invoked both in legal and popular discourse, and as such, continues to present a normative counterpoint to the imagination of a totalitarian State.

Shock Doctrine: Favouring Capital and Arming the State

Disasters are utilised by those in power to augment the interests of the owners of capital and further disempower the working class, argues writer and activist Naomi Klein. In *The Shock Doctrine,* she posits a close relationship between shocks—be they coups, natural disasters, war or terrorist attacks—and a radical pro-corporate agenda. The 'shock' disorients and distracts people, and it is precisely at this moment that the capitalist State chooses to push through far-reaching economic changes which further the interests of capitalists, disadvantage labour, and set back climate justice and environmental justice.[137]

The COVID-19 pandemic has presented those in power with precisely that kind of 'shock', which has 'disoriented the public' and allowed for the introduction of measures that in normal times would have met with tremendous pushback. The singularity of the shock produced by COVID-19, apart from the stress on the health system, is that the key institutions of democracy are in a state of suspended animation. The imposition of lockdown by countries around the world as a public health measure has meant that the normal functioning of the institutions of democracy, such as Parliament, courts and media, as well as the exercise of the right to assembly through protests and demonstrations and the expression of opinion by student activism has been affected.

Executive power has been augmented with parliamentary oversight being compromised. When the pandemic hit the country in March 2020, Parliament could work for only thirty-four days. The winter session had to be cancelled, while three others were cut short.[138] One of the causes for the reduced working of Parliament, apart from disruptions by the Opposition, was the decision of the Speaker of the Lok Sabha and the chairperson of the Rajya Sabha to not continue functioning online or have hybrid sessions, as was being done in other parts of the world.

The Speaker of the lower house and the chairman of the upper house have also not allowed for the online convening of the various parliamentary standing committees which examine legislations and bills when Parliament is not in session, thereby virtually bringing the working of Parliament to a standstill. The secretariats of both houses have maintained that committee meetings cannot be held via videoconferences since that would violate the confidentiality clause. A Lok Sabha official told the media, 'The government reveals crucial information at these meetings. How can anyone ensure that the member at the other end of the video call is alone and no one else is sitting in the meeting other than him or her.'[139]

Despite demands from Opposition members to allow online functioning of the committees[140] and despite this being the global practice during the pandemic, India alone among the democracies has decided to totally suspend the working of parliamentary committees. Parliament has been a shadow of its normal self during the pandemic, with the result that executive action has been shielded from any effective scrutiny.[141]

The importance of parliamentary oversight in a time of crisis has been recognised globally. Resolution 2209 (2018) of the Council of Europe has noted, 'Fundamental safeguards of the rule of law, in particular legality, effective parliamentary oversight, independent judicial control and effective domestic remedies, must be maintained even during a state of emergency.' Transparency International has applied this standard to the COVID-19 crisis to argue that 'with elections, meetings of parliament and other political activities now suspended over safety concerns in some countries, many normal oversight and accountability processes have been severely disrupted. Governments should therefore go to extra lengths to act with integrity and be open with the public. Access to information is key so that there can be accountability in the future for the decisions made now'.[142]

However, in India, the current administration has not appreciated the vital importance of Parliament in a time of crisis and has allowed this institutional safeguard to wither away, thereby entrenching executive supremacy.

Other important actors in a democracy, be it civil society or political parties, have also been seriously hobbled and have been unable to play the watchdog role, which is crucial for upholding democratic values. Protests and demonstrations, which are a way of expressing public opinion in a democracy, have stood suspended, especially during the lockdown.

The Supreme Court, which could have adapted itself to the changed circumstances and played its role in ensuring that the executive functioned within the limits of the Constitution, did not do so, especially during the first wave of COVID-19, as seen in the lack of response to the migrant crisis.

It is in such a time that the current regime in India has carried out far-reaching changes in areas of social, economic and political life, which would not have been possible without strong pushback if the institutions of democracy had been able to function.

The government rolled out a draft proposal in March 2020 to amend the environment impact assessment (EIA) procedures that would place many projects outside the purview of public hearings, effectively rendering local communities voiceless in such decisions.[143] The timing of this decision was widely criticised. As the Centre for Policy Research noted in a letter to the government, 'The EIA notification is an important regulation through which the impacts of land use change, water extraction, tree felling, pollution, waste and effluent management for industrial and infrastructure projects are to be studied and used in developmental decision making. Any change in this law has a direct bearing on the living and working conditions of people and the ecology.'[144] The EIA notification elicited a strong response in spite of the restrictions during the lockdown, with 'over two million comments, most asking to retract the draft'.[145]

In September 2020, the Karnataka High Court issued a stay order prohibiting the Ministry of Environment, Forest and Climate Change from publishing the final notification. However, as environmental activists Meenakshi Kapoor and Krithika A. Dinesh argue in an article in the *Wire*, the government is getting the draft notification into operation by making piecemeal amendments to the EIA notification, 2006, removing crucial environmental safeguards.[146]

A media report on the website *BehanBox* noted, 'During the nationwide lockdown from 24 March to 30 June 2020, the Forest and Expert Appraisal Committees within the Ministry of Environment, Forests and Climate Change went on a project-clearing spree for large-scale industrial, mining, hydropower, roads and highway construction projects, without any due diligence and in absolute disregard of environmental laws and the FRA [Forest Rights Act 2006].' The consent of gram sabhas was not taken, as mandated by the FRA, in the auction of forty-one coal blocks across five states in central India, announced in June 2020 by the prime minister. For instance, according to an amendment made to Section 8A of the Mines and Minerals (Regulation and Development) Act, 1956, a successful bidder for an existing mining lease which is expiring does not need the otherwise mandatory gram sabha consent for forest diversion, as the modification to the Act deems the new lessee to have obtained the mandatory gram sabha consent.[147]

An analysis of Expert Appraisal Committee (a Centre-appointed committee which evaluates coal, hydro and river valley, thermal, non-coal mining, infrastructure, coastal regulations zones and industrial projects) and Forest Advisory Committee meeting minutes during the lockdown—about forty of them, with some meetings as short as ten minutes and others up to five hours—reveal that approximately 120 projects were recommended, ninety were deferred, thirty returned for reconsideration and only two were rejected. A quarter of the recommended projects fell in Fifth Schedule districts, in which transfer of land can be restricted keeping in mind the interests of Scheduled Tribes.

The pandemic has also been used by several state governments to suspend labour laws in the garb of protecting businesses. Uttar Pradesh and Madhya Pradesh, both BJP-ruled states, promulgated ordinances to relax certain aspects of existing labour laws. The Uttar Pradesh Temporary Exemption from Certain Labour Laws Ordinance, 2020, states that 'All factories and establishments engaged in manufacturing process shall be exempted from the operation of all Labour laws for a period of three years', with the relaxation specifically allowing for the working day to be extended to twelve hours. Another notification dated 8 May 2020 exempts all factories registered under the Factories Act, 1948, from provisions regulating weekly hours, daily hours, overtime, intervals of rest, etc., of all adult workers. Thus, Uttar Pradesh has in effect suspended thirty-five of the thirty-eight labour laws for three years, including laws related to industrial disputes, trade unions and contract workers.[148]

Further, BJP-ruled Gujarat, Haryana, Uttarakhand, Himachal Pradesh, Assam, Goa and Madhya Pradesh as well as Congress-ruled Rajasthan have notified an increase in the length of work hours to twelve hours.[149] In July 2020, Karnataka, another BJP-ruled state, approved a labour ordinance which aimed at 'improving the ease of doing business'. The ordinance increased the labour threshold for key labour legislations such as the Industrial Disputes Act, 1947, Contract Labour Regulation and Abolition Act, 1970, and Factories Act to even be applicable. Thus, under Section 25K of the Industrial Disputes Act, the worker threshold has been increased from 100 to 300. This means that only those establishments that employ 300 or more persons will have to seek government permission for closure, retrenchment or layoff. With the increase in the threshold from twenty employees to fifty employees, the Contract Labour Act will now apply only to establishments with more than fifty employees.[150]

As Maitreyi Krishnan and Clifton D' Rozario, both lawyers and trade union activists, and I wrote for *Firstpost*:

> While the history of the neo-liberal era is about the progressive whittling down of labour law protections, these amendments in one fell swoop attempt to take Indian labour back to the unregulated laissez-faire days of 19th-century European capitalism. These ordinances are not only illegal and unconstitutional but also starkly indicative of the larger designs of a state determined to take advantage of the pandemic to push the working class to the situation of rightlessness.[151]

The Central government has also used the cover of the pandemic to push through three labour codes, bringing about fundamental changes to labour law and further weakening the rights of organised labour. The reorganising of a century of labour jurisprudence began with the passing of the Code on Wage in 2019. In September 2020, three more codes, namely the Social Security Code, the Industrial Relations Code and the Occupational Safety, Health and Working Conditions Code were passed with little debate in Parliament. 'The Rajya Sabha passed all three within two hours,' as per an article in *Seminar* by well-known trade union leader and labour law jurist Babu Mathew and co-author Kavya Bharadkar.[152]

Under the Industrial Relations Code, if workers want to go on strike against their employer, they must serve strike notice to their employer at least fourteen days in advance. On the other hand, if within that period the labour commissioner calls a meeting with the employer/management and the workers' union to find a solution to the problem, then strikes cannot be held for sixty days. This law makes it highly difficult, if not impossible, for workers to strike. If workers do not give the notice to strike fourteen days in advance, the strike will be declared illegal.[153]

The Occupational Safety Code becomes applicable only when ten or more workers are employed in an establishment. As Mathew and Bharadkar note, '... a very small minority of Indian establishments cross this threshold'. If there was one important labour context in which the reforms were passed, it was the mass migration of thousands of migrant labourers, sometimes on foot, when the unplanned lockdown was declared. Migrant labour suffered during the lockdown due to non-payment of wages, non-availability of food and rations and lack of medical care. However, the code, instead of increasing the protections for migrant labour, further dilutes the existing ones by increasing the threshold for the applicability of the code from five migrant workers in an establishment, according to the Inter-State Migrant Workers Act, 1979, to ten.

The Social Security Code replaces nine laws related to social security, including Employees' Provident Fund Act, 1952, Maternity Benefit Act, 1961, and the Unorganized Workers Social Security Act, 2008. Under the code, the Central government may notify various social security schemes for the benefit of workers. These include an Employees' Provident Fund Scheme, an Employees' Pension Scheme and an Employees' State Insurance Scheme. However, as Mathew and Bharadkar note, this code at best creates 'enabling provisions' for 'progressive extension of better social security measures to the working class—it is neither guaranteed, nor can be demanded legally'.

The passing of the labour codes during the pandemic shows that the government was not prepared to debate such far-reaching changes to labour law nor was it concerned about the impact of the pandemic on the working class. In fact, as Mathew and Bharadkar note, '... post pandemic, the working class requires stronger legal protection—not more neglect and precarity'. However, the labour codes demonstrate a striking indifference to the needs of 90 per cent of India's labourers, who are in the unorganised sector, and weaken legal protections for the working class as a whole.

The Centre also utilised the pandemic to attempt to push through what have come to be known as the Farm Laws, even though, constitutionally, it did not have the legislative competence to do so, as agriculture is a state subject. This was the Centre's most drastic effort yet to fundamentally alter the relationship between the farmer and the State, with the farmer being abandoned, in effect, to the full strength of market forces.[154] The effect of the laws, as apprehended by farmers, was that the State would move towards dismantling the Agricultural Produce Marketing Committees as well as the minimum procurement price, leaving small farmers in the uneven bargaining position of having to negotiate the sale of their produce with larger corporations.[155] Farmers saw this as an unmitigated disaster as it would only increase corporate control over Indian agriculture. While farmers had been demanding changes in agricultural laws and policies in line with the recommendations of the 2006 M.S. Swaminathan Commission, including providing minimum support price to all crops, the government had embarked on a mission of dismantling any State support to the agricultural sector.[156]

Though the Central government chose the time of the pandemic to introduce these laws, calculating that farmers would be silent due to the pandemic, it was proved wrong. The massive and organised protests against these laws under the banner of the *Samyukta Kisan Morcha,* which began in November 2020, continued through 2021. There was massive mobilisation with rallies of more than 100,000 persons, which finally resulted in the government being forced to repeal the laws almost a year after they were enacted.[157]

The changes briefly touched upon above are to some of the fundamental laws of the land. Some of the laws that are sought to be changed are themselves the outcome of determined and long-term struggles by labour, farmers, forest-dwellers and the rural poor.

Klein's perceptive analysis that capitalism thrives on disaster provides a good pointer to understand why the government chose to undertake such extreme measures during a global health crisis: capitalism remakes the world to benefit capital owners while further attenuating the rights to health, food, clean air and water as well as diluting the rights of labour.

This trampling of the rights of the marginalised calls to mind a State which can afford to ignore the voices of its people. Rosenberg, citing the example of fascist Italy, notes:

> In November, 1921, at the third congress of his party, Mussolini assured them [capitalists] that while he was of course opposed to liberalism in the political sense, he was unconditionally in favour of economic liberalism: 'If possible, I would be even inclined to hand over railways and post and telegraph back to private enterprise in order to relieve the state of economic functions that are really quite uneconomical.' In this way fascism returned to an unconditional defence of private capitalism.[158]

While the regime makes no bones about its espousal of a majoritarian project, it is essential to understand that this is no less about an 'unconditional defence of private capitalism'. The dismantling of labour laws, environmental laws and farm laws under cover of the pandemic speak to this project, which should be subjected to searching and critical scrutiny. Moreover, the 'shock doctrine' as applied to India is not only meant to advantage capital interests but also to further the agenda of the majoritarian State. The BJP government's majoritarian agenda had not been significantly challenged till the eruption of the anti-CAA protests towards the end of 2019. Led by Muslim women, Shaheen Bagh, a Muslim neighbourhood in Delhi, became the iconic face of these protests. Students were inspired by the movement, with Aligarh Muslim University, Jamia Millia Islamia University and Jawaharlal Nehru University becoming significant centres of resistance. The State was not able to formulate an adequate response to the countrywide protests which reclaimed the language of nationalism, positing an inclusive nationalism against the State's version of an exclusivist one.

However, the lockdown provided the State with the opportunity to abruptly terminate the protests. Not content with this, the Central government used the lockdown period to arrest thousands of protestors. The combination of the reduced functioning of the courts and the repressive laws under which protestors have been arrested has made access to bail difficult, if not impossible. The spiteful nature of State action is demonstrated by the arrest under the UAPA of young anti-CAA protestor Safoora Zargar in the middle of the pandemic when she was pregnant. She was denied bail by the sessions court and eventually granted bail by the high court after spending three months in jail.[159]

While some of the FIRs lodged against anti-CAA protestors do not indicate any crime, even under a law as stringent as the UAPA, other FIRs have vindictively sought to pin the crimes of violence during the Delhi pogrom of 2020 on peaceful anti-CAA protestors and even the victims.[160] The State has sought to change the narrative of the Delhi pogrom from one which was incited by speeches made by BJP leaders and largely led by right-wing mobs to one led by peaceful anti-CAA protestors.

In its utterly cynical methodology of blaming the victims for their own losses, the State seems to have taken a leaf out of the Nazi playbook. The night called Kristallnacht, The Night of the Broken Glass, was when Nazi organisations took the law into their own hands and destroyed over 267 synagogues, 7,000 Jewish businesses and arrested 30,000 Jewish men and incarcerated them in concentration camps. The horrors of Kristallnacht were followed not by any accounting for the wrongs done but by further punishment of those who had suffered in the pogrom. As the German historian Volker Ullrich writes:

> Jews were required to pay an 'atonement contribution' of one billion reichsmarks for the Paris assassination.[161] In addition, as of 1 January, 1939, they were prohibited from running businesses or working as tradesmen and required to pay for all the damage to their businesses

and residences during the pogrom themselves. The sums due to them from insurance policies was confiscated by the Reich.[162]

The Central government continues to use the pandemic to further strengthen itself by seeking to alter the criminal law regime in the country. A committee was constituted by the home ministry under Ranbir Singh, director of the National Law University, Delhi, to consider 'reforms' of the IPC, CrPC and the Indian Evidence Act on 4 May 2020. The unrepresentative all-male committee did not publish its terms of reference; neither did it have any stakeholders from those communities most intimately affected by the criminal law, nor was the level of autonomy of the committee from the home ministry clear. The questionnaires circulated by the committee, which seemed to indicate that all of criminal law was up for reform, raised red flags among many stakeholders.

Eminent judges and senior advocates raised substantive objections to the committee's proposals.[163] Members of civil society sent a representation to the committee, critiquing the government's intent to carry out 'far reaching changes in the entire legal framework which operates around crime' when the country is 'going through one of the most serious crises it has ever faced in the form of the COVID-19 pandemic'.[164] They took serious objection to 'the Committee's intent to open up settled principles of jurisprudence which have a constitutional sanction including questions such as the requirement of proof beyond a reasonable doubt, shifting of burden of proof, re-examining Actus Reus and Mens Rea requirements under the I.P.C and re-examining the need and framework for strict and absolute liability'. They also expressed their apprehension that the criminal justice reforms would ultimately 'authorize and legitimize a dangerous new penal system which will see the unconstitutional principles which are the heart of the UAPA become the ordinary criminal law of this land'.

The representation by fourteen retired judges and fifty-two advocates expressed alarm that 'the Committee appears to be labouring under some pre-conceived ideas on the law, crime control and the

Constitution'. They asserted that 'Changing time-honoured principles such as those that govern the burden of proof and proof beyond reasonable doubt should not even be contemplated.' They, in fact, called for the suspension of 'the functioning of the committee while India remains in the grip of the COVID-19 pandemic'.[165]

The previous chapter on the undeclared emergency highlighted the troubling challenges faced by those concerned about the future of Indian democracy. Many of the challenges related to the authoritarianism of the State have deeper roots in Indian history. However, as this chapter argues, the challenges of an authoritarian State are compounded by a movement towards totalitarianism. The ambitions of the State go beyond the pursuit of power for its own sake and encompass a vision of a wider societal transformation in line with Hindutva ideology. It is this coming to power of a deeply authoritarian regime imbued with an ideological mission that poses a fundamental challenge to the constitutional imagination of India.

5

What Is to Be Done?

Political prisoners know the meaning of hope but they do not know the meaning of despair. Chera called me a frightful optimist for this, and yet I must honestly admit that although I have known pain, suffering and anxiety along with hope, happiness and enthusiasm, never have I been plunged into despair and frustration even in the most trying times.

In personal matters, I have felt a sorrowful indifference at moments and said, 'Let troubles and hardships come if they must.' I have felt detachment, but have never yielded in to cynicism even for a moment in my solitary cell.[1]

– Varavara Rao

Histories of Resistance

How does one confront an authoritarian State that openly uses repressive laws to shut down dissent? And what if the State is not just authoritarian but also potentially has totalitarian ambitions? That such a regime is in power in India today makes the insistent Leninist question, 'What is to be done?', very important to ask and very difficult to answer.

In some ways, the answer must be gathered from what is already being done. There is dissatisfaction with the actions of the regime, and it has found a voice in acts of resistance, both big and small, spanning every field—from culture to law to politics. Such resistance could draw sustenance both from contemporary forms of activism as well as global histories of dissent, and be nourished by a deeper historical, cultural and political understanding. But this is essential: a strong and united resistance must emerge.

Defence of the Normative State

In contemporary India, as noted earlier in the book, the prerogative State has made significant inroads into the normative State. Interestingly, Ernst Fraenkel has argued that the Nazi State was a 'dual state' comprising both normative and prerogative elements. International relations scholar Jens Meierhenrich, in his excellent introduction to Fraenkel's book *The Dual State*, argues that 'Fraenkel's great achievement' was to 'have countered, in the substantive parts of his analysis, the scholarly trend of treating the German polity as if it were a totalitarian "black box", to have resisted the moral urge to depict the emergent racial order as a monolithic garrison state that emerged fully formed'.[2] Meierhenrich posits that, for Fraenkel, the normative State had to coexist alongside the expanding prerogative State in Nazi Germany because 'capitalism presupposes a high degree of legal regularity and, hence, some features of the liberal rule of law. Insofar as German fascism remains capitalist, Fraenkel concludes, it preserves certain minimum characteristics of modern rational authority that can be identified in the sphere of private law.'[3]

If the normative State continued to exist in Nazi Germany, then undoubtedly it will persist in India as well, regardless of the continuing growth of the prerogative State. And it is these elements of the normative State that could form the basis of resistance.

Just as nine high courts upheld their constitutional duty during the Emergency era—Justice Khanna too acknowledged that he was reaffirming the high courts' position in his dissent—in the contemporary era as well, when there was growing concern about the Supreme Court, several high courts took seriously their role in ensuring that the government's actions were in conformity with the Constitution. The high courts of Karnataka, Bombay, Tamil Nadu, Andhra Pradesh, Uttar Pradesh and Gujarat passed orders to protect the rights of migrant workers post the lockdown. The courts exercised a dialogic jurisdiction, nudging the State to fulfil its constitutional obligations.

In the context of the COVID-19 pandemic, the high courts by admitting petitions of various marginalised groups, such as street sweepers, poor persons and prisoners, gave visibility and voice to their concerns, nudged states into being transparent about what they were doing to protect the rights of those affected by the pandemic and subjected the claims of the State that the rights of these groups were being protected to verification. By regular monitoring, they ensured that the State brought into force policies that would fulfil its constitutional responsibilities.

The Karnataka High Court, for example, monitored the functioning of the state when it came to ensuring the rights of migrants, food security, the running of anganwadis, the rights of street sweepers, transgender persons as well as prisoners. The court's intervention and monitoring ensured that Karnataka ran free trains to transport migrants back to their homes, distributed rations without requiring ration cards and protected the health and safety of street sweepers during the pandemic.

As senior advocate Mihir Desai notes, the response of some of the high courts offers a telling contrast to the Supreme Court's response to the migrant crisis. The Supreme Court had accepted the claim of the Central government that there were no migrants on the road in spite of the migrant crisis being the largest mass migration since Partition. He also observes that while the Supreme Court disposed of a petition to ensure food security during the lockdown, stating that it was a policy matter, the high courts of Karnataka and Bombay continued to hold the state accountable when it came to ensuring food security.[4]

Justices Abhay Shreeniwas Oka and B.V. Nagarathna of the Karnataka High Court repeatedly asserted during oral arguments that, while the manner of the Karnataka government's response to COVID-19 was a policy matter in which there would be no interference, the court would look into the way the policy was implemented. The court implied that it would not substitute its wisdom for the government's and take over its functioning, but was committed to ensuring that executive action and policy conformed to the Constitution.[5]

While this is heartening, the far more difficult question to answer is, what does one do when the decisions of the apex court appear to be more aligned with the prerogative State?

The work that Ernst Fraenkel did in Nazi Germany, or anti-apartheid lawyers did in South Africa, or Israeli and Palestinian lawyers continue to do in Israel, is to uphold the spirit of the normative State. Even if it means certain defeat, the continuous and daily assertion of the rule of law keeps it alive in the common imagination till such time as the normative State is re-established wholly.

Such assertions are never in vain and can, even in the heyday of a totalitarian regime, shake its legitimacy. One such moment was the custodial death of Steve Biko, leader of the Black Consciousness Movement in apartheid South Africa. As Meierhenrich notes in *The Legacies of Law*, the response in the Afrikaner press to Biko's murder was 'a turning point ... For the first time, some Afrikaner journalists openly criticised the government on moral grounds.' Meierhenrich cites one such example that showed the 'rift in Afrikanerdom':

> It is not only opponents of the Government who have grave misgivings about detention without trial and the dimensions it has assumed. ... [I]t is obvious that one cannot keep on locking up people one after the other.

He concludes that 'this apparent cleavage cutting through Afrikanerdom underlines how important the legal way of doing things had become in South Africa.'[6]

In the occupied territories of Palestine, the work of human rights activists and lawyers goes a long way in asserting that the occupation is illegal. Painstaking legal work continues to demonstrate that the policies followed by the Israeli State in the name of security—be it the occupation of Palestinian land, assassinations, torture, administrative detention or the demolition of Palestinian homes—are both illegal and immoral. The victories in the courts are few and far between, but each time a particularly egregious violation is litigated, the legal, ethical and moral opposition to the State is emphasised. A pre-eminent human rights lawyer in Israel, Avigdor Feldman, argued in an op-ed in an Israeli paper that the numerous litigations against the occupation resulted in a jurisprudence of the Israeli High Court that has become 'the great library of the occupation'. This paper trail is important, as 'A regime of evil writes itself to oblivion. It leaves behind, with historic generosity, not a paper trail but a highway of words that will feed PhD theses, master's theses, and scholarly conventions until kingdom come.'[7]

Another Israeli human rights lawyer, Michael Sfard, argues that human rights lawyering against the Israeli apartheid state is about going to court every day and 'writing an indictment of the status quo'.[8] In a compelling account of the need for normative assertion of the rule of law, even when not favoured by the Israeli public or by the courts, Sfard asserts in *The Wall and the Gate*:

> The significance of this legal fight for Israel's society is greater than the sum of its victories and successes. Based as it is on moral and ethical values, the fight preserves an alternative to the policies of settlement, belligerence, and dispossession, even when no one seems to be interested in that alternative. It is not only lawyers who do the work of preservation, but also public figures, artists and academics, journalists and politicians, all of those who fight for democratic values and against the occupation. However, the critical, cautionary, educating voice of legal activists has a special role and importance, constantly defining and articulating the evil to be uprooted and the good that should come in its stead.[9]

Sfard goes on to argue that 'one day the occupation will end, like apartheid in South Africa, like the fall of the Berlin Wall'. These were not events which were 'predicted', but yet they happened. It is the role of human rights lawyers to persist with their work, holding their 'heads high', knowing that 'they have a role in the appearance of cracks in the occupation'.[10]

There is a long history to this kind of legal work. Legal scholar Jules Lobel argues in *Success Without Victory* that, based on the experience of repeated legal failures in the United States, one needs to think of victory as beyond the question of a win or a loss, and that 'success inheres in the creation of a tradition, of a commitment to struggle, of a narrative of resistance that can inspire others similarly to resist'.[11]

What is unpredictable is when the inflection point might arrive and the ideas put forward by a minority begin to have a wider public resonance. In recent Indian history, the brutal rape and murder of Nirbhaya triggered a mass protest, forcing the Indian State to reform the rape law.[12] More recently, the custodial torture and death of the father-and-son duo of Jayaraj and Bennix Felix in Tamil Nadu triggered mass outrage against the police. In this case, the Chennai High Court monitored the police investigation, which, in turn, led to the arrest of the concerned police officers.[13] This opens up the possibility of conviction for custodial murder, which rarely happens in the Indian context. A Human Rights Watch report notes that 591 people died in police custody between 2010 and 2015, but not a single officer was convicted for a custodial death in this time frame.[14] While the Jayaraj–Bennix trial is yet to conclude, the proceedings hold out the hope that police impunity for custodial deaths can be breached. These are only a few examples of unpredictable moments of inflection, which point to why it is important to keep asserting normative positions such as that sexual violence and custodial deaths are unacceptable within a rule-of-law framework.

These changes would not have come about if the normative State had not been kept alive, even if only through legal 'failures'. It is important that injustices are not allowed to disappear into 'holes of oblivion'.[15] Keeping constitutionalism alive, even when institutions abdicate their constitutional responsibility, is vital. As legal scholar Gautam Bhatia puts it in his blog, *Indian Constitutional Law and Philosophy*:

... it remains important at all times to articulate and defend *the rule of law* as an independent value, and to record and demonstrate how the actions of the Court fall short in that respect; in other words, there must at all times be an active struggle to preserve the *idea* of the rule of law, despite—or even because of—what happens in the Courts.[16]

The defence of the normative State requires one to have an imagination that can see beyond immediate 'victory' or 'loss'. It is about invoking and keeping alive the norms that govern the constitutional State through hostile times in the hope of a more propitious time to come.

Cultivating Constitutional Values

Since the challenges of the contemporary era include both the authoritarianism of the State and an intolerant society, it is important that society be equally the focal point of activism. The constitutional values embedded in the Preamble, of liberty, equality, dignity and fraternity, need to take deeper roots in society. Undoubtedly, all four values that underlie the Constitution are under threat today.

These values are articulated not only in the text of the Constitution but also in the Constituent Assembly Debates, the history of the freedom struggle as well as in literature and dissenting Indian traditions. Kabir and Basavanna, the poets from the north and south of India respectively, are only two examples of thinkers who articulated fraternity centuries before the French Revolution. More recently, writers such as Mahasweta Devi from Bengal and Girish Karnad from Karnataka have given expression to humanist values which find an echo in the Constitution. These values can be communicated through a wide range of mediums, be it literature, myth, history or popular culture.

When it comes to liberty, especially the freedom of speech, expression and association, an exemplary defender was Gandhi. He was the strongest critic of the sedition law and vociferously defended the right to dissent. When he was being tried for sedition by the colonial government for his anti-government writing, he famously defended his right to be seditious, arguing that the governement could not compel him to have affection for it:

> Section 124-A under which I am happily charged is perhaps the prince among the political sections of the Indian Penal Code designed to suppress the liberty of the citizen. Affection cannot be manufactured or regulated by law. If one has no affection for a person or system, one should be free to give the fullest expression to his disaffection, so long as he does not contemplate, promote or incite violence. ... I have no personal ill will against any single administrator; much less can I have any disaffection towards the King's person. But I hold it to be a virtue to be disaffected towards a Government which in its totality had done more harm to India than any previous system.[17]

The exercise of the freedom of speech is important, as silent complicity provides the foundation for an authoritarian State. A sense of pervasive fear prevents citizens from exercising this right. As Ravish Kumar writes, 'If you can't speak up before friends, how will you ever stand before the government to criticize it? You will have to start practicing speaking up somewhere. Things aren't so bad yet that no one can speak out.'[18] The cultivation of liberty demands that you overcome the culture of fear and express your opinions even if they go against a prevailing societal and political consensus.

Cultivating constitutional values is also about challenging inequalities embedded in society, with relation to caste, gender, sexual orientation or gender identity. This is sometimes more difficult than standing up to the State, for challenging the norms of the society in which one lives can mean facing criticism, alienation and ostracisation. Ambedkar understood this:

> Most people do not realize that society can practise tyranny and oppression against an individual in a far greater degree than a Government can. The means and scope that are open to society

for oppression are more extensive than those that are open to Government, also they are far more effective. What punishment in the penal code is comparable in its magnitude and its severity to excommunication?[19]

Challenging these social orthodoxies, all of which constrain human freedoms, is a key aspect of a transformative constitution. To defend the transformative constitution is not to defend the status quo, but is instead a dynamic call to challenge the inequalities embedded in society.

The defence of constitutional values is, at its heart, about the non-negotiability of the dignity of the individual. It is a difficult concept to define, but Ambedkar hinted at its essence by contrasting it with economic want:

> If I may say so, the servile classes do not care for social amelioration. The want and poverty which has been their lot is nothing to them as compared to the insult and indignity which they have to bear as a result of the vicious social order. Not bread but honour is what they want.[20]

To lead a dignified life is to experience the fullness of what it is to be human. What demeans one's dignity is scorn, ostracism and humiliation, all of which attempt to strip a person of their humanity. We get a sense of the deeper philosophical significance of this in B.N. Rau's formulation—on Ambedkar's insistence, as Akash Singh Rathore persuasively argues—during the drafting of the Indian Constitution, that 'dignity of the individual' should precede 'unity of the nation' in the Preamble. Rau notes (again, mirroring Ambedkar's preoccupations), '... the reason for putting the dignity of the individual first is that unless the dignity of the individual is assured, the nation cannot be united'.[21]

What Ambedkar posits is the idea that individuals are not means to an end but ends in themselves. He insists that the individual is the fundamental unit on which rights are conferred. The lexical priority of the individual is really a key to the philosophical centring of the individual in the Indian Constitution, as philosopher Akash Singh

Rathore notes in *Ambedkar's Preamble*.[22] It is on the dignity of the individual (including the autonomy of expression, the freedom of choice and the freedom from humiliation) that the 'unity and integrity of the nation' is premised.

This concept of dignity also speaks to the struggles of marginalised communities. In *Navtej Singh Johar v Union of India*,[23] in which the apex court read down Section 377 of the IPC, the court saw dignity as linked to the idea of autonomy and intimate choice.

> Section 377 insofar as it curtails the personal liberty of LGBT persons to engage in voluntary consensual sexual relationships with a partner of their choice, in a safe and dignified environment, is violative of Article 21. It inhibits them from entering and nurturing enduring relationships. As a result, LGBT individuals are forced to either lead a life of solitary existence without companion, or lead a closeted life as 'unapprehended felons'.

Finally, a cultivation of constitutional values has to be about the defence of fraternity. According to Ambedkar:

> Fraternity means a sense of common brotherhood of all Indians. ... It is the principle which gives unity and solidarity to social life. It is a difficult thing to achieve. ... In India there are castes. The castes are anti-national. In the first place because they bring about separation in social life. They are anti-national also because they generate jealousy and antipathy between caste and caste. But we must overcome all these difficulties if we wish to become a nation in reality. For fraternity can be a fact only when there is a nation. Without fraternity, equality and liberty will be no deeper than a coat of paint.[24]

Defending fraternity will have to involve defending inter-caste marriage, the living together of communities and castes, and all such practices that can enhance fellow-feeling between Indians—a proposition that could be dangerous in this country. As Ravish Kumar puts it, 'I wouldn't know how it is in other places but in India, to love is to battle with innumerable strictures imposed by society and religion.'[25] The roll call of lovers who have been killed by their own family is unfortunately too long to record here. 'The way things are in India, couples invariably find little love and far more hatred in the course of their love. That they still dare to love is worthy of our salutations.'[26] In the India of today, a defence of the right to love is an essential dimension of nurturing constitutional values.

This task of cultivating the values of liberty, equality, fraternity and dignity gets to the heart of the meaning of the freedom struggle. Although India is a 'free' country and has been so for seventy-five years, the seeding of these values remains an unfinished project, even more so as we struggle to defend them from an authoritarian State. Again, one cannot but recall Ambedkar on the difficult yet absolutely necessary task of seeding constitutional morality in the country:

> The question is, can we presume such a diffusion of constitutional morality? Constitutional morality is not a natural sentiment. It has to be cultivated. We must realise that our people have yet to learn it. Democracy in India is only a top dressing on an Indian soil which is essentially undemocratic.[27]

In an interview, Jean Drèze notes that this task is vital, as merely addressing the State can never be enough. There is, he says, a desperate need to 'rebuild commitment to democracy among people who are privileged'.[28] The flourishing of democracy depends on these values taking deeper roots in Indian society.

Revival of Forms of Dissent Rooted in Culture and Religion

One of the challenges that contemporary activism faces is the dismissal of 'human rights' as 'Western', without any roots in Indian culture. To some extent, activists themselves have ceded ground when it comes to culture and religion, even as they seek to defend humanist values, justice and rights using the language of the Constitution. As historian Ramachandra Guha notes in an article in the *EPW*, this arises from the fall of the 'bilingual intellectual' like Ambedkar, who 'knew his Tukaram, but also his John Stuart Mill',[29] and the rise of the English-speaking intellectual with roots in Antonio Gramsci and Karl Marx but not in the Mahabharata or the vachanas of Basavanna. This loss of 'intellectuals who are properly linguidextrous' has meant that the conceptual vocabulary of protest, originating from the monolingual activist and academic, is often impoverished.[30]

It is important that activists are able to employ cultural metaphors that arise from, and speak to, the experience of the common person. To put it simply, the reference to Nero when one means an authoritarian ruler may not be grasped as easily as the metaphor of Kamsa. To give another example, the lassitude of a politician who refuses to respond to your concerns may be better invoked through Kumbhakarna rather than Rip Van Winkle.

Further, it should be noted that writing in English and in journals has a limited reach. As Guha notes in another article, 'dexterity in multiple languages' is 'a tool' for 'reaching out to more people, and expanding the ambit of the debate, and consequently increasing the number of participants in the debate'.[31]

Ambedkar, for instance, never relied solely on texts with Western provenance, making a sustained effort, especially in the later part of his life, to return to texts and traditions with Indian lineage and producing such work as his celebrated re-interpretation of Buddhism in *Buddha and His Dhamma*.[32] His extensive engagement with religion and his conversion to Buddhism may have come from an understanding of the limitations of the constitutional argument's form, and the necessity for also thinking of dissent within the 'idiom of religion', as historian Romila Thapar writes in *Voices of Dissent*.[33] It could be said that this was the spirit in which Ambedkar moved away from attributing the idea of fraternity to the French Revolution, as he did during the Mahad Satyagraha in 1927, to stating that fraternity was not alien to India as it was nothing other than the Buddhist principle of maitreyi.[34]

However, it is not only a question of greater 'reach' through finding appropriate cultural metaphors but also, more importantly, about recovering a cultural memory of dissent. As Thapar demonstrates, dissent is an Indian tradition, with texts such as the Mahabharata encoding dissenting viewpoints within.[35] Her larger argument is that there is a 'narrowness' to the 'contemporary definition of Indian culture' as it 'excludes … assenting and dissenting dimensions that are inevitable in the creation of any expansive culture'.[36]

Apart from the scope for creative interpretations of mainstream traditions and texts, there are also entire traditions in India that arose as a form of dissent. Perhaps the most powerful of these was the emergence of the Bhakti tradition in south India, which was based on a critique of Brahminical Hinduism's acceptance of hierarchy and inequality. It was a truly subaltern revolt, with the 'religious rebels' including 'boatmen, washermen, watermen, tanners, cobblers, tailors, barbers, shepherds, labourers, basket weavers, fishermen, toddy sellers and peasants', notes author Mukunda Rao in *Sky-clad*.[37] The Bhakti tradition also critiqued notions of gender and sexuality, and nobody embodied this critique better than the well-known poet Akka Mahadevi, who walked naked, 'breast to breast' with the cosmos.[38]

The challenge to Brahminism was not only in terms of radical thoughts and ideas but also how these transmuted into radical action. Basavanna's life is an exemplar of revolutionary provocation, such as when he blessed a wedding between a Brahmin girl and a boy from the cobbler caste, both of whom were his followers. The explosive potential of this wedding is described in Karnad's play *Taledanda* quite simply: '… this is not a wedding, it is a revolution'. Basavanna, in Karnad's retelling, goes on to say that 'the orthodox will see the mingling of castes as a blow at the very roots of varnashrama dharma. Bigotry has not faced such a challenge in two thousand years.'[39]

This wedding across lines of caste has since formed the basis of several contemporary Kannada plays, such as *Sankranti* by P. Lankesh and *Mahachaitra* by H.S. Shivaprakash. We must now draw upon this tradition—from Basavanna's revolutionary act in the twelfth century to contemporary attempts to remember and recreate his life—to critique, for instance, the anti-love laws of Yogi Adityanath's governance in Uttar Pradesh.

In August 2020, during the inauguration pooja for the Ram temple in Ayodhya—to be constructed over the ruins of the Babri masjid—Prime Minister Modi was quoted as saying that finally a grand temple would be built for 'our Ram Lalla who had to live under a tent for years'.[40]

For those who vested their faith in the Constitution, the day was one of sadness, loss, hurt and betrayal. The language of the Constitution on secularism and justice can capture this shock. However, there is another critique available of the prime minister's words, rooted in the spiritual traditions of India.

> The rich
> Will make temples for Shiva
> What shall I,
> A poor man, do?
> My legs are pillars,
> The body the shrine,
> The head a cupola of God
> Listen oh lord of the meeting rivers,
> Things standing shall fall
> But the moving ever shall stay[41]

Basavanna's critique was of the 'priestly dictatorship over spiritual matters and, more importantly, against the institutionalisation of God(s) grace and the Sacred', writes Rao.[42] This remarkable verse, according to the eminent translator A.K. Ramanujan, 'dramatizes several of the themes and oppositions characteristic of the protest movement called Virashaivism'.[43] The movement was a 'social upheaval by and for the poor, the low caste and the outcaste against the rich and the privileged; it was the rising of the unlettered against the literate pundit, flesh and blood against stone'.[44]

Basavanna's vachana evokes a tradition that views the true

relationship between God and human as being intimate and personal, and worship as being an offering of the self. He would have been shocked at the spiritual poverty of a world view which, like the 'rich', takes pride in building a 'magnificent temple'.

There is an Indian culture that has radical and dissenting strands, and is often at odds with what is taken to be 'Indian' culture. Any activism for the future should be able to draw from these dissenting strands to shape a broader humanistic vision of freedom and justice.

Humour as Dissent

Humour has emerged as a potent form of dissent in many parts of the world. In India, the emergence of stand-up comedy has been aided by digital media, and today, there are a number of comedians who are YouTube sensations with followings in the lakhs, like Varun Grover, Kunal Kamra and legions of others.

Comedy has the ability to shame the State into performing its constitutional obligations. Nothing embodies this better than the story of Munawar Faruqui, a young man originally from Gujarat whose family was affected by the 2002 pogrom and later shifted to Mumbai. Faruqui makes his living as a comedian. His stand-up routines posted on social media include a number of jokes about growing up Muslim, and satire on the current political scenario, from the way elections are run to the government's failure during the migrant crisis.[45] Faruqui also pokes fun at political figures as diverse as Nehru and Amit Shah. His humour is 'tongue in cheek' and 'unapologetically political', and includes such one-liners as 'making bomb is not easy, I think it's as difficult as building a mandir'.[46]

On a fateful day in Indore in January 2021, a local BJP leader disrupted Faruqui's show before it could even begin, accusing him of disrespecting Hindu gods. The comedian responded that he was not targeting Hinduism and in fact he mostly made fun of the Muslim community, with jokes on 'triple talaq' and so on. Not satisfied with

Faruqui's assertion of being an 'equal opportunity offender', the vigilantes, who included the son of a BJP MLA, marched him to the police station, where he was arrested on the charge of hurting religious sentiments.

In an irony of Kafkaesque proportions, Faruqui was arrested for a joke he did not even crack. He had to spend thirty-seven days in jail, with the Madhya Pradesh High Court denying him bail. Eventually, he had to approach the Supreme Court for relief. Faruqui's spirit was not dimmed by this unfair treatment, and he played upon his own detention by releasing a video in which he said he was not 'leaving comedy' but 'living comedy'. He would not quit comedy, he asserted, because it kept him alive.[47]

Faruqui may have been suggesting that a lightness of spirit is vital for coping in difficult times. However, comedy is also a political force, and authoritarian rulers, cognisant of its power, strive to nip it in the bud.

Another humourist worth recalling is Mahatma Gandhi. Endlessly deified and sanctified on the one hand and reviled on the other, his impish sense of humour is now quite forgotten. The PUCL, in 2021, in a statement on Martyrs' Day, 30 January, remembered the Gandhi whom 'Sarojini Naidu jokingly called Mickey Mouse, because of the way his ears stuck out'. 'Gandhi himself was not averse to cracking jokes' and 'when he met King George V and a reporter reportedly asked him why he had so little clothes on, Gandhi is said to have remarked, "The king has enough clothes on for both of us."' The PUCL wrote that they would 'like to remember the mischievous Gandhiji especially today … because Munawar Farooqui, a young comedian from Gandhiji's own state, languishes in jail because he dares to crack jokes at the current political establishment. … It is a sad commentary of our democracy that today comedians of all stripes and hues find themselves under unprecedented attack as the state has lost its sense of humour and comedy is criminalised'.[48]

To be playful about serious subjects can be a meaningful act of dissent and a way of reducing the gap between the powerful and the powerless. Charlie Chaplin's film *The Great Dictator*, which mercilessly parodies the power and pomp of fascism, shows how humour can effortlessly skewer authority, reducing its power in the eyes of the people by rendering it an object of ridicule.

Preserving a sense of humour and enlarging the space for public humour remain vital tasks in combating an aspirationally totalitarian regime in India. It is part of the fight to preserve the freedom of speech and expression, not least on the internet, where irreverent political humour flourishes, with many stand-up comedians having their own YouTube channels. Recently, the Centre notified the Information Technology (Intermediary Guidelines and Digital Media Ethics Code) Rules, 2021, which attempts to specifically bring social media under tighter State control. Intermediaries will have to exercise 'due diligence' to ensure that the content posted by users does not, among other things, threaten the 'unity, integrity and sovereignty of India'. If they fail to take action to remove such content, they can be prosecuted under criminal law. This could have a chilling impact on online comedy as the State could consider virtually any content as coming within the restricted clauses and intermediaries might self-censor user content, fearing criminal action by the State. The State's attempt to monitor, control and take down content online as facilitated by the Information Technology Rules will have to be successfully challenged before the courts to preserve the freedom of speech.[49]

Bureaucratic Dissent

Dissent in its flamboyant avatar takes the form of a Salman Rushdie fleeing a death threat but standing by his book or a Pratap Bhanu Mehta being forced to resign from a university rather than keeping silent. However, this performative register is only one of many forms of dissent.

Academician Shiv Visvanathan writes in *Seminar* about the dissent of the bureaucrat through the story of R.B. Sreekumar. As the additional director general of police (intelligence) of Gujarat, Sreekumar was requested to follow what he considered to be 'illegal' or 'unethical' directions issued by his higher-ups in the Gujarat administration in the aftermath of the pogrom in Gujarat in 2002. He kept a diary of these instructions and submitted extracts from it in the affidavit he filed, against the wishes of his superiors, before the Nanavati Commission. Visvanathan gives an example of the content and tenor of the Sreekumar affidavits in his article:

> ... on 16 April 2002, the Chief Minister called a meeting of the DGP, himself [Sreekumar], and P.K. Mishra, Principal Secretary to the Chief Minister. Modi argued that certain Congress leaders were responsible for the continuing communal incidents in Ahmedabad. Sreekumar, as head of SIB, responded that he did not have any information to this effect. Modi asked him to immediately start tapping Shankarsinh Waghela's phone. Sreekumar replied that this was not legal or ethical for as yet there was no information regarding Waghela's involvement in crime. P.K. Mishra, Principal Secretary also tried to persuade Sreekumar to do so. Sreekumar's column on 'further action' has this terse sentence: 'The Chief Minister's instruction being illegal and immoral not complied with.'[50]

For Visvanathan, the dissent by the bureaucrat, which manifested in an 'official note' or an 'affidavit', is not a 'scream, a challenge or a human rights protest' but rather 'appears as something more banal, as a policeman performing his duty. Bureaucratic dissent is expressed not in the 'poetics of rights' but in the 'everyday prose of duty'.[51]

When most of the bureaucracy in Gujarat post 2002 went along with the opinion of the government, where did Sreekumar find his conviction? The rewards for following the government line were clear and the punishment implicit.[52] However, Sreekumar dissented.

His refusal to toe the government line was firmly grounded in his conception of his duty as well as in the oath he had taken to preserve, protect and defend the Constitution. As he put it, '... if the CM's policies are in contravention of the letter, spirit and ethos of the Constitution of India, no government officer is bound to follow such policies.'[53] Sreekumar was one of a tribe of bureaucrats in Gujarat, which included Rahul Sharma,[54] Sanjiv Bhatt and Rajnish Rai.[55] They had to pay a high price for their dissent. All of them were subjected to harassment and prosecution by the State.

Bhatt, then an IPS office in Gujarat, paid the highest price of all for having claimed he was present in a meeting held at the chief minister's office on 27 February 2002, where he heard Modi directing the police and the state administration to refrain from taking any strict action and permit members of the majority community to express anger against the minority community.[56] The SIT set up to probe Modi's complicity in the violence discarded Bhatt's evidence as 'ill motivated because he thought he was being denied a promotion'. Raju Ramachandran, the amicus in the matter appointed by the Supreme Court, disagreed and said that the 'evidence of Sanjiv Bhatt could not be summarily discarded, particularly in the light of other circumstantial evidence'.[57] Bureaucratic dissent bears testimony to the fact that even in hostile circumstances, when the pressure to conform is huge, the human urge to act in accordance with one's conscience cannot be underestimated. The fact that such dissenters exist, that individuals still act in accordance with their conscience, nurtures the hope that another world is possible.

Bhatt was maliciously prosecuted by the State, which revived an old and false charge of custodial death and followed through to ensure a conviction and a sentence of life imprisonment in June 2019. Since then, he has been in prison. As his children Aakashi and Shantanu Bhatt poignantly noted in a social media post on his birthday in 2020:

An example was made of an upright officer, and you, the people of this nation stood in silence. He was incessantly targeted and victimised, and the nation looked the other way. His home was broken down, and the nation shut its eyes and ears. He was falsely framed and vindictively incarcerated in a fabricated case, ripping him away from his family, sentenced to languish behind bars for a crime he did not commit, and the nation still watched as silent spectators ... Our father, Mr Sanjiv Bhatt stood up to this totalitarian regime at great personal and professional cost, and today, he is paying the heavy price for being, honest, upright and courageous. As our father spends yet another year incarcerated for a crime he did not commit, his only crime that he did not buckle under political pressure and vindictive victimisation; I implore you all, to be the citizens, the nation that our father believes exists.[58]

While the State may have succeeded in clamping down on the bureaucracy in Gujarat, the idea of dissent as duty is difficult to suppress entirely.

There have been judges too, who have performed their constitutional duty without fear or favour, even in very difficult times. One such extraordinary, yet unsung and forgotten story is that of Justice Jyotsna Yagnik, who in an exemplary judgement convicted those accused of murder and looting in the neighbourhood of Naroda Patiya in Ahmedabad in 2002.[59] As journalist Ashish Khetan notes in *Undercover*, Justice Yagnik wrote a letter to the SIT, informing them that she had 'received as many as twenty-two threatening letters and blank phone calls at her home when she was presiding over the Naroda Patiya case and after her verdict'. He goes on to say that 'right-wing commentators have even demanded her prosecution' and she was subjected to a 'campaign of vilification on social media'.[60] When she was asked 'what kept her going when so many in the system had failed the victims of the Gujarat riots', she responded, 'To keep my head high before my own conscience. To truly observe the oath of upholding the constitution I had taken when I became a judge. That's what kept me going.'[61]

In December 2020, in an unprecedented move, a sessions court judge in Srinagar recused himself from hearing a bail application after he received a call from a Jammu and Kashmir High Court judge's secretary and was directed not to grant bail. The sessions judge, Abdul Rashid Malik, recorded in his order that he had received a call from the secretary to Justice Javed Iqbal Wani on the morning when the bail plea moved by one Sheikh Salman was scheduled to be heard. Judge Malik stated that the secretary to Justice Wani told him, 'I have been directed by the Hon'ble Mr. Justice Javed Iqbal Wani to convey to you to make sure that no bail is granted to Sheikh Salman. If there is any Anticipatory bail pending, the direction is the same.'

Expressing his inability to hear the matter, the judge directed that the bail application be submitted to the registrar (judicial) of the high court, so that the case may be placed before the chief justice as it involved the liberty of a person.[62] According to media reports, the chief justice sent the matter back to the sessions judge and the accused was released on bail.[63]

As retired high court judge Anjana Prakash notes in an article in the *Wire*, '... the sessions judge called out the high court judge and that too in a judicial order, putting his career at stake. I salute him and commend the chief justice of the J&K high court for having taken prompt action upon it.' Justice Prakash also recommends that Judge Malik's career be tracked 'a few years hence to see what effect this act has had upon him or his career'.[64]

Bureaucratic dissent is never easy—the dissenter is often alone in their action and surrounded by a hostile system. But it can be of the greatest consequence, as an analysis of what bureaucratic dissenters have achieved shows us.

Edward Snowden was a contractor with the National Security Agency in the US, who chose to expose the organisation's wrongdoings, setting off a stormy global debate on State surveillance and the violation of the right to privacy.

In France, in the late nineteenth century, there was the instance of the injustice suffered by Alfred Dreyfus, a military officer who had been wrongly convicted of espionage merely because he was Jewish. Dreyfus's unjust conviction came to light because of Georges Picquart, an intelligence officer whose investigation revealed that he had been wrongly convicted, and who, in spite of pressure from within the military, refused to withdraw his report.

Picquart's dissent led to a national campaign launched by intellectuals such as French writer Émile Zola, which finally resulted in Dreyfus being pardoned. This would never have come to pass without the quintessential bureaucratic dissenter. As Hannah Arendt observes:

> [Picquart] was no hero and certainly no martyr. He was simply that common type of citizen with an average interest in public affairs who in the hour of danger (though not a minute earlier) stands up to defend his country in the same unquestioning way as he discharges his daily duties.[65]

For his pains, Picquart was arrested. The dissent of Bhatt, India's own forgotten Picquart, is invaluable despite his incarceration. The paper trail left by a bureaucrat ensures that there are no 'holes of oblivion' into which all deeds good and evil will disappear. As Arendt writes, 'nothing can ever be "practically useless", at least, not in the long run'. For Arendt, the lesson of dissent is simple. It is that, under 'conditions of terror', 'most people will comply, but some people will not ... Humanly speaking, no more is required, and no more can reasonably be asked, for this planet to remain a place fit for human habitation'.[66]

Defending an Inclusive Nationalism

Nationalism is based on an affective identification with the nation. It has been criticised because it is the passions unleashed by nationalism which were responsible for the horrors of the two world wars. However, it was equally the passions unleashed by nationalism which were responsible for successful anti-colonial struggles around the world.

In India, in recent times, the idea of the nation has been sought to be monopolised by the Hindu Right. From the Ram Janmabhoomi campaign to cow protection to the 'protection' of Hindu girls from Muslim men, there are many symbols of an aggressive Hindu nationalism in evidence.

There is a need to move away from such an aggressive, xenophobic and exclusive idea of the nation to an inclusive one based on the 'ability to see full and equal humanity in another person', as US political philosopher Martha Nussbaum writes in *Political Emotions*. To the extent that such an idea of the nation exists in constitutional democracies, it must count as one of 'humanity's most difficult and fragile achievements'.[67]

In recent Indian history, it was the anti-CAA protests that best invoked the symbolism of the nation as an inclusive entity. At the protest sites, people energetically waved the national flag and carried posters of Gandhi and Ambedkar. Speakers at these sites recalled the history of the Indian national movement while protestors sang songs and recited poetry about liberty, equality and fraternity from the country's radical literary traditions. Thus, the deeply felt identification with the nation was channelled towards a critical, humanist and inclusive sense of belonging. This became an important counterpoint to the exclusivist understanding of nationhood.

To build a public culture with the nation as the object of love, one might well start with the author of India's national anthem, Rabindranath Tagore.

The national anthem is the first stanza of a five-stanza song written by Tagore. It reads:

You are the ruler of the minds of all people,
Dispenser of India's destiny.
Thy name rouses the hearts of Punjab,
Sindh, Gujarat and Maratha,
Of the Dravida and Orissa and Bengal;
It echoes in the hills of the Vindhyas and Himalayas,
Mingles in the music of Jamuna and Ganges
and is chanted by the waves of the Indian Ocean.
They pray for your blessings and sing your praise.

The saving of all people waits in your hand,
You dispenser of India's destiny.
Victory, victory, victory, victory to you. [68]

The second stanza of the song goes as follows:

Your call is announced continuously,
we heed Your gracious call
The Hindus, Buddhists, Sikhs, Jains, Parsees, Muslims, and Christians,
The East and the West come, to the side of Your throne,
And weave the garland of love.
Oh! You who bring in the unity of the people!
Victory be to You, dispenser of the destiny of India![69]

The national anthem, the first stanza of the poem, invokes a feeling of being one. By referring to the geographical diversity of the country as the object of love and veneration, it shows what inclusive nationalism can mean. The second stanza, by referring to the various religious communities who inhabit the land, also sets up the idea of an inclusive nation.

Uniquely, the author of the national anthem was also one of the strongest critics of nationalism. He wrote that 'with the growth of nationalism, man has become the greatest menace to man'.[70] Tagore went on to write three articles on nationalism in Japan, India and the West, all of which read as dire warnings against the dangers of nationalism. He saw the 'idea of the nation' as 'one of the most powerful anaesthetics that man has invented', under the influence of which 'the whole people can carry out its systematic programme of the most virulent self-seeking without being in the least aware of its moral perversion—in fact being dangerously resentful if it is pointed out'.[71]

However, Tagore, in spite of his critique of nationalism, was not opposed to the idea of building a common sentiment amongst the people. While opposing Japanese nationalism, he continued to affirm the commonality among the citizens of Japan based on their common reverence for the beauty of their land:

This spiritual bond of love she [Japan] has established with the hills
of her country, with the sea and the streams, with the forests in all
their flowerly moods and varied physiognomy of branches; she
has taken into her heart all the rustling whispers and sighing of the
woodlands and sobbing of the waves; ... this opening of the heart to
the soul of the world is not confined to a section of your privileged
classes, it is not the forced product of exotic culture, but it belongs
to all your men and women of all conditions. ... It is a civilisation of
human relationship.[72]

We can read Tagore's patriotism as the call for a 'civilisation of
human relationship' built on a common reverence for the beauty of
the native land. One of India's best-known cultural theorists, Ashis
Nandy, elaborates on the 'large, plural concept of India' and reaffirms
the universalism in Tagore's 'moral universe' in his book *The Illegitimacy
of Nationalism*. He quotes Tagore as saying, 'Because we have missed
the character of India as one related to the whole world, we have in
our action and thought given a description of India which is narrow
and faded.'[73] Nandy writes:

[Tagore's] version of patriotism rejected the violence propagated by
terrorists and revolutionaries, it rejected the concept of a single ethnic
Hindu Rasthra as anti-Indian and even anti-Hindu, and it dismissed
the idea of the nation-state as being the main actor in Indian political
life. His critics rightly guessed that Janaganamana could only be the
anthem of a state rooted in the Indian civilisation, not of an Indian
nation-state trying to be the heir to British-Indian empire.[74]

The national anthem is not based on the creation of an enemy, but
rather on an invocation of diversity; the country's unity lies precisely
in this diversity. If the national anthem is read with Tagore's corpus,
what you get is an aspirational image of the nation as it should be.
This is perhaps best exemplified in his famous poem 'Where the Mind
Is Without Fear'.

Where the mind is without fear and the head is held high
Where knowledge is free
Where the world has not been broken up into fragments
By narrow domestic walls
Where words come out from the depth of truth
Where tireless striving stretches its arms towards perfection
Where the clear stream of reason has not lost its way
Into the dreary desert sand of dead habit
Where the mind is led forward by thee
Into ever-widening thought and action
Into that heaven of freedom, my Father, let my country awake.

Here, Tagore speaks of a value of great importance: freedom from fear; fearlessness as an inviolable aspect of human dignity. He invokes the ideal of universalism by counterposing a free world to a world fragmented by 'narrow domestic walls'. He invokes the importance of public reasoning by invoking the counter-image of 'the dreary desert sand of dead habit'. For Tagore, nothing should be taken for granted and everything should be subjected to critique. At the same time, thought and action have to be linked together to achieve freedom. This is a Tagore-inflected notion of nationalism: it is not worship of power, nor an invocation of strength, but the invocation of a commonality based on the above values. Needless to say, all these values lie at the core of the Constitution.

Addressing Inequality

The defence of constitutional values, while important, does not address the reasons why totalitarianism is on the rise, not only in India but globally as well. Some thinkers, like French economist Thomas Picketty, would locate the rise of authoritarian states in economic factors.

In his book *Capital and Ideology*, Picketty takes a long view of history and locates the catastrophe of the two world wars in economic causes, particularly the rise of inequality. In his analysis, in the period before the First World War, between 1880 and 1914, the world underwent an 'inegalitarian turn'.[75] Ironically, the period post the French Revolution produced one of the most inegalitarian societies, with the highest levels of inequality the world had ever experienced. Picketty argues that this was unsustainable and the 'excessive concentration of wealth exacerbated social and nationalist tensions',[76] which in turn were exploited by the fascists, who went on to capture power in both Italy and Germany.

In Piketty's analysis, the world is facing a similar crisis of inequality today.

> The top decile's share [of income] has risen almost everywhere. Take for example, India, the United States and Russia, China, and Europe. The share of the top decile in each of these five regions stood at around 25–35 percent in 1980 but by 2018 had risen to between 35–55 percent. ... In India the change from 1980 to 2018 is among the largest moving from 32 to 55 percent with 10 percent of the population now earning over 55 percent of all income.[77]

The social instability generated by high levels of economic inequality in the contemporary world is becoming increasingly evident. The UN Special Rapporteur on Extreme Forms of Poverty, Phillip Alston, stresses this point in his 2015 report to the Human Rights Council, in which he says:

> Economic inequalities, especially when extreme, can also be closely linked to social unrest and conflict. The Secretary-General has noted that when people perceive inequality to be unfair and excessive, protests and social unrest can result, such as those seen around the world in recent years.[78]

According to Piketty, we are on the precipice of a similar threshold as before the outbreak of the First World War. The levels of inequality are unsustainable, and the disruptions caused in the social order are because the world is in thrall to what he calls the ideology of 'neoproprietarianism', which demands absolute respect for the right to private property.[79]

If, then, economic inequality is one of the root causes of the rise of totalitarianism, what can we do to address it?

Piketty proposes a new social compact to this end: a challenge to the fetish for private property. There have to be new forms of social ownership of property and the idea of permanent ownership has to be replaced with temporary ownership. He calls this 'participatory socialism', one of the key elements of which is a progressive tax on property, inheritance and income. By curtailing the rights of property owners through progressive tax regimes, 'permanent ownership' is converted into 'temporary ownership'. 'Each generation is allowed to accumulate considerable wealth, but parts of that wealth must be returned to the community at that generation's passing, or shared with other potential heirs, who thus get a fresh start in life.' A taxation regime more in line with a commitment to equality of opportunity, he writes, will make it 'increasingly difficult to perpetuate large fortunes across generations'.[80]

Piketty also stresses on capping large shareholder voting rights, heavier investment in the social sectors of health and education and providing a basic income to all persons.[81] He sees his book as a trigger to thinking about policy proposals to combat inequality and sees the need for greater citizen engagement with more debates on inequality.[82] And, certainly, this is one lens through which to find a way forward.

In the context of the US, a policy programme that aims to address the multiple crises of economic inequality and climate change has taken the form of the Green New Deal, which is a State-led transition to a low-carbon economy combined with the creation of thousands of new jobs in new sectors, such as solar and wind energy, as well as those that aid the transition to a zero-carbon economy. This has begun a new conversation in the US around futures that take into account multiple systemic injustices. A similar policy conversation, which addresses environmental, social and economic injustices on one platform, needs to begin in India.

While the Piketty proposal of increasing taxation of the wealthy and the US conversation around the Green New Deal have not yet found political salience in India, there is an emerging discussion around cash transfers or income support to the marginalised. During the 2019 election, the Congress Manifesto proposed a cash transfer of Rs 72,000 as part of the Minimum Income Support Programme (MISP) or Nyuntam Aay Yojana (NYAY) to a 'target population' of 5 crore families who constituted the poorest 20 per cent of all families.[83]

While policy proposals such as NYAY are important for addressing the harsher manifestations of inequality, the conversation needs to advance much further, to tackling the root causes of inequality and thinking through policy solutions. In India, the debate around inequality cannot be fully addressed without tackling the social determinants of inequality, especially gender and caste. Jean Drèze and Amartya Sen argue that in the Indian context, policy proposals need to account for these specific determinants of inequality as well.[84]

While there may be no clear answers as to the best way inequality can be addressed, public debate is vital. As Piketty says, 'Justice [can only be] the result of ongoing collective deliberation.'[85]

Cultivating Hope, Breaking Isolation, Addressing Loneliness

Arendt describes isolation and loneliness as psychological states on which totalitarianism thrives. For her, all tyrannical governments strive to keep people isolated so that they cannot come together and take action. As she puts it, '... power always comes from men acting together, "acting in concert" (Burke); isolated men are powerless by definition'.[86] She writes, 'Isolation is that impasse into which men are driven when the political sphere of their lives, where they act together in the pursuit of a common concern, is destroyed.'[87]

Tyrannical States have always found ways to create a feeling of isolation in their subjects. One of these, deeply relevant to our contemporary context, is the arbitrary use of the power of arrest to target protestors and dissenters in particular. The person who I remember as putting forward this insight was the inspirational civil liberties activist K. Balagopal. In a speech delivered in Bangalore about the arrest of Binayak Sen under the sedition law in 2007, he made the point that, at one level, arresting Sen was about silencing the voice that was uniquely his. But at another level, it was about sending a message that dissent has costs. The psychological objective of Sen's arrest, in Balagopal's analysis, was to make people afraid that if they were ever to dissent, like Binayak Sen, they could be arrested.[88]

Vasanth Kannabiran, the feminist writer, captured this feeling of isolation vividly when speaking about her husband K.G. Kannabiran's role in representing those arrested during the Emergency.[89] She said that there was a widespread feeling that he was on the list of people who would soon be arrested for their work. This translated into a feeling of fear of being associated with him. As she puts it, 'people stopped wishing him, people stopped talking to him, people were afraid of being seen talking to him'. The number of people who would associate with Kannabiran drastically reduced, making it difficult for him to effectively oppose the Emergency.

Through arrests, the State creates a climate of fear that strangles human solidarity and forces human beings into a state of isolation. This, according to Arendt, is 'the murder of the moral person in man'. According to her, the true genius of the Nazis was to destroy the belief of people that 'a protest has even historic importance'. Writing about the police wing of Nazi Germany, she notes, 'This scepticism is the real masterpiece of the SS. Their great accomplishment. They have corrupted all human solidarity. Here the night has fallen on the future.'[90]

According to Arendt, loneliness is the 'experience of not belonging to the world at all, which is among the most radical and desperate experiences of man'. It is a fundamental inability to connect to the world and linked to a feeling of 'uprootedness and superfluousness'. 'To be uprooted means to have no place in the world, recognized and guaranteed by others; to be superfluous means not to belong to the world at all.'[91]

People who are vulnerable to the pull of totalitarian ideology are usually those whose lives are marked by such a feeling of superfluousness. Their sense of alienation leads them to take refuge in right-wing ideologies that appear to provide a sense of belonging, give one an identity and provide a sense of meaning to life.

The challenge, then, is to factor in these psychological states of being and strive to redress them in practice. Understanding that totalitarian States strive to 'corrupt human solidarity'[92] and create a sense of hopelessness allows us to truly comprehend the importance of why people need to come together. Activities ranging from attending discussions to participating in protests are ways of breaking the sense of isolation. Once people begin to meet each other, the possibility of acting together opens up. When people begin to act together, the process of change is set in motion. Human solidarity creates an environment in which it is possible to actualise the World Social Forum slogan that 'another world is possible'.[93]

Redressing loneliness is more complicated, as the condition has deep roots in the modern world and the current model of social and economic life is arranged to produce 'atomized, isolated individuals.'[94] The process of redressal has to begin with a critique of capitalism and offering alternatives to it. This structural response is important. For instance, historical studies of Nazi Germany have shown that Hitler's star was on the ascendant while the lives of the large majority of Germans worsened due to the Great Depression.

At a more immediate level, the problem is, how do people find meaning in their existence so that they don't become vulnerable to far-right ideologies? The liberal response seems unable to make the necessary emotional connect. As Yeats poignantly put it:

The best lack all conviction
The worst are full of passionate intensity[95]

An effort in this direction of infusing a deeper sense of meaning to the liberal defence of human rights was made philosopher Martha

Nussbaum, who looks to the literature of Tagore and Walt Whitman and the public speeches of Martin Luther King and Nehru to find a deeper emotional connect based on the 'cultivation of a wide range of deep emotions, ranging from compassion to deep grief to, of course, a boundless joy in both nature and human beings'.[96] The most effective way to redress loneliness is to be a part of a vibrant society that encourages forms of association, be it sports, music, dance or a pursuit of literature. What is required is a return to a 'public poetry of humanity that would use art, emotion, and the humanities to craft a pluralistic public culture'.[97]

In the Indian context, Balagopal points out the need for a strategy founded not on opposition alone, but on the creation of what he calls 'moral values'. As he put it in an article in the EPW, 'The alternative values and norms can emerge from struggles against Hindu fanaticism; or rather, they can be recalled through the struggles from the moral storehouse of the human species.' He also calls for a rethinking of Marxism, which has failed to account for the 'moral life of the human species'. There is, he says, 'a need to build 'democratic tolerance and the acceptance of social equality as a principle' and appeal to 'the sense of justice that human cultures equally possess'. Philosophies such as Marxism fail to do this, and Balagopal notes that 'these moral possibilities are intrinsic to human beings as much as they are a product of history', and hence it is vital for the emergence of a radical political practice which stresses on cultivating 'qualities such as empathy and love'.[98]

In a sense, Balagopal's ideas echo Nussbaum's. She writes, 'A democracy must learn how to cultivate the inner world of human beings, equipping each citizen to contend against the passion for domination and to accept the reality and the equality of others.'[99]

Building a United Front Against Totalitarianism

Lenin argued in his essay 'What Is to Be Done?'[100] that the way forward for a political party in Tsarist Russia had to be based on an 'all-sided political indictment of autocracy'. The role of the social democrats, according to him, was to draw the people into opposition to 'each and every manifestation of police oppression and autocratic outrage'. In the time of the Tsarist autocracy, this included fighting on behalf of all oppressed groups for basic political freedoms, including fighting against 'extortion of taxes', 'corporal punishment of peasants', 'persecution of sectarians', 'harsh treatment of soldiers and students', and so on.[101]

The political imperative was clear. One had to go beyond a narrow programme of looking only at the economic issues faced by workers, to oppose the Tsarist autocracy in toto by working to 'deepen, broaden and intensify political indictments and political agitation'.[102] The task of the political party was, therefore, to 'get people to think' of how a solution to their specific problems might link back to the end of the Tsarist autocracy. The purpose of the political party would be to 'sum up and generalise each and every flicker of ferment and active struggle'.[103] Lenin's point was that there had to be a way to 'concentrate all those droplets and streams of popular indignation that percolate out of Russian life in vastly greater quantities than we think of or can conceive but which indeed must be merged into one gigantic flood'.[104]

Obviously, we do not live in Lenin's era. The world is different today, and the regime we face in India is vastly different. While Lenin lived in an autocratic Tsarist State that could be opposed by broad and diverse strata of society, that is not the reality in contemporary India, in which a significant number of people support the current government. Nonetheless, the idea of building a wider unity of those affected by the current regime is absolutely vital.

For an effective resistance against totalitarianism, or the possibility of it, one has to first recognise the existential threat posed by such a regime to all forms of diversity, be it religion, caste, class, sexuality or political opinion and ideology. This has to be followed by the coming together of all those who feel threatened by the new regime. However, as history has taught us, those in the middle of the furious flow of events are sometimes blind to the contours of the emerging beast. If the present were to be solely analysed through the lens of the immediate past, it would fail to account for the birth of something unprecedented. It is not easy to recognise the nature of totalitarianism, and it is very difficult for even those who face an existential threat to come together till it is too late.

In Nazi Germany, the Opposition failed to both recognise the nature of the threat and to come together to prevent it. Volker Ullrich outlines how the conservatives paved the way for Hitler to take control. The first critical failure was their inability to understand the nature of the Nazi Party. This led to the grave mistake of Hindenburg inviting Hitler to become chancellor as part of a 'government of national concentration'.[105] Once the Nazi Party was in, there was no looking back, and the conservatives who had hoped to pin Hitler down in the cabinet ended up ceding complete power.

Once he got control over the levers of power, Hitler went about the 'destruction and eradication of Marxism',[106] 'removing the cancerous damage of democracy' and preparing for war.[107] He opportunistically used the Reichstag Fire, when the German Parliament came under an arson attack, to promulgate an emergency decree and suspend constitutional protections on the basis that it was required as a 'defensive measure against Communist acts of violence endangering the state'.[108] Then came the 'brutal persecution of the communists', with the arrest of all their leading functionaries and parliamentarians, and the banning of all communist papers. Over '10,000 political opponents of Nazism were arrested in Prussia alone'.[109] This persecution of the communists, including the arrest of elected deputies to the Parliament (which had eighty-one communist deputies out of a total of 647), did not 'draw any condemnation from the middle class'.[110]

Once the communists were disposed of, Hitler went after parliamentary democracy itself. He proposed the Enabling Bill, which divested Parliament of its legislative authority. The Enabling Act, as William Shirer puts it in *The Rise and Fall of the Third Reich*, was the 'cloak of legality' under which the seizure of absolute power was shrouded.[111]

With the communist representatives eliminated and the conservatives in support of Hitler, the Nazis succeeded in getting the Enabling Act passed. This was in spite of the sole, brave opposition from the Social Democratic Party of Germany (SDP). To the accompaniment of jeers from the Nazis, the chairman of the SDP, Otto Wels, said:

> German Social Democrats pledge ourselves to the principles of humanity and justice, of freedom and socialism. No Enabling Law can give you the power to destroy ideas which are eternal and indestructible. ... From this new persecution too German social democracy can draw new strength. We send greetings to the persecuted and oppressed. We greet our friends in the Reich. Their steadfastness and loyalty deserve admiration. The courage with which they maintain their convictions and their unbroken confidence guarantee a brighter future.[112]

With the passing of the Act, total power passed into the hands of the Nazis and Hitler. The SDP was soon 'dissolved' as being 'subversive and inimical to the state', and a law was passed declaring the formation of political parties an offence. Wels emigrated to Prague and became one of the chairmen of the Social Democratic Party in Exile (SOPADE).[113] Germany became a 'one party totalitarian state'.[114]

If history has an element of contingency to it, the question to ask is: would this have happened had the communists and the socialists been able to foresee the existential threat posed by Hitler and formed an alliance to resist him? It is worth remembering that the electoral popularity of the communists and the socialists put together, even at the height of the repression, was greater than the popularity of the Nazi party by '6 percentage points', as Ullrich records in his book *Hitler*.[115]

Is there any awareness of the existential threat posed by the current regime in India today? As far as political parties go, the BJP's battle cry of a 'Congress-mukt Bharat' indicates that the liberal constitutionalism of the Congress is the 'enemy'. All factions of the Left too have always been seen as the 'enemy' by the BJP, ever since the seminal text by Golwalkar identified the three 'internal threats' as 'Muslims, Christians and Communists'.[116]

Regionalism and regional parities too threaten the ideology of religious nationalism by identifying fault lines of language and ethnicity. Over a period of time, the BJP has lost many of its alliance partners, including the Shiromani Akali Dal in Punjab and the Shiv Sena in Maharashtra. However, in Parliament, other regional parties have not been averse to allying with it. Further, the revocation of Article 370 in Kashmir and the curbing of the powers of the Delhi government by using the lieutenant governor as the cat's paw[117] show that federalism is under threat. While there is strong resistance to the BJP's subsumption of regional identities from state parties like the Mamata Banerjee-led Trinamool Congress in West Bengal, Stalin's Dravida Munnetra Kazhagam in Tamil Nadu and Uddhav Thackeray's Shiv Sena, there are a number of other regional parties such as K. Chandrashekar Rao's Telangana Rashtra Samithi, Jaganmohan Reddy's YSR Congress in Andhra and Naveen Patnaik's Biju Janata Dal in Orissa which continue to align with the BJP.

At the same time, Hindutva aspires to weld all Hindus into a homogenous Hindu community without fundamentally challenging the caste system. Ambedkar was prescient in seeing the threat of a Hindu Raj and said, '... if a Hindu Raj does become a fact, it will, no doubt, be the greatest calamity for this country. No matter what the Hindus say, Hinduism is a menace to liberty, equality and fraternity. On that account it is incompatible with democracy. Hindu Raj must be prevented at any cost.'[118] The Hindutva world view cannot tolerate an Ambedkarite ideology, based as it is on 'annihilating caste'. The prosecution of those who organised the Bhima Koregoan celebrations, and especially those who dared to call the BJP's regime the rule of the 'New Peshwas', is indicative of the existential threat to Ambedkarism from Hindutva.

A totalitarian ideology affects the everyday life of the citizen, in seemingly intimate yet everyday matters such as the choice of God, lovers, and even friends and associates. The ambition of a totalitarian ideology is to control all aspects of a person's life, and that ambition should deeply concern citizens who care about their basic freedoms. The intensified persecution and pogroms against religious minorities make it quite clear that they, and the rest of the country, face a very real threat.

While the Hindutva ideology may seem concerned with only cultural and social matters, it also allows for the unchecked growth of the interests of capital at the expense of the interests of labour. If any illustration is needed, according to Oxfam, 'the wealth of [Indian] billionaires increased by 35% during the lockdown'.[119] This was at a time of unprecedented misery for millions of people, who saw their livelihoods shrink during the pandemic. The policies of the ruling power are clearly aligned against the interests of the working poor.

The economic policies of the current regime, which unfairly benefit a few, have also put at risk the environment, again impacting millions. The perception that the government's policies unfairly favour just a powerful few is gaining ground, as was apparent in the sustained anti-farm-law protests that brought farmers into the ranks of the dissatisfied. The final repeal of these laws is also a tribute to how sustained and organised protests, even in adverse circumstances, can succeed in putting the state on the defensive.

In short, those who have reason to fear the current dispensation span the diversity of India: those who are in favour of a federal polity; those of an Ambedkarite ideology; those who want to protect personal liberties of food, clothing, marriage and worship; those of minority faiths; those who are opposed to the pro-corporate tilt of government policy, including farmers and fisherfolk; those concerned about the environment; those concerned about labour rights and those in civil society concerned about human rights. All these affected groups have the incentive to come together and demand a change in government-policy orientation.

When the US freedom fighters signed the Declaration of Independence, they did so knowing that it was an act of war and they would be killed if they did not win. As Benjamin Franklin is reputed to have said, 'We must all hang together, or assuredly we shall all hang separately.'[120] In a similar sense, if at this moment, political parties, civil society groups, social movements and individuals who are existentially threatened by the totalitarian project do not come together to try and prevent it, the project will succeed.

The famous poem by Martin Niemöller, written during the Nazi capture of Germany, has never seemed more urgent and appropriate:

> First they came for the socialists, and I did not speak out—because I was not a socialist.
> Then they came for the trade unionists, and I did not speak out—because I was not a trade unionist.
> Then they came for the Jews, and I did not speak out—because I was not a Jew.
> Then they came for me—and there was no one left to speak for me.[121]

Notes

Introduction

1.   Christophe Jaffrelot and Pratinav Anil, *India's First Dictatorship* (HarperCollins, New Delhi: 2021), p. 17. The displacement was due to the callous and brutal programme of beautification of the city which inevitably involved demolition of thousands of slums around the country, but with the epicentre of demolitions being New Delhi.

2.   Gyan Prakash, *Emergency Chronicles: Indira Gandhi and Democracy's Turning Point* (Penguin Viking, New Delhi: 2018), p. 167.

3.   'Let us identify and confront "Undeclared Emergency"!: Press Note on Anti-Emergency Day with two Resolutions', PUCL Gujarat, 26 June 2018, pucl.org/press-statements/let-us-identify-and-confront-undeclared-emergency.

4.   Mrudula Bhavani, 'Some Oxygen For Siddique Kappan, Please?', *Outlook*, 12 May 2021, outlookindia.com/website/story/opinion-some-oxygen-for-siddique-kappan-please/382579.

5.   H.M. Seervai, *The Emergency: Future Safeguards and the Habeas Corpus Case: A Criticism* (N.M. Tripathi Pvt Ltd, Bombay: 1978), p. 8.

6.   Tarunabh Khaitan, 'Killing the Constitution with a Thousand Cuts: Executive Aggrandizement and Party-State Fusion in India', *Law and Ethics of Human Rights* (forthcoming), papers.ssrn.com/sol3/papers.cfm?abstract_id=3367266.

NOTES   237

7. Shah Commission of Inquiry, 'Interim Report I' (11 March 1978), countercurrents.org/shah-commission-interimreport%201.pdf.

8. 'Upendra Kushwaha's strongly worded resignation letter: Full text', *DNA*, 10 December 2018, dnaindia.com/india/report-upendra-kushwaha-s-strongly-worded-resignation-letter-full-text-2694312.

9. Sudheendra Kulkarni, '1975 Emergency: Indian Democracy Needs "Vertical Men" Like Advani', *The Quint*, 25 June 2018, thequint.com/voices/opinion/1975-emergency-lk-advani-critique-of-indian-media-rings-true.

10. *ADM Jabalpur v Shivakant Shukla* (April 1976), indiankanoon.org/doc/1735815/.

11. *Anuradha Bhasin v Union of India* (January 2020), indiankanoon.org/doc/82461587/.

12. Apart from Varavara Rao, who is out on medical bail, and Stan Swamy, who passed away in judicial custody.

13. Juan Linz, *Totalitarian and Authoritarian Regimes* (Lynne Rienner Publishers, London: 2000), p. 151.

14. Christophe Jaffrelot and Pratinav Anil, *India's First Dictatorship*, p. 70.

15. Ibid., p. 69.

16. Ibid., p. 70.

17. Ibid., p. 145.

18. Ibid., p. 127.

19. Ibid., p. 21.

20. Gyan Prakash, *Emergency Chronicles* (Penguin Viking, New Delhi: 2018), p. 197.

21. Smriti Kak Ramachandra, 'BJP resolution lauds agri laws, Covid fight', *Hindustan Times*, 22 February 2021, hindustantimes.com/india-news/bjp-resolution-lauds-agri-laws-covid-fight-101613953911657.html.

22. Christophe Jaffrelot (ed.), *Hindu Nationalism: A Reader* (Penguin, New Delhi: 2007), pp. 116–117.

23. Ibid., p. 177–201.

24. Walter Andersen and Shridhar D. Damle, *Messengers of Hindu*

Nationalism (C. Hurst and Co., London: 2019), pp. 258–59.

25. P.K. Datta, 'Dying Hindus—Production of Hindu Communal Common Sense in Early Twentieth Century Bengal', *Economic and Political Weekly* (19 June 1993), p. 1,307.

26. 'The Wages of Hate: Journalism in Dark times, 2020' (A report by Campaign Against Hate Speech), hatespeechbeda.wordpress. com/2020/09/08/report-wages-of-hate-journalism-in-dark-times/.

27. Harsh Mander, 'Junaid, my son', *The Indian Express*, 1 July 2017, indianexpress.com/article/opinion/columns/junaid-my-son-4729828/.

28. The Wire Staff, 'COVID-19 Sharpened Inequalities in India, Billionaires' Wealth Increased by 35%: Report', *The Wire*, 25 January 2021, https://thewire.in/rights/covid-19-sharpened-inequalities-in-india-billionaires-wealth-increased-by-35-report.

29. Rohan Venkataramakrishnan, 'Interview: Christophe Jaffrelot on understanding the Emergency and its relevance to Modi's India', *Scroll*, 7 November 2020, scroll.in/article/977814/interview-christophe-jaffrelot-on-understanding-the-emergency-and-its-relevance-to-modis-india.

30. Juan Linz, *Totalitarian and Authoritarian Regime*, p. 92.

31. Special Correspondent, 'Emergency was a mistake, says Rahul Gandhi', *The Hindu*, 3 March 2021, thehindu.com/news/national/emergency-was-a-mistake-says-rahul/article33974721.ece.

32. Bhikhu Parekh, *Hannah Arendt and the Search for a New Political Philosophy* (Macmillan Press, London: 1981), p. ix.

33. Hannah Arendt, *The Origins of Totalitarianism* (Harcourt Brace and Company, London: 1979), p. vii.

34. Peter Baehr (ed.), *The Portable Hannah Arendt* (Penguin Books, London: 2003), p. xxi.

1. Authoritarian Rule

1. Hannah Arendt, *The Origins of Totalitarianism* (Harcourt, Brace and Company, London: 1979), p. viii.

2. Venkat Iyer, *States of Emergency: The Indian Experience* (Butterworth: New Delhi, 2000), p. 157.

3. See Article 353A and B

4. Constituent Assembly Debates, Book no. 2 (Lok Sabha Secretariat, New Delhi: 1999), pp. 34–35.

5. See Article 358.

6. See Article 359.

7. Constituent Assembly Debates, Book no. 4, p. 106.

8. Ibid., p. 112.

9. Ibid., p. 196.

10. Ibid., p. 123.

11. Christophe Jafferlot and Pratinav Anil, *India's First Dictatorship: The Emergency, 1975—1977* (Harper Collins, New Delhi: 2021), p. 17.

12. Granville Austin, *Working a Democratic Constitution: A History of the Indian Experience* (Oxford University Press, New Delhi: 1999), p. 303.

13. Balraj Puri, 'A Fuller View of the Emergency', *Economic and Political Weekly*, Vol. 3, No. 28 (15 July 1995), pp. 1736–1744.

14. K.G. Kannabiran, *The Wages of Impunity: Power Justice and Human Rights* (Orient Longman, New Delhi: 2004), p. 47.

15. Ibid., p. 49.

16. Section 8 of MISA mandated that the grounds for detention was to be communicated to the detainee within five days and no later than fifteen days. As per Sec 3(4), a state government's orders to detain a person and its reasons were to be reported to the Central government within seven days. Under 11(2), the detention orders were also required to be referred to an advisory board which had to 'report' to the concerned government its 'opinion' on whether there was 'sufficient cause for the detention of the person concerned', and if there were no sufficient cause, under 12(2), the state government was mandated to revoke the detention order and release the person. Under Section 13, the law also had a maximum period of detention which was 'twelve months from the date of

detention or until the expiry of the Defence and Internal Security of India Act, 1971, whichever is later'.

17. Section 9(2) of MISA.

18. Section 16A(4) of MISA.

19. Shah Commission of Inquiry, 'Third and Final Report' (6 August 1978), p. 40, countercurrents.org/Shah-commission-of-Inquiry-3rd-Final-Report.pdf.

20. Ibid., p. 41.

21. Shah Commission, 'Third and Final Report', p. 41.

22. Ibid., p. 46.

23. Ibid., p. 42.

24. Ibid., p. 42.

25. Ibid., p. 42.

26. Ibid., p. 43.

27. Shah Commission, 'Interim Report I' (11 March 1978), p. 83, https://www.countercurrents.org/shah-commission-interimreport%201.pdf.

28. Ibid., p. 84.

29. Ibid., p. 85.

30. Shah Commission, 'Third and Final Report', p. 44.

31. Gyan Prakash, *Emergency Chronicles: Indira Gandhi and Democracy's Turning Point* (Penguin Viking, New Delhi: 2018), p. 16.

32. youtube.com/watch?v=6Ep7QP_6wZA (video).

33. T.V. Eachara Varier, *Memories of a Father* (Asian Human Rights Commission, Hong Kong: 2004).

34. Varier, *Memories of a Father*, p. 29.

35. Ibid., p. 28.

36. *T.V. Eachara Varier v Secretary to the Ministry of Home Affairs* (April 1977), indiankanoon.org/doc/783127/; Varier, *Memories of a Father*, pp. 77–108,

37. *T. V. Eachara Varier v Secretary to the Ministry of Home Affairs*; Varier, *Memories of a Father*, p. 46.

38. *T.V. Eachara Varier v Secretary to the Ministry of Home Affairs*; Varier, *Memories of a Father*, p. 31.

39. Shah Commission, 'Third and Final Report', p. 44.

40. Ibid., 'Third and Final Report', p. 43.

41. The Shah Commission culls out the following four circumstances from *Khudi Ram Dass v State of Bengal* when 'subjective satisfaction of the detaining authority would stand vitiated'. They are:

    Where the authority has not applied its mind at all

    Where the power is exercised dishonestly or for an improper purpose, i.e., purpose not contemplated by the Statute or where the order is passed mala fide

    Where the satisfaction is not the satisfaction of the authority itself

    Where the satisfaction is based upon the application of a wrong test on misconstruction of the statute

42. Shah Commission, 'Third and Final Report', p. 44.

43. Ibid., p. 45.

44. Ibid., p. 45.

45. Shah Commission, 'Interim Report I', p. 34.

46. Ibid., p. 38.

47. Ibid., p. 38.

48. Ibid., p. 36.

49. Ibid., pp. 39–40.

50. Ibid., p. 35.

51. Ibid., p. 35.

52. Ibid., p. 35.

53. H.M. Seervai, *The Emergency, Future Safeguards and the Habeas Corpus Case: A Criticism* (N.M. Tripathi Pvt. Ltd, Bombay: 1978), p. vii.

54. Hannah Arendt, *The Origins of Totalitarianism* (Harcourt Brace and Company, London: 1976), p. 434.

55. See Section(3) of the Parliamentary Proceedings (Protection of Publication) Act, 1956.

56. Shah Commission, 'Interim Report I', p. 39.

57. Shah Commission, 'Third and Final Report', p. 153.

58. Ibid., p. 154.

59. Ibid., p. 159.

60. Ibid., p. 155.
61. Ibid., p. 156.
62. Ibid., p. 159.
63. Ibid., p. 162.
64. Ibid., p. 165.
65. Ibid., p. 179.
66. Ibid., p. 179.
67. Ibid., p. 180.
68. Ibid., p. 196.
69. Ibid., p. 183.
70. Ibid., p. 197.
71. Ibid., p. 29.
72. Ibid., p. 29.
73. John Dayal and Ajoy Bose, *For Reasons of State: Delhi Under Emergency* (Penguin, New Delhi: 2018), p. 44.
74. Emma Tarlo, *Unsettling Memories: Narratives of the Emergency in Delhi* (University of California Press, Berkeley: 2003) p. 55.
75. Shah Commission, 'Third and Final Report', p. 208.
76. Ibid., p. 209.
77. Ibid., p. 209.
78. Ibid., p. 209.
79. Ibid., p. 210.
80. Shah Commission, 'Third and Final Report', p. 212.
81. Ibid.
82. Prashant Bhushan, *The Case that Shook India: The Verdict that Led to the Emergency* (Penguin, New Delhi: 2017), pp. 29–110.
83. See Section 329A(4) of the 39th Amendment.
84. Prashant Bhushan, *The Case that Shook India*, p. 139.
85. Constitution (42nd Amendment) Act, 1976.
86. See Section 144A of the Constitution (42nd Amendment) Act, 1976.
87. *Bharati Nayyar v Union of India* (September 1975), indiankanoon.org/doc/1149398/.
88. Shah Commission, 'Interim Report I', p. 51.

89. Ibid., p. 52.

90. Ibid., p. 54.

91. Seervai, *The Emergency, Future Safeguards and the Habeas Corpus Case*, p. vii.

92. Seervai, *The Emergency, Future Safeguards and the Habeas Corpus Case*, p. vii ; The nine high courts are: (1) Delhi (2) Karnataka (3) Bombay (Nagpur Bench) (4) Allahabad (5) Madras (6) Rajasthan (7) Madhya Pradesh (8) Andhra Pradesh (9) Punjab and Haryana. Justice Khanna's dissent in *ADM Jabalpur v Shivkant Shukla* begins by referencing the decision of the high courts. As Justice Khanna notes, '... the Presidential order did not create an absolute bar to the judicial scrutiny of the validity of the detention', indiankanoon. org/doc/1735815/.

93. *ADM Jabalpur v Shivkant Shukla* (April 1976), indiankanoon.org/ doc/1735815/.

94. Austin, *Working a Democratic Constitution*, p. 339.

95. Seervai, *The Emergency, Future Safeguards and the Habeas Corpus Case*, p. 6.

96. Austin, *Working a Democratic Constitution*, p. 339.

97. Ibid., p. 340.

98. Ibid., p. 339.

99. *ADM Jabalpur v Shivkant Shukla*.

100. Seervai, *The Emergency, Future Safeguards and the Habeas Corpus Case*, p. 1.

101. Ibid., p. 2.

102. Ibid., p. vii.

103. H.M. Seervai, The Emergency: Future Safeguards and the Habeas Corpus Case: A Criticism, (NM Tripathi Pvt. Ltd, Bombay: 1978) p. viii.

104. indianexpress.com/article/opinion/columns/january-30-1977-forty-years-ago-4497986/; *Puttaswamy v Union of India*, cf. Opinion of Justice Nariman who cites Palkhivala's opinion piece on Justice Khanna's supersession, main.sci.gov.in/supremecourt/ 2012/35071/35071_2012_Judgement_24-Aug-2017.pdf.

105. main.sci.gov.in/supremecourt/2012/35071/35071_2012_
     Judgement_24-Aug-2017.pdf.

106. 1941(3) ALLER 338

107. Speech delivered by Justice Yatindra Singh, Chief Justice,
     Chhattisgarh High Court, at the valedictory function of the
     Regional Judicial Conference on 'Role of Courts in Upholding
     the Rule of Law' at Bilaspur on 30 March 2014, 164.100.179.45/
     artical/RuleofLaw.pdf.

108. Prakash, *Emergency Chronicles*, p. 303.

109. Shah Commission, 'Third and Final Report', pp. 1–12.

110. Prakash, *Emergency Chronicles*, p. 204.

111. Puri, 'A Fuller View of the Emergency', p. 1743.

112. Ibid., p. 1742.

113. Varier, *Memories of a Father*, p. 46.

114. Ibid., p. 58.

115. youtube.com/watch?v=1GmHRscNl6I (video).

116. Varier, *Memories of a Father*, p. 74.

117. Constitution (44th Amendment) Act, 1978.

118. Ibid., 1978.

119. Section 3 of the Constitution (44th Amendment) Act, 1978.

120. *A.K. Roy v Union of India* (December 1981), indiankanoon.org/
     doc/875590/.

121. Arendt, *The Origins of Totalitarianism*, p. vii.

2. Roots of the Emergency

1. Article 22 reads:

    (1) No person who is arrested shall be detained in custody
        without being informed, as soon as may be, of the grounds
        for such arrest nor shall he be denied the right to consult, and
        to be defended by, a legal practitioner of his choice.

    (2) Every person who is arrested and detained in custody shall
        be produced before the nearest magistrate within a period of
        twenty-four hours of such arrest excluding the time necessary

for the journey from the place of arrest to the court of the magistrate and no such person shall be detained in custody beyond the said period without the authority of a magistrate.

(3) Nothing in clauses (1) and (2) shall apply—

    (a) to any person who for the time being is an enemy alien; or

    (b) to any person who is arrested or detained under any law providing for preventive detention.

(4) No law providing for preventive detention shall authorise the detention of a person for a longer period than three months unless—

    (a) an Advisory Board consisting of persons who are, or have been, or are qualified to be appointed as, Judges of a High Court has reported before the expiration of the said period of three months that there is in its opinion sufficient cause for such detention:

    Provided that nothing in this sub-clause shall authorise the detention of any person beyond the maximum period prescribed by any law made by Parliament under sub-clause (b) of clause (7); or

    (b) such person is detained in accordance with the provisions of any law made by Parliament under subclauses (a) and (b) of clause (7).

(5) When any person is detained in pursuance of an order made under any law providing for preventive detention, the authority making the order shall, as soon as may be, communicate to such person the grounds on which the order has been made and shall afford him the earliest opportunity of making a representation against the order.

(6) Nothing in clause (5) shall require the authority making any such order as is referred to in that clause to disclose facts which such authority considers to be against the public interest to disclose.

(7) Parliament may by law prescribe—

        (a)   the circumstances under which, and the class or classes of cases in which, a person may be detained for a period longer than three months under any law providing for preventive detention without obtaining the opinion of an Advisory Board in accordance with the provisions of sub-clause (a) of clause (4);

        (b)   the maximum period for which any person may in any class or classes of cases be detained under any law providing for preventive detention; and

        (c)   the procedure to be followed by an Advisory Board in an inquiry under [sub-clause (a) of clause (4)].

2.   A.R. Desai, (ed.), *Violation of Democratic Rights in India* (Popular Prakashan, Bombay: 1986), p. 73.

3.   Further safeguards are provided in Article 22(4) and (7). The first states that a law authorising preventive detention cannot be for more than three months, unless the detainee is produced before an advisory board consisting of members who are, have been or are qualified to be appointed as judges of the high court and such a board comes to the conclusion that 'there is sufficient cause for such detention'. Clause (7) qualifies the limited protection of clause (4) by allowing Parliament to make a law authorising the detention of persons beyond three months without obtaining the opinion of an advisory board. However, it adds in the caveat that such a law has to specify the 'circumstances' as well as the 'class of cases' for which detention is prescribed.

    Additionally, Article 22(5) puts in the safeguard that when a person is preventively detained, 'the authority making the order shall ... communicate' to the person detained 'the grounds on which the order has been made', 'as soon as possible'. However, Article 22(6) immediately qualifies this already limited right by prescribing that the authority shall not be required to disclose 'facts' which it 'considers to be against the public interest to disclose'.

4.   The debates on draft Article 15 began on 6 December 1948.

5. Article 15 reads:

    No person shall be deprived of his life or personal liberty except according to procedure established by law, nor shall any person be denied equality before the law or the equal protection of the laws within the territory of India.

    constitutionofindia.net/historical_constitutions/draft_constitution_of_india__1948_21st%20February%201948.

6. Constituent Assembly Debates, Book no. 2 (Lok Sabha Secretariat, New Delhi: 1999), p. 847.

7. Ibid., p. 852.

8. Speech by Bakhshi Tek Chand on 15 September 1949, Constituent Assembly Debates, Book no. 4, p. 1,532.

9. Speech by Chand, Constituent Assembly Debates, Book no. 4, p. 1,533.

10. Constituent Assembly Debates, Book no. 2, pp. 1,000–1,001.

11. Article 15A read:

    (1) No person who is arrested shall be detained in custody without being informed, as soon as may be, of the grounds for such arrest nor shall he be denied the right to consult a legal practitioner of his choice.

    (2) Every person who is arrested and detained in custody shall be produced before the nearest magistrate within a period of twenty-four hours of such arrest excluding the time necessary for the journey from the place of arrest to the court of the magistrate and no such person shall be detained in custody beyond the said period without the authority of a magistrate.

    (3) Nothing in this article shall apply—

        (a) to any person who for the time being is an enemy alien, or

        (b) to any person who is arrested under any law providing for preventive detention;

            Provided that nothing in sub-clause (b) of clause (3) of this article shall permit the detention of a person for a longer period than three months unless—(a) an

Advisory Board consisting of persons who are or have been or are qualified to be appointed as judges of a High Court has reported before the expiration of the said period of three months that there is in its opinion sufficient cause for such detention, or (b) such person is detained in accordance with the provisions of any law made by Parliament under clause (4) of this article.

(4) Parliament may by law prescribe the circumstances under which and the class or classes of cases in which a person who is arrested under any law providing for preventive detention may be detained for a period longer than three months and also the maximum period for which any such person may be so detained. Constituent Assembly Debates, Book no. 4, pp. 1,000–1,001. This was introduced on 15 September 1949.

12. Constituent Assembly Debates, Book no. 4, p. 1,500.
13. Ibid., p. 1,543.
14. Ibid., p. 1,537.
15. Ibid., p. 1,506.
16. Ibid., p. 1,509.
17. Ibid., p. 1,519.
18. Ibid., pp. 1,521 and 1,543.
19. Constituent Assembly Debates, Book no. 4, p. 1,549.
20. Constituent Assembly Debates, Book no. 4, p. 1,521.
21. Seventh Schedule List 1—Union List entry 9 reads: Preventive Detention for reasons connected with Defence, Foreign Affairs, or the security of India; persons subjected to such detention; List 3—Concurrent List entry 3 reads: Preventive detention for reasons connected with the security of a State, the maintenance of public order, or the maintainance of supplies and services essential to the community; persons subject to such detention.
22. Constituent Assembly Debates, Book no. 4, p. 1,561.
23. Ibid., p. 1,561.
24. Ibid., p. 1,538.

25. Ibid., p. 1,552.

26. Ibid., p. 1,566.

27. A.K. Gopalan, *In the Cause of the People: Reminiscences by A.K. Gopalan* (Orient Longman, New Delhi: 1956), p. 168.

28. K.G. Kannabiran, *The Wages of Impunity: Power, Justice and Human Rights* (Orient Longman, New Delhi: 2004), p. 31.

29. Gopalan, *In the Cause of the People*, p. 168.

30. Kannabiran, *The Wages of Impunity*, p. 36.

31. *A.K. Gopalan v State of Madras* (May 1950), indiankanoon.org/doc/1857950/.

32. Justice Kania's opinion held:

> As to the meaning of the word 'law' it was argued that it meant principles of natural justice. It meant 'jus', i.e., law in the abstract sense of the principles of natural justice, as mentioned in standard works of Jurisprudence, and not 'lex', i.e., enacted law. Against the contention that such construction will leave the meaning vague, it was argued that four principles of natural justice recognised in all civilized countries were covered, in any event, by the word 'law'. They are: (1) An objective test, i.e., a certain, definite and ascer- tainable rule of human conduct for the violation of which one can be detained; (2) Notice of the grounds of such detention; (3) An impartial tribunal, administrative, judicial or advisory, to decide whether the detention is justified; and (4) Orderly course of procedure, including an opportunity to be heard orally (not merely by making a written representation) with a right to lead evidence and call witnesses.
>
> In my opinion, this line of approach is not proper and indeed misleading.

The majority position on why law was 'lex' and not 'jus' was also lucidly expressed by Justice Patanjali Shastri.

> Mr. Nambiar urged that the word 'law' in article 21 should be understood, not in the sense of an enactment but as signifying the immutable and universal principles of natural justice--the jus naturale of the civil law--and that the expression 'procedure

established by law' meant the same thing as that famous phrase 'due process of law' in the American Constitution in its procedural aspect. Giving full effect to these principles, however, I am unable to agree that the term 'law' in article 21 means the immutable and universal principles of natural justice. 'Procedure established by law' must be taken to refer to a procedure which has a statutory origin, for no procedure is known or can be said to have been established by such vague and uncertain concepts as 'the immutable and universal principles of natural justice.' In my opinion, 'law' in article 21 means 'positive' or State-made law.

33. Section 14 of the act read:

No court shall, except for the purposes of a prosecution for an offence punishable under sub-section (2) allow any statement to be made, or any evidence to be given, before it of the substance of any communication made under section 7 of the grounds on which a detention order has been made against any person or of any representation made by him against such order; and, notwithstanding anything contained in any other law, no court shall be entitled to require any public officer to produce before it, or to disclose the substance of, any such communication or representation made, or the proceedings of an Advisory Board or that part of the report of an Advisory Board which is confidential.

34. Kannabiran, *The Wages of Impunity*, p. 35.

35. *S. Krishnan v State of Madras* (May 1951), indiankanoon.org/doc/1879676/.

36. Kannabiran, *The Wages of Impunity*, p. 38.

37. George Gadbois, *Supreme Court of India: The Beginnings* (Oxford University Press, New Delhi: 2017), p. 169.

38. Gopalan, *In the Cause of the People*, p. 172.

39. Ibid., p. 173.

40. [1941] UKHL 1.

41. *K.S. Puttaswamy v Union Of India* (August 2017), indiankanoon.org/doc/91938676/.

42. Ibid.

43. *R.C. Cooper v Union of India* (February 1970), indiankanoon.org/doc/513801/.

44. *Maneka Gandhi v Union of India* (January 1978), indiankanoon.org/doc/1766147/.
45. *A.K. Roy v Union of India* (December 1981), indiankanoon.org/doc/50294192/.
46. *Kartar Singh v State of Punjab* (1994), indiankanoon.org/doc/1813801/.
47. *PUCL v Union of India* (December 2013), indiankanoon.org/doc/110957682/.
48. Venkat Iyer, *States of Emergency: Moderating Their Effects on Human Rights* (Butterworth, New Delhi: 2000), p. 282.
49. Kannabiran, *The Wages of Impunity*, p. 50.

3. The Modi Era

1. Gautam Navlakha, 'Dare I hope to be freed from the burden of yet another conspiracy trial?', *The Caravan*, 16 March 2020, https://caravanmagazine.in/noticeboard/gautam-navlakha-letter-bhima-koregaon-bail-rejected. Also see: Leonard Cohen, 'Anthem', https://www.youtube.com/watch?v=c8-BT6y_wYg.
2. Ramachandra Guha, *India After Gandhi: The History of the World's Largest Democracy* (Macmillan, New Delhi: 2017), pp. 751–783.
3. Ibid., p. 753.
4. Ibid., pp. 770–982.
5. 'Press Note on Anti-Emergency Day with two Resolutions', pucl.org/press-statements/let-us-identify-and-confront-undeclared-emergency.
6. Pratap Bhanu Mehta, 'There is no Emergency', *The Indian Express*, 5 November 2016, indianexpress.com/article/opinion/columns/emergency-period-india-ndtv-ban-media-freedom-3737771/.
7. Ramachandra Guha, 'Via Virus Crisis, Modi Furthers Cult Of His Personality', NDTV, 30 April 2020, ndtv.com/opinion/modi-uses-the-pandemic-to-squeeze-states-by-ramachandra-guha-2220885.
8. 'What You See in India Is Less an Undeclared Emergency and More Sultanism: Christophe Jaffrelot', youtube.com/watch?v=EXoDaxOfHWY (video).

9.   A.P. Shah, 'Supreme Court Then and Now', *Economic and Political Weekly*, Vol. 55, No. 40 (3 October 2020), pp. 31–37 at p. 31; Madan B. Lokur, 'Supreme Court Deserves an "F" Grade For Its Handling of Migrants', The Wire, 28 May 2020, thewire.in/law/after-humanitarian-law-died-a-million-deaths-the-supreme-courthas-finally-stirred-itself; Sevanti Ninan, 'How India's news media have changed since 2014: Greater self-censorship, dogged digital resistance', Scroll, 5 July 2019, scroll.in/article/929461/greater-self-censorshipdogged-digital-resistance-how-indias-news-media-have-changedsince-2014.

10. Rajinder Sachar, *In Pursuit of Justice: An Autobiography* (Rupa, New Delhi: 2020), p. 118.

11. Web Desk, 'Atmosphere of fear: Rahul Bajaj criticises Centre in presence of Amit Shah at award function', *The Week*, 1 December 2019, theweek.in/news/india/2019/12/01/atmosphere-of-fear-rahul-bajaj-criticises-centre-in-presence-amit-shah-award-function.html.

12. Numerous special rapporteurs as well as the Office of the High Commission of Human Rights have expressed concern over the state of human rights in India, but have not been able to theorise what these violations put together mean, news.un.org/en/story/2020/10/1075792, theprint.in/diplomacy/stan-swamys-death-stain-on-indias-human-rights-record-says-un-expert-mary-lawlor/697788/.

13. Mihir Desai, 'Terror laws under a Proto-fascist regime', Public lecture on the fourth death anniversary of Gauri Lankesh, 5 September 2021, https://fb.watch/7Qqe7-NNsv/.

14. News Desk, '11 years in jail, Kashmiri man returns home after acquitted of UAPA charge by Gujarat court', *India TV*, 2 July 2020, indiatvnews.com/news/india/kashmiri-man-bashir-ahmed-baba-11-years-in-jail-returns-home-acquitted-uapa-charge-by-gujarat-court-716253.

15. Mustafa Shaikh, 'Two men, cleared of UAPA charges, regret the 9 years they lost in jail', *India Today*, 17 June 2021, indiatoday.in/cities/mumbai/story/two-men-acquitted-uapa-charges-tajola-jail-navi-mumbai-1816255-2021-06-17.

16. Justice Aftab Alam, 'A Performance Audit and Some Thoughts on UAPA', *LiveLaw*, 7 August 2021, livelaw.in/columns/justice-aftab-alam-former-sc-judge-speech-for-democracy-dissent-and-draconian-law-uapa-and-sedition-webinar-by-cjar-hrda-livelaw-179093.

17. Special Correspondent, 'Parliament proceedings | Over 72% rise in number of UAPA cases registered in 2019', *The Hindu*, 9 March 2021, https://www.thehindu.com/news/national/parliament-proceedings-over-72-rise-in-number-of-uapa-cases-registered-in-2019/article34029252.ece.

18. 'SLL Crimes (Crime Head-wise) - 2017-2019', ncrb.gov.in/sites/default/files/crime_in_india_table_additional_table_chapter_reports/Table%201.3_3.pdf.

19. Special Correspondent, 'Parliament proceedings | Over 72% rise in number of UAPA cases registered in 2019', *The Hindu*, 9 March 2021, https://www.thehindu.com/news/national/parliament-proceedings-over-72-rise-in-number-of-uapa-cases-registered-in-2019/article34029252.ece.

20. N.C. Asthana, 'India's Bogey of "Hurt Sentiments" is a Ploy to Persecute the "Others"', *The Wire*, 7 March 2021, thewire.in/government/indian-government-uapa-sedition-cases-bhaybheet-bharat.

21. 'Seventeenth Series, Vol. III, First Session, 2019/1941 (Saka)', https://eparlib.nic.in/bitstream/123456789/786392/1/lsd_17_01_24-07-2019.pdf.

22. V. Suresh, 'UAPA: Law As Instrumentality of State Tyranny and Violence' in *Sudha Bharadwaj Speaks* (ed. Arvind Narrain), A report by PUCL, 2020, pucl.org/writings/sudha-bharadwaj-speaks-life-law-and-activism.

23. https://twitter.com/ManishTewari/status/1153988182133760000. Also see: Deeptiman Tiwary, 'Congress denies Amit Shah charge on POTA, slams changes to UAPA', *The Indian Express*, 24 July 2019, https://indianexpress.com/article/india/congress-denies-amit-shah-charge-on-pota-slams-changes-to-uapa-5846261/.

24. *Kartar Singh v State of Punjab*, https://indiankanoon.org/doc/1813801/.

25. *PUCL v Union of India* (December 2003), indiankanoon.org/doc/110957682/.

26. Annual Report 2002–2003, National Human Rights Commission, https://nhrc.nic.in/sites/default/files/AR02-03ENG.pdf.

27. Mihir Desai's public lecture, 'Terror laws under a Proto-fascist regime'.

28. See Section 60 of POTA.

29. Justice Alam, 'A Performance Audit and Some Thoughts on UAPA'. Also see: 'Pre-charge detention in terrorism cases', *Justice*, https://justice.org.uk/pre-charge-detention-terrorism-cases/.

30. V. Suresh, 'UAPA: Law as Instrumentality'.

31. *PUCL v Union of India*, https://indiankanoon.org/doc/110957682/.

32. See Section 13 of the National Security Act, 1980.

33. Section 13 of the Maintenance of Internal Security Act, 1971.

34. Section 11A of the Preventive Detention Act, 1950.

35. Diva Rai, 'The Rowlatt Act and preventive detention laws in India', iPleaders, 3 August 2021, https://blog.ipleaders.in/the-rowlatt-act-and-preventive-detention-laws-in-india/.

36. *Zahoor Ahmad Shah Watali v National Investigating Agency* (December 2003), indiankanoon.org/doc/124771365/.

37. V. Suresh, 'UAPA: Law as Instrumentality'. Also see: *National Investigating Agency v Zahoor Ahmad Shah Watali* (April 2019), https://indiankanoon.org/doc/117627977/.

38. *K.A. Najeeb v Union of India* (February 2021), livelaw.in/pdf_upload/union-of-india-vs-ka-najeeb-ll-2021-sc-56-388472.pdf.

39. *Varavara Rao v NIA* (February 2021), indiankanoon.org/doc/95912324/.

40. *Asif Iqbal Tanha v State of Delhi NCT* (June 2021), indiankanoon.org/doc/73074664/.

41. *Natasha Narwal v State of Delhi NCT* (June 2021), livelaw.in/pdf_upload/natasha-narwal-bail-order-delhi-high-court-395020.pdf.

42. *Devangana Kalita v State of Delhi NCT* (June 2021), https://www.livelaw.in/pdf_upload/devangana-kalita-bail-order-395018.pdf.

43. *Devangana Kalita v State of Delhi NCT* (June 2021), livelaw.in/pdf_upload/136002021443728073order18-jun-2021-395190.pdf.

44. *Bikramjit Singh v State of Punjab* (October 2020), https://indiankanoon.org/doc/10807134/.

45. *Akhil Gogoi v NIA* (July 2021), livelaw.in/pdf_upload/display-12-1-395867.pdf; *Bikramjit Singh v State of Punjab* (October 2020), https://indiankanoon.org/doc/10807134/; *Mohammad Shariq v State of Karnataka*, (July 2021), https://www.livelaw.in/pdf_upload/only-special-courts-can-extend-custody-beyond-90-days-in-uapa-cases-karnataka-hcwatermark-400317.pdf.

46. *Akhil Gogoi v NIA* (July 2021), livelaw.in/pdf_upload/display-8-395337.pdf.

47. From 21–23 January 2021, the PUCL online consultation on UAPA and repressive laws was conducted. Below are the links to the three days:

    i. On 21 January 2021, activists from Delhi, Telangana, Andhra Pradesh shared their experiences and analysis of the UAPA. Day 1: https://fb.watch/7Y7cO5a9rL/.

    ii. On 22 January 2021, activists from Karnataka, Maharashtra, Punjab, Haryana, Assam and Kerala shared their viewpoints. Day 2: https://fb.watch/7Y7hgv8rGj/.

    iii. On 23 January 2021, activists from Chhattisgarh, Jharkhand, Utttar Pradesh, Kashmir shared their viewpoints. Day 3: https://fb.watch/7Y7gns3Ui9/.

48. 'TAAA to UAPA', Facebook Live, https://fb.watch/7Y7cO5a9rL/. Also see: Parvathi Sajiv, 'PUCL and 100 Organisations demand the repeal of the UAPA', *The Leaflet*, 21 January 2021, theleaflet.in/pucl-and-100-organisations-demand-the-repeal-of-the-uapa/#.

49. 'TAAA to UAPA', Facebook Live.

50. They were, however, acquitted under the UAPA because the technical requirement of sanction from the Central government was not complied with. *State v Arwinder Singh*, Sessions Case

No. 15 of 2017, Judgement of the Additional Sessions Judge, delivered on 31 January 2019.

51. 'Repeal UAPA: Day Two', Facebook Live, https://fb.watch/7Y7hgv8rGj/. Also see: Megha Katheria, 'Under UAPA, anything can be an offence based on flimsy evidence', *The Leaflet*, 22 January 2021, https://www.theleaflet.in/under-uapa-anything-can-be-an-offence-based-on-flimsy-evidence/. See also the reporting by *The Wire* on the rampant misuse of UAPA in Punjab: Pawanjot Kaur, 'Rampant Arrests, Rare Convictions: In Punjab, the UAPA Is Ripe for Misuse', *The Wire*, 13 February 2021, https://thewire.in/rights/rampant-arrests-rare-convictions-in-punjab-the-uapa-is-ripe-for-misuse.

52. Ibid.

53. Fact-finding Report, 'Communalising Violence in Bangalore D.J. Halli', *Countercurrents*, 17 September 2020, https://countercurrents.org/2020/09/communalising-violence-in-bangalore-d-j-halli/.

54. Megha Katheria, 'Under UAPA, anything can be an offence based on flimsy evidence'.

55. 'Repeal UAPA: Day Three', Facebook Live, https://fb.watch/7Y7gns3Ui9/.

56. 'Repeal UAPA: Day Three'; Quratulain Rehbar, '"Just a Cricket Match": 10 J&K Men Booked Under UAPA For Playing in Memory of Slain Militant', *The Wire*, 9 September 2020, https://thewire.in/rights/nazneenpora-shopian-ruban-militant-cricket-match-uapa.

57. TNN, '151 UAPA cases registered in Kerala in five years', *The Times of India*, 6 November 2019, https://timesofindia.indiatimes.com/city/kochi/151-uapa-cases-registered-in-state-in-5-years/articleshow/71929825.cms.

58. TNM Staff, 'Kerala HC sets aside bail granted to Thaha Fasal in the UAPA case', TheNewsMinute, 4 January 2021, https://www.thenewsminute.com/article/kerala-hc-sets-aside-bail-granted-thaha-fasal-uapa-case-140805.

59. 'Repeal UAPA: Day Two', Facebook Live.

60. 'A Brief History of CBI', https://cbi.gov.in/About-Us/History.

61. Delhi Special Police Establishment Act, 1946, Section 6 states: Consent of State Government to exercise of powers and jurisdiction. Nothing contained in section 5 shall be deemed to enable any member of the Delhi Special Police Establishment to exercise powers and jurisdiction in any area in a State not being a Union Territory or railways area, without the consent of the Government of that State.

62. See Section 6 of the National Investigation Agency Act.

63. Parliamentary Debates, Rajya Sabha, 17 July 2019, 26 Ashadha, 1941 (Saka), https://rajyasabha.nic.in/Documents/Official_Debate_Nhindi/Floor/249/F17.07.2019.pdf.

64. Parliamentary Debates, Rajya Sabha, 17 July 2019.

65. See Section 273 of the CrPC, which mandates that, 'evidence is to be taken in presence of accused'.

66. See Section 178 of the CrPC, which specifies that offences shall be inquired into by a court within whose local jurisdiction the offence was committed.

67. See Section 327 of the CrPC.

68. The adversary system is one in which a decision is arrived at by having each side to a dispute present its case and then mandating the judge to determine the facts and apply the law after hearing both sides. By contrast, in an inquisitorial system, the court is actively involved in investigating the facts of the case. The Indian legal system is adversarial and the judge is expected to arrive at their decision based on the presentation by both sides.

69. See Section 16(5) of the National Investigation Agency Act.

70. Ibid., Section 12.

71. Ibid., Section 17(1).

72. Ibid., Section 17(2).

73. Ibid., Section 17(3)(d).

74. Special laws are those enacted to address special situations which may not have been contemplated or dealt with under the existing criminal law framework of the IPC, CrPC and Evidence Act, such as child sexual abuse, terrorism or drug-related offences.

75. Kunal Ambasta, 'Designed for Abuse: Special Criminal Laws and Rights of the Accused', *NALSAR Student Law Review*, Vol. 14, pp. 1–19 at p. 4, nslr.in/wp-content/uploads/2020/07/NSLRVolume-XIV.pdf.

76. Committee for Reforms in Criminal Laws: https://criminallawreforms.in/substantive-criminal-law/; https://criminallawreforms.in/procedural-criminal-law/; https://criminallawreforms.in/law-of-evidence/.

77. Imran Khan, 'Activists raise concerns over reforms in criminal laws', *Times Now*, 9 July 2020, timesnownews.com/mirror-now/crime/article/activists-raise-concerns-over-reforms-in-criminal-laws/618657.

78. Since its inception and till date, the Central government has entrusted 319 cases to the NIA for investigation. Out of the cases registered, charge sheets have been filed in 237 cases. Judgement has been pronounced in 62 cases, in which 56 cases have resulted in convictions. A total of 276 persons have been convicted in these cases. The conviction rate is 90.32 per cent, Union Minister of State for Home Affairs G. Kishan Reddy stated in the written reply to a question in the Lok Sabha. https://pib.gov.in/PressReleasePage.aspx?PRID=1604976.

79. https://twitter.com/ManishTewari/status/1153988182133760000. Also see: Deeptiman Tiwary, 'Congress denies Amit Shah charge on POTA, slams changes to UAPA'.

80. Press release, 'NIA achieves a Conviction Rate of over 90% in the cases entrusted to it: Shri G. Kishan Reddy', https://pib.gov.in/PressReleasePage.aspx?PRID=1604976.

81. Kunal Ambasta, 'Designed for Abuse', p. 13.

82. *Union of India v K.A. Najeeb*, livelaw.in/pdf_upload/union-of-india-vs-ka-najeeb-ll-2021-sc-56-388472.pdf.

83. Justice Alam, 'A Performance Audit and Some Thoughts on UAPA'.

84. See Section 4 of the National Investigation Agency Act.

85. See Section 4A of the Delhi Special Police Establishment Act, 1946.

86. Arshu John, 'The Professional Fortunes Of Cops, Bureaucrats and SIT Members Associated With the 2002 Godhra Investigation',

The Caravan, 22 September 2017, https://caravanmagazine.in/
vantage/postings-cops-bureaucrats-sit-members-godhra-2002-
investigation; 'Sit Volume II 459-541', https://www.scribd.com/
doc/93082121/Sit-Volume-II-459-541.

87.   'Pakistan calls for justice in 2007 train blast case', Anadolu Agency,
      19 February 2021, aa.com.tr/en/asia-pacific/pakistan-calls-for-
      justice-in-2007-train-blast-case/2150001.

88.   *National Investigation Agency v Naba Kumar Sarkar @ Swami
      Aseemanand and Others* (March 2019), https://drive.google.com/
      viewerng/viewer?url=https://www.livelaw.in/pdf_upload/
      pdf_upload-359520.pdf.

89.   Editorial, 'Terror and the Course of Law', *Economic and Political
      Weekly*, 30 March 2019, p. 9.

90.   Parliamentary Debates, Rajya Sabha, 17 July 2019.

91.   Ibid.

92.   Ibid.

93.   Special Correspondent, 'Samjhauta Express blast case case lacked
      proof, says Amit Shah', *The Hindu*, 17 July 2017, https://www.
      thehindu.com/news/national/samjhauta-express-blast-case-case-
      lacked-proof-says-amit-shah/article28524850.ece.

94.   *National Investigation Agency v Naba Kumar Sarkar @ Swami
      Aseemanand and Others* (March 2019), https://drive.google.com/
      viewerng/viewer?url=https://www.livelaw.in/pdf_upload/
      pdf_upload-359520.pdf.

95.   'Takeover of the Elgar case by the NIA', *Economic and Political
      Weekly*, 1 February 2020, p. 7.

96.   PUCL, Repeal UAPA Campaign, Forthcoming publication.

97.   Ibid.

98.   Vijayta Lalwani, 'Delhi Police claims February riots were a
      conspiracy by CAA protestors – but where is the evidence?', *Scroll*,
      19 July 2020, https://scroll.in/article/967881/delhi-polices-grand-
      riots-conspiracy-where-is-the-evidence.

99.   PTI, 'Maharashtra bandh: Sixteen-year-old boy crushed to death
      while fleeing police in Nanded during protests', *FirstPost*, 4 January

2018, firstpost.com/india/maharashtra-bandh-sixteen-year-old-boy-crushed-to-death-while-fleeing-police-in-nanded-during-protests-4286251.html.

100. 'Sambhaji Bhide & Milind Ekbote, The Men Behind Caste Clashes In Maharashtra', youtube.com/watch?v=o-_g9AAUUm0 (video).

101. Apoorvanand, 'If we do not speak up now against the arrest of Professor Hany Babu, we may lose India forever', *Scroll*, 30 July 2020, scroll.in/article/968949/if-we-do-not-speak-up-now-against-the-arrest-of-professor-hany-babu-we-may-lose-india-forever.

102. Tony P.M. and Peter Martin, 'Adivasi rights activist Stan Swamy's life and work demonstrate why the powerful want him silenced', *Scroll*, 21 October 2020, scroll.in/article/976136/arrested-adivasi-rights-activist-stan-swamys-life-demonstrates-why-the-powerful-want-him-silenced.

103. Aarefa Johari, 'Bhima Koregaon: What has happened to the five activists who were arrested a year ago', *Scroll*, 6 June 2019, scroll.in/article/925929/bhima-koregaon-what-has-happened-to-the-five-activists-who-were-arrested-a-year-ago.

104. *Romila Thapar v Union of India* (September 2018), indiankanoon.org/doc/52834611/.

105. Arvind Narrain and Saumya Uma (eds), *Passion for Justice* (Friends of Mukul Sinha), p. 19.

106. Ashish Khetan, *Undercover* (Westland Books, New Delhi: 2021), p. 58; 'Amit Shah Arrested', youtube.com/watch?v=p-inRH5cDUw (video).

107. As noted above, see Section 43 D(5) of the UAPA.

108. Martand Kaushik and Anjaneya Sivan, 'Bhima Koregaon case: Prison-rights activist Rona Wilson's hard disk contained malware that allowed remote access', *The Caravan*, 12 March 2020, https://caravanmagazine.in/politics/bhima-koregaon-case-rona-wilson-hard-disk-malware-remote-access.

109. Arsenal Consulting, *In the Court of Special Judge NIA, Mumbai Special Case No. 414/2020 National Investigating Agency v Sudhir Pralhad Dhawale & others*, Report I, 8 February 2021, https://arsenalexperts.com/.

110. Ibid., Report III, 21 June 2021.

111. Ibid.

112. Mihir Desai's public lecture, 'Terror laws under a Proto-fascist regime'.

113. B.R. Ambedkar, *Babasaheb Ambedkar: Writings and Speeches*, Vol. 8 (Govt of Maharashtra, Mumbai: 2014), p. 358.

114. Anand Teltumbde, 'Ghar Wapsi: Welcome to the Hellhole of Hinduism', *Economic and Political Weekly*, Vol. 50, No. 1 (3 January 2015), pp. 10–11.

115. Anand Teltumbde, 'Saffron Science', *Economic and Political Weekly*, Vol. 50, No. 6 (7 February 2015), pp. 10–11.

116. Anand Teltumbde, 'The Holy Cow', *Economic and Political Weekly*, Vol. 50, No. 14 (4 April 2015), pp. 10–11.

117. Anand Teltumbde, 'Gujarat 2002 and Modi's Misdeeds', *Economic and Political Weekly*, Vol. 47, No. 11 (17 March 2012), pp. 10–11.

118. Anjani Kumar's interview with Sudhir Dhawale, 'No one can kill the dream for democracy', http://sanhati.com/excerpted/15898/.

119. Aarefa Johari, 'Who are the three Kabir Kala Manch artistes arrested in the Bhima Koregaon case this week?', *Scroll*, 12 September 2020, https://scroll.in/article/972791/who-are-the-three-kabir-kala-manch-artistes-arrested-in-the-bhima-koregaon-case-this-week.

120. Ibid.

121. 'PUCL Press Conference against Illegal arrests in Bhima Koregaon conspiracy case', https://www.youtube.com/watch?v=NuhHxjI_BDA.

122. Kainat Sarfaraz, 'Jailed DU professor GN Saibaba terminated by Ram Lal Anand College', *Hindustan Times*, 3 April 2021, https://www.hindustantimes.com/india-news/jailed-du-professor-gn-saibaba-terminated-by-ram-lal-anand-college-101617387964098.html.

123. Aarefa Johari, 'A poet, a lawyer, a professor: These are the five activists held for sparking Bhima Koregaon clashes', *Scroll*, 8 June 2018, https://scroll.in/article/881849/a-poet-a-lawyer-a-

professor-these-are-the-five-activists-held-for-sparking-bhima-koregaon-clashes.

124. 'Who is Surendra Gadling?', https://indiacivilwatch.org/issues-b12/surendra-gadling/.

125. *Sudha Bharadwaj Speaks* (ed. Arvind Narrain), p. 108.

126. Ibid., p. 23.

127. Ibid., p. 96. Arun Ferreira, Colours of the Cage, (Aleph, New Delhi: 2014), p. 103.

128. Sagar Abraham-Gonsalves, '"Don't worry, said father. Mother served the constables tea": A son describes a police raid at dawn', *Scroll*, 30 August 2018, https://scroll.in/article/892495/dont-worry-said-father-mother-served-the-constables-tea-a-son-describes-a-police-raid-at-dawn.

129. Arun Ferreira, *Colours of the Cage* (Aleph, New Delhi: 2014), p. 103.

130. 'An Adivasi activist against corporate greed and state violence: A profile of Hidme Markam', *The Polis Project*, 11 May 2021, thepolisproject.com/an-adivasi-activist-against-corporate-greed-and-state-violence-a-profile-of-hidme-markam.

131. Sonam Saigal, 'Bhima Koregaon: Mahesh Raut turns 33 inside jail', *The Hindu*, 2 July 2020, https://www.thehindu.com/news/national/other-states/bhima-koregaon-mahesh-raut-turns-33-inside-jail/article31966682.ece.

132. The Polis Project and Maraa, 'The youngest accused in the Bhima Koregaon violence case: A profile of Mahesh Raut', *The Polis Project*, 26 October 2020, https://thepolisproject.com/the-youngest-accused-in-the-bhima-koregaon-violence-case-a-profile-of-mahesh-raut/#.YCJ6HF5S-Iw; 'Petition to the Government of India: Mahesh Raut Needs to be Free', Socialist Party (India), https://spi.org.in/letters-and-petitions/petition-to-the-government-of-india-mahesh-raut-needs-to-be-free/.

133. Ibid.

134. John Dayal, 'Jailed activist Stan Swamy has spent half a century making Adivasi struggles his own', *Scroll*, 14 Ocotober 2020, https://scroll.in/article/975693/jailed-activist-stan-swamy-has-spent-half-a-century-making-adivasi-struggles-his-own.

135. *Samatha v State of Andhra Pradesh*, https://indiankanoon.org/doc/1969682/.

136. Bagaicha Research Team, *Deprived of rights over natural resources, impoverished Adivasis get prison: A study of undertrials in Jharkhand* (Bagaicha, Jharkhand), http://sanhati.com/wp-content/uploads/2016/02/Undertrials.in_.Jharkhand.pdf.

137. Stan Swamy and Sudha Bhardwaj, 'Illegal Solitary Confinement', *Economic and Political Weekly*, Vol. 53, No. 14 (7 April 2018), p. 4.

138. E.P. Thompson, *Writing by Candlelight* (Merlin, London: 1980), p. 156.

139. Josy Joseph, *The Silent Coup: A History of India's Deep State* (Context/Westland, New Delhi: 2021).

140. E.P. Thompson, *Writing by Candlelight*, p. 176.

141. Gautam Navlakha, 'A Savage War for "Development"', *Economic and Political Weekly*, Vol. 52, No. 21 (27 May 2017), pp. 61–65.

142. Among the numerous writings on Kashmir, see Gautam Navlakha, 'Redeeming Ourselves as People in Jammu and Kashmir', *Economic and Political Weekly*, Vol. 51, No. 39 (24 September 2016), pp. 14–17.

143. Gautam Navlakha, 'Private Corporations in Defence Production', *Economic and Political Weekly*, Vol. 52, No. 44 (4 November 2017), pp.16–17.

144. Gautam Navlakha, 'A hard look at national security', *Economic and Political Weekly*, Vol. 51, No. 29 (16 July 2016), pp. 32–37.

145. 'A History of Criminal Laws in India', Dalit Camera, https://www.youtube.com/watch?v=p_rXmpwer_o.

146. Ibid.

147. 'Rona Wilson', https://indiacivilwatch.org/issues-b12/rona-wilson/.

148. PTI, 'Hard work is more powerful than Harvard : Modi', *The Hindu*, 1 March 2017, thehindu.com/elections/uttar-pradesh-2017/hard-work-more-powerful-than-harvard-narendra-modi/article17387381.ece.

149. Ngũgĩ wa Thiong'o, 'Foreword', in *Captive Imagination* by Varavara Rao (Penguin Viking, New Delhi: 2010), p. x.

150. Shoma Sen, 'Class Struggle and Patriarchy: Women in the Maoist

Movement', *Economic and Political Weekly*, Vol. 52, No. 21 (27 May 2017), pp. 56–60.

151 Ibid., p. 59.

152. 'Shoma Sen', https://indiacivilwatch.org/issues-b12/shoma-sen/.

153. 'Shoma Sen – Demonising a Beloved Teacher and Life-long Activist', https://www.kractivist.org/shoma-sen-demonising-a-beloved-teacher-and-life-long-activist/.

154. G.N. Saibaba is a professor of English who was arrested under the UAPA on grounds of being a member of an unlawful association, convicted by a Maharashtra Sessions Court and sentenced to life imprisonment.

155. DU professor Hany Babu on the witch-hunt of academics in India, https://www.youtube.com/watch?v=9s4EVfKB6fw.

156. Ibid.

157. Hannah Arendt, *Men in Dark Times* (Harcourt, Brace & World: 1968), p. ix.

158. *The Wire* has also extensively covered the BK-16. For an example, see: Rajshree Chandra, 'Bhima Koregaon Case: Trying Without a Trial Is the Intent of Draconian UAPA Law', *The Wire*, 9 July 2021, https://thewire.in/rights/bhima-koregaon-case-trying-without-a-trial-is-the-intent-of-draconian-uapa-law.

159. For a profile of Arun Ferriera, see: Aarefa Johari, 'After almost five years in jail, alleged Maoist leader is found innocent', *Scroll*, 3 February 2014, https://scroll.in/article/655295/after-almost-five-years-in-jail-alleged-maoist-leader-is-found-innocent.

160. For a profile of the Kabir Kala Manch trio, see: The Polis Project and Maraa, 'The crushing power of street performances from the margins: A profile of Kabir Kala Manch's Sagar Gorkhe, Jyoti Jagtap and Ramesh Gaichor', *The Polis Project*, 2 September 2021, https://thepolisproject.com/the-crushing-power-of-street-performances-from-the-margins-a-profile-of-kabir-kala-manchs-sagar-gorkhe-jyoti-jagtap-and-ramesh-gaichor/#.YTiSdMbhUcQ. There are similar profiles of each of the other BK arrestees.

161. Milan Kundera, *The Book of Laughter and Forgetting* (Perennial, New York: 1999), p. 13.

162. Kanishk Bhawsar, 'Lessons from anti-CAA protests', *The Indian Express*, 11 December 2020, indianexpress.com/article/opinion/lessons-from-anti-caa-protests-7101411/; scroll.in/article/980474/what-the-bjps-differing-reactions-to-anti-caa-and-farmers-protests-tell-us-about-how-it-sees-india.

163. Bureaus/PTI, 'Anti-CAA protests escalate across India', *BusinessLine*, 19 December 2019, thehindubusinessline.com/news/national/anti-caa-protest-internet-shut-down-in-parts-of-delhi/article30346740.ece.

164. Citizens Against Hate, 'Everyone Has Been Silenced', 2020, citizensagainsthate.org/wp-content/uploads/2020/03/Citizens-Against-Hate-Everyone-Has-Been-Silenced.pdf.

165. Staff Reporter, '24-year-old protester arrested in Bengaluru', *The Hindu*, 22 February 2020, thehindu.com/news/national/karnataka/24-year-old-protester-arrested-in-bengaluru/article30884838.ece.

166. Sukanya Shantha, 'After 110 Days in Jail for Saying "Pakistan Zindabad", 19-Year-Old Activist Gets "Default Bail"', *The Wire*, 11 June 2020, thewire.in/rights/amulya-leona-bail-bengaluru.

167. Arvind Narrain, 'Like Indians battled to overturn law criminalising homosexuality, we must fight sedition statute', *Scroll*, 11 February 2020, scroll.in/article/952758/like-indians-battled-to-overturn-law-criminalising-homosexuality-we-must-fight-sedition-statute; PTI, 'Mumbai Student Urvashi Chudawala Booked For Sedition Gets Interim Protection From Arrest', *NDTV*, 11 February 2020, ndtv.com/india-news/mumbai-student-urvashi-chudawala-booked-for-sedition-gets-interim-protection-from-arrest-2178668.

168. 'The Night of The Broken Glass: Testimonies From Jamia Millia Islamia', scribd.com/document/458087289/The-Night-of-the-Broken-Glass-Testimonies-from-Jamia-Millia-Islamia.

169. 'An Account of Fear and Impunity', A fact-finding report by the Youth for Human Rights Documentation, February 2020, hrfn.org/wp-content/uploads/2020/03/An-Account-of-Fear-Impunity.pdf.

170. 'Report of the DMC Fact-finding Committee on Northeast Delhi Riots of February 2020' (henceforth DMC report), https://ia801906.us.archive.org/11/items/dmc-delhi-riot-fact-report-2020/-Delhi-riots-Fact-Finding-2020.pdf; Seemi Pasha, 'Delhi Police Chargesheet Misses Key Fact: Riots Killed the Anti-CAA Protest', *The Wire*, 18 June 2020, thewire.in/rights/delhi-police-chargesheet-riot-media-coverage.

171. DMC report.

172. Ibid.

173. Ibid.

174. The Wire Analysis, 'Delhi Police Riot "Plot" Has Trump Present When He Can't Have Been, Kapil Mishra Absent', *The Wire*, 12 June 2020, thewire.in/government/delhi-police-riots-chargesheet-trump-umar-khalid-conspiracy-loophole; Tarique Anwar, 'Delhi Riots: Police Spin Conspiracy Theory, Accuse Anti-CAA Protesters of Planning "Blast" Ahead of Trump's Visit', *NewsClick*, 13 June 2020, newsclick.in/Delhi-Riots-Police-Spins-Conspiracy-Theory-Accuses-Anti-CAA-Protesters-Planning-Blast-Trump-Visit.

175. Dheeraj Mishra, 'Why Is the Police Stonewalling The Wire's RTI Queries on the Delhi Violence?', *The Wire*, 19 April 2020, thewire.in/government/delhi-riots-police-rti.

176. The Wire Staff, '"Delhi Riots Began With Kapil Mishra's Speech, Yet No Case Against Him': Minority Commission Report', *The Wire*, 16 July 2020, thewire.in/communalism/delhi-riots-kapil-mishra-minority-commission-report.

177. Asmita Bakshi, 'The Curious Case of "Humanitarian Grounds" in Zafoora's Bail Order', *Mint*, 23 June 2020, livemint.com/mint-lounge/features/the-curious-case-of-humanitarian-grounds-in-safoora-zargar-s-bail-order-11592916696953.html.

178. Sharjeel Usmani, 'Charting history of Indian Muslims and the police: From British era to AMU violence, a story of injustice', *FirstPost*, 27 April 2020, firstpost.com/india/charting-history-of-indian-muslims-and-the-police-from-british-era-to-amu-violence-a-story-of-injustice-8303531.html.

179. N.D. Jayaprakash, 'Delhi Riots 2020: There Was a Conspiracy, But Not the One the Police Alleges', *The Wire*, 15 July 2020, thewire. in/communalism/delhi-riots-2020-there-was-a-conspiracy-but-not-the-one-the-police-alleges.

180. Narendra Jadhav, (ed.), *Ambedkar Speaks*, Vol. I (Konark publisher, New Delhi: 2013), p. 294.

181. 'What Is Article 370?', *Business Standard*, https://www.business-standard.com/about/what-is-article-370.

182. 'Imprisoned Resistance: 5th August and Its Aftermath', A report by PUCL, 2019, pucl.org/reports/imprisoned-resistance-5th-august-and-its-aftermath.

183. 'Imprisoned Resistance', PUCL.

184. PTI, 'Over 5,000 arrested in Kashmir valley since Aug 4: Govt', *Deccan Herald*, 20 November 2019, https://www.deccanherald. com/national/north-and-central/over-5000-arrested-in-kashmir-valley-since-aug-4-govt-778001.html.

185. LiveLaw News, '99% Of Habeas Pleas Filed Before Jammu and Kashmir HC Since Abrogation Of Article 370 Are Still Pending: J&K HC Bar Association Writes To CJI', LiveLaw, 29 June 2020, livelaw.in/top-stories/99-of-habeas-pleas-filed-before-jammu-and-kashmir-hc-since-abrogation-of-article-370-are-still-pending-jk-hc-bar-association-writes-to-cji-read-letter-159059.

186. 'Imprisoned Resistance', PUCL.

187. Naveed Iqbal, '2,300 booked under UAPA in J&K since 2019, nearly half still in jail', *The Indian Express*, 5 August 2021, indianexpress. com/article/india/2300-booked-under-uapa-in-jk-since-2019-nearly-half-still-in-jail-7438806/.

188. Ibid.

189. 'Media, Democracy and Democratic Institutions', Facebook Live, facebook.com/watch/live/?v=2489512174527989&ref=w atch_permalink (video).

190. Vindu Goel and Jeffrey Gettleman, 'Under Modi, India's Press Is Not So Free Anymore', *The New York Times*, 6 May 2020, nytimes. com/2020/04/02/world/asia/modi-india-press-media.html.

191. Sevanti Ninan, 'How India's news media have changed since 2014: Greater self-censorship, dogged digital resistance', *Scroll*, 5 July 2019, scroll.in/article/929461/greater-self-censorship-dogged-digital-resistance-how-indias-news-media-have-changed-since-2014.

192. Sonia Faleiro, 'Fact-checking Modi's India', Rest of World, 12 May 2021, restofworld.org/2021/fact-checking-modis-india/.

193. Apoorvanand, 'It's Clear Why NewsClick Is Being Targeted, and Why it Was Viewed as a Threat', *The Wire*, 14 February 2021, thewire.in/media/newsclick-enforcement-directorate-raid-target.

194. Vidhi Doshi, 'World Media On CBI Raids On NDTV', NDTV, 7 June 2017, ndtv.com/india-news/world-media-on-cbi-raids-on-ndtv-1708744.

195. Sonia Faleiro, 'Fact-checking Modi's India'.

196. Sudheendra Kulkarni, '1975 Emergency: Indian Democracy Needs "Vertical Men" Like Advani', *The Quint*, 25 June 2018, thequint.com/voices/opinion/1975-emergency-lk-advani-critique-of-indian-media-rings-true.

197. 'Jug Suraiya's Column That Was Dropped From Times of India's Print Edition', *The Wire*, 14 May 2021, thewire.in/humour/jug-suraiya-times-of-india-covid-column.

198. 'Intermediary Liability in India: Chilling Effects on Free Expression on the Internet', Report by the Centre for Internet and Society, 2012, cis-india.org/internet-governance/chilling-effects-on-free-expression-on-internet.

199. 'Constitutional questions against unconstitutional Rules', internetfreedom.in/constitutional-questions-against-unconstitutional-rules/.

200. 'Tandav is a Case Study for OTT censorship under the IT Rules, 2021 #LetUsChill', internetfreedom.in/tandav-case-study/.

201. Shobhana K. Nair, 'India again placed at 142nd rank in press freedom', *The Hindu*, 21 April 2021, thehindu.com/news/national/india-again-placed-at-142nd-rank-in-press-freedom/article34377079.ece.

202. 'Modi tightens his grip on the media', Reporters Without Borders, rsf.org/en/india.

203. Sevanti Ninan, 'How India's news media have changed since 2014'.

204. Garvita Khybri, 'How Threats on Twitter Manifest In Real Life: Indian Troll Tales', *The Quint*, 28 August 2018, thequint.com/neon/gender/trolling-women-journalists-rana-ayyub#read-more.

205. Amy Kazmin, '"I Am a Troll" by Swati Chaturvedi', *Financial Times*, 20 February 2017, https://www.ft.com/content/6dd90462-e3bd-11e6-8405-9e5580d6e5fb.

206. Rollo Romig, 'Railing Against India's Right-Wing Nationalism Was a Calling. It Was Also a Death Sentence', *The New York Times*, 14 March 2019, nytimes.com/2019/03/14/magazine/gauri-lankesh-murder-journalist.html.

207. PTI, 'Man, Wanted In Gauri Lankesh's Murder, Arrested in Jharkhand', NDTV, 11 January 2020, ndtv.com/india-news/gauri-lankesh-murder-case-man-wanted-in-gauri-lankesh-murder-arrested-in-dhanbad-jharkhand-2162251; PTI, 'Same group behind killings of Narendra Dabholkar, M M Kalburgi, Gauri Lankesh: Official', *The Economic Times*, 16 September 2018, economictimes.indiatimes.com/news/politics-and-nation/same-group-behind-killings-of-narendra-dabholkar-m-m-kalburgi-gauri-lankesh-official/articleshow/65828022.cms.

208. Geeta Seshu and Urvashi Sarkar, 'Getting away with Murder', https://www.thakur-foundation.org/report-on-attacks-on-journalists-in-india-2014-2019.pdf.

209. A.P. Shah, 'Supreme Court Then and Now', *Economic and Political Weekly*, Vol. 55, No. 40 (3 October 2020), pp. 31–37.

210. Madan B. Lokur, 'Supreme Court Deserves an "F" Grade For Its Handling of Migrants', *The Wire*, 28 May 2020, thewire.in/law/after-humanitarian-law-died-a-million-deaths-the-supreme-court-has-finally-stirred-itself.

211. Ashok Bagriya, 'A year after landmark press conference, little has changed in Supreme Court's running', *Hindustan Times*, 12 January 2019, hindustantimes.com/india-news/a-year-after-landmark-

press-conference-little-has-changed-in-supreme-court-s-running/story-ZtTyvwIyFTCJLDxngrOQuL.html.

212. PTI, 'SC to hear over 140 pleas challenging CAA today', *India Today*, 22 January 2020, indiatoday.in/india/story/supreme-court-hear-over-pleas-challenging-citizenship-amendment-act-caa-today-1638948-2020-01-22.

213. Murali Krishnan, 'Kashmir and Article 370: A look at the cases in Supreme Court and where do they stand', *Hindustan Times*, 4 August 2020, hindustantimes.com/india-news/kashmir-and-article-370-a-look-at-the-cases-in-sc-and-where-do-they-stand/story-SLNajzn1cL3JNXuHH4eVdO.html.

214. 'Electoral Bonds, the Great Fraud, Nitin Sethi at Manthan', youtube.com/watch?v=m5HIgiDuIVU.

215. 'Electoral Bonds: *Association for Democratic Reforms v. Union of India*', Supreme Court Observer, scobserver.in/court-case/electoral-bonds.

216. Justice Gopala Gowda, 'A supreme failure', *Deccan Herald*, 25 May 2020, deccanherald.com/opinion/main-article/a-supreme-failure-841803.html.

217. Madan B. Lokur, 'Supreme Court Deserves an "F" Grade For Its Handling of Migrants'.

218. The Wire Staff, 'Loya Case the Tipping Point, Four SC Judges Say Democracy Is in Danger', *The Wire*, 12 January 2018, thewire.in/law/sc-justices-hold-historic-press-conference-triggered-judge-loya-case; V. Venkatesan, 'How Justice Arun Mishra Rose to Become the Most Influential Judge in the Supreme Court', *The Wire*, 1 September 2020, thewire.in/law/justice-arun-mishra-judgments-analysis.

219. TNM Staff, '"Then-CJI Dipak Misra was being controlled from outside": Justice Kurian Joseph', *The News Minute*, 3 December 2018, thenewsminute.com/article/then-cji-dipak-misra-was-being-controlled-outside-justice-kurien-joseph-92636.

220. Justice A.P. Shah, 'Supreme Court Then and Now'.

221. *Shanti Bhushan v Supreme Court* (July 2018), indiankanoon.org/doc/51165139/.

222. Manu Sebastian, 'Master of Roster Case- Summary of Judgment', LiveLaw, 6 July 2018, livelaw.in/master-of-roster-case-summary-of-judgment/.

223. *Navtej Singh Johar v Union of India* (September 2018), indiankanoon. org/doc/168671544/.

224. Ibid.

225. *Joseph Shine v Union of India* (September 2018), indiankanoon.org/ doc/42184625//.

226. *Indian Young Lawyers Association v State of Kerala* (September 2018), indiankanoon.org/doc/163639357/.

227. *Kamlesh Verma v Mayawati* (August 2013), casemine.com/ judgement/in/56e6687b607dba6b53433113.

228. *Kantaru Rajeevaru v Indian Young Lawyers Association* (November 2019), indiankanoon.org/doc/120364030/.

229. Shaju Philip, 'Amit Shah asks on Sabarimala: Why issue orders that can't be enforced?', *The Indian Express*, 28 October 2018, indianexpress.com/article/india/amit-shah-asks-on-sabarimala-why-issue-orders-that-cant-be-enforced-5421715/.

230. Ibid.

231. US Chief Justice Charles Even Hughes cited by Justice Nariman in *Puttaswamy v Union of India* (August 2017), indiankanoon.org/ doc/91938676/.

232. *M. Siddiq v Mahant Suresh Das* (November 2019), indiankanoon. org/doc/107745042/.

233. *Mahant Raghobar Dass v Secy of State for India*, No. 122 of 1886, in the Court of the Judicial Commissioner of Oudh. Cf. A.G. Noorani, ed., *The Babri Masjid Question, 1528-2003* (Tulika Books, New Delhi: 2003), p. 188.

234. *Gopal Singh Visharad and others v Zahoor Ahmad and others + Nirmohi Akhara and others v Baboo Priya Datt Ram and others + The Sunni Central Board of Waqfs, UP v Gopal Singh Visharad and others + Bhagwan Sri Ram Lala Virajman v Rajendra Singh and others*, http:// elegalix.allahabadhighcourt.in/elegalix/ayodhyafiles/honsukj.pdf.

235. Sruthisagar Yamunan, 'How Ram Lalla became a party to the

Ayodhya dispute – and who might actually benefit from it', *Scroll*, 19 August 2019, https://scroll.in/article/934029/how-ram-lalla-become-a-party-to-the-ayodhya-dispute-and-who-might-actually-benefit-from-it.

236. Report of the Liberhan Commission of Inquiry, para 160.10.

237. Justice A.P. Shah, 'Supreme Court Then and now', p. 34.

238. *M. Siddiq v Mahant Suresh Das*, https://indiankanoon.org/doc/107745042/.

239. Ismat Ara, '"Cloud on Ayodhya Verdict": Mosque Moves SC to Intervene in PIL Challenging Places of Worship Act', *The Wire*, 22 March 2021, thewire.in/law/lucknow-mosque-moves-sc-to-intervene-in-pil-against-places-of-worship-act.

240. Justice A.P. Shah, 'Supreme Court Then and Now'.

241. 'Supreme Court holds Prashant Bhushan guilty of contempt for tweets against court, CJI SA Bobde', *Hindustan Times*, 14 August 2020, hindustantimes.com/india-news/supreme-court-holds-prashant-bhushan-guilty-of-contempt-of-court-for-tweets-against-cji-sa-bobde-sc/story-mChDvJ23SOIjQE5rMdDbUP.html.

242. Affidavit filed by Prashant Bhushan on 2 August 2020 in *In Re Prashant Bhushan*, livelaw.in/pdf_upload/pdf_upload-380215.pdf.

243. *In Re Prashant Bhushan* (August 2020), indiankanoon.org/doc/172868218/.

244. Affidavit filed by Prashant Bhushan.

245. The Wire Staff, 'Ex SC/HC Judges Lead Support by 3,000 Eminent Persons for Prashant Bhushan', *The Wire*, 17 August 2020, thewire.in/rights/prashant-bhushan-solidarity-statement-contempt-supreme-court.

246. 'Contempt case: Statement by Prashant Bhushan', *The Hindu*, 20 August 2020, thehindu.com/news/resources/contempt-case-statement-by-prashant-bhushan/article32402905.ece.

247. The Wire Staff, 'Ex SC/HC Judges Lead Support by 3,000 Eminent Persons for Prashant Bhushan'.

248. *In Re Prashant Bhushan* (August 2020).

249. The Wire Staff, 'Ex SC/HC Judges Lead Support by 3,000 Eminent Persons for Prashant Bhushan'.

250. Quratulain Rehbar, 'Meet Anuradha Bhasin, a Vocal Journalist Facing Government Crackdown', *The Wire*, 21 October 2020, thewire.in/media/anuradha-bhasin-kashmir-time-crackdown.
251. Ibid.
252. *Foundation for Media v Union Territory of Jammu and Kashmir* (May 2020), indiankanoon.org/doc/123992151/.
253. Ratnadip Choudhury, 'Ex-Chief Justice Ranjan Gogoi On Why He Accepted Rajya Sabha Nomination', NDTV, 17 Marh 2020, ndtv.com/india-news/former-chief-justice-of-india-ranjan-gogoi-tells-media-will-speak-on-why-i-accepted-rajya-sabha-nomi-2196042.
254. Debayan Roy, 'Former CJI Ranjan Gogoi nominated to Rajya Sabha, less than 6 months after retirement', *The Print*, 16 March 2020, theprint.in/india/former-cji-ranjan-gogoi-nominated-to-rajya-sabha-less-than-6-months-after-retirement/382089/.
255. Pratap Bhanu Mehta, 'The Gogoi betrayal: Judges will not empower you, they are diminished men', *The Indian Express*, 20 March 2020, indianexpress.com/article/opinion/columns/ranjan-gogoi-supreme-court-rajya-sabha-6320869/.
256. Srinivasan Jain, '"Death Knell For Power Separation": Retired Judge On Ranjan Gogoi's New Role', NDTV, 17 March 2020, ndtv.com/india-news/on-former-cji-ranjan-gogois-new-role-as-mp-justice-ap-shahs-reservations-2196290.
257. Gautam Bhatia, '"A little brief authority": Chief Justice Ranjan Gogoi and the Rise of the Executive Court', *Indian Constitutional Law and Philosophy*, 17 November 2019, indconlawphil.wordpress.com/2019/11/17/a-little-brief-authority-chief-justice-ranjan-gogoi-and-the-rise-of-the-executive-court/.
258. Gautam Bhatia, 'The Troubling Legacy of Chief Justice Ranjan Gogoi', *The Wire*, 16 March 2020, thewire.in/law/chief-justice-ranjan-gogoi-legacy.
259. Ibid.
260. ANI, 'SC accepts JK juvenile justice committee's report on illegal detention', *Business Standard*, 13 December 2019, https://www.business-standard.com/article/news-ani/sc-accepts-jk-juvenile-

justice-committee-s-report-on-illegal-detention-119121300778_1.
html.

261. Madan B. Lokur, 'Judicial Independence: Three Developments
that Tell Us Fair is Foul and Foul is Fair', *The Wire*, 23 March 2020,
thewire.in/law/judicial-independence-three-developments-that-
tell-us-fair-is-foul-and-foul-is-fair.

262. Ernst Fraenkel, *The Dual State: A Contribution to the Theory of
Dictatorship* (Oxford University Press: 2017), p. xv.

263. Ibid., p. xv.

264. Ibid., p. 46.

265. Ibid., p. lxiii.

266. Jens Meierhenrich, *The remnants of the Rechtsstaat* (Oxford
University Press, Oxford, 2018), p.186.

267. Fraenkel, *The Dual State*, p. lxiii.

268. 'Reichstag Fire Decree', United Nations Holocaust Memorial
Museum, ushmm.org/learn/timeline-of-events/1933-1938/
reichstag-fire-decree.

269. Fraenkel, *The Dual State*, p. lxiv.

270. Ibid., p. lxvii.

271. See Section 10(1)(b) of the Act, prsindia.org/files/bills_acts/
bills_states/uttar-pradesh/2020/Uttar%20Pradesh%20Special%20
Security%20Force%20Ordinance%20Text.pdf.

272. 'Repeal UAPA: Day Three'. https://ms-my.facebook.com/
peoples.union.for.civil.liberties/videos/repeal-uapa-day-three/
412960196481735/ along with te Footnote 272.

273. See Section 16 of the Act.

274. S. Farman Ahmad Naqvi, 'Reincarnation of the Gestapo in
Uttar Pradesh', naqvifarman.wordpress.com/2020/10/01/
reincarnation-of-gestapo-in-uttar-pradesh/.

275. Niranjan Takle, 'A Family Breaks Its Silence: Shocking details
emerge in death of judge presiding over Sohrabuddin trial',
The Caravan, 20 November 2017, caravanmagazine.in/vantage/
shocking-details-emerge-in-death-of-judge-presiding-over-
sohrabuddin-trial-family-breaks-silence.

276. Abhinav Sekhri, 'Guest Post: Preventive Detention and the Dangers of Volcanic, Ever-Proximate, Ideologies', *Indian Constitutional Law and Philosophy*, 29 May 2020, https://indconlawphil.wordpress.com/2020/05/29/guest-post-preventive-detention-and-the-dangers-of-volcanic-ever-proximate-ideologies//.

277. *Mian Abdul Qayoom v State of Jammu and Kashmir* (May 2020), jkhighcourt.nic.in/doc/upload/orders&cir/kashmir/28052020/LPA%20No.282020%20in%20%5bWP(Crl.)%20No.2512019%5d.pdf.

278. *Puttaswamy v Union of India*.

279. Gautam Bhatia, 'ICLP Turns 7 || A Constitutionalism Without the Court', *Indian Constitutional Law and Philosophy*, 1 August 2020, indconlawphil.wordpress.com/2020/08/01/iclp-turns-7-a-constitutionalism-without-the-court/.

280. Fraenkel, *The Dual State*, p. 53.

4. Slouching Towards a Totalitarian Future

1. W.B. Yeats, 'The Second Coming', poetryfoundation.org/poems/43290/the-second-coming.

2. Juan Linz, *Totalitarian and Authoritarian Regimes* (Lynne Rienner Publishers, London: 2000), p. 4.

3. Ibid., p. 16.

4. Gyan Prakash, *Emergency Chronicles: Indira Gandhi and Democracy's Turning Point* (Penguin Viking, New Delhi: 2018), p. 197.

5. Harsh Mander, 'New hate crime tracker in India finds victims are predominantly Muslims, perpetrators Hindus', *Scroll*, 13 November 2018, scroll.in/article/901206/new-hate-crime-tracker-in-india-finds-victims-are-predominantly-muslims-perpetrators-hindus.

6. Harsh Mander, 'Junaid, My Son', *The Indian Express*, 1 July 2017, indianexpress.com/article/opinion/columns/junaid-my-son-4729828/.

7. Ravish Kumar, *The Free Voice: On Democracy, Culture and the Nation* (Speaking Tiger, New Delhi: 2018), p. 23.

8. 'Violent Cow Protection in India', Human Rights Watch, 18
    February 2019, hrw.org/report/2019/02/18/violent-cow-
    protection-india/vigilante-groups-attack-minorities.

9. Harsh Mander, 'Four months after Oraon man is lynched in
    Jharkhand, bafflement at how neighbours could be so brutal',
    Scroll, 6 September 2019, scroll.in/article/936397/four-months-
    after-oraon-man-is-lynched-in-jharkhand-bafflement-at-how-
    neighbours-could-be-so-brutal.

10. Harsh Mander, 'One morning, returning from visiting his sister,
    an 80-year-old Muslim man was lynched in Sitamarhi', *Scroll*, 5
    November 2019, scroll.in/article/942671/one-morning-returning-
    from-visiting-his-sister-an-80-year-old-muslim-man-was-lynched-
    in-sitamarhi.

11. *Tehseen S. Poonavala v Union of India* (July 2018), indiankanoon.
    org/doc/71965246/.

12. Alok Pandey, '"Cancel Bail Of Accused": Family Of Police Officer
    Killed In UP Violence', NDTV, 26 August 2019, ndtv.com/india-
    news/bulandshahr-violence-family-of-police-officer-killed-in-
    up-violence-say-cancel-bail-of-accused-2090785?pfrom=home-
    topscroll.

13. FP Staff, 'Who was Subodh Kumar Singh? Slain Bulandshahr cop
    was chief investigating officer in 2015 Dadri lynching', *FirstPost*,
    4 December 2018, firstpost.com/india/bulandshahr-violence-
    up-police-inspector-subodh-kumar-singh-was-chief-investigating-
    officer-in-dadri-lynching-case-in-2015-5666991.html.

14. Web Desk, 'Bulandshahr violence: Five charged with murder of
    inspector Subodh Kumar Singh, 38 named in chargesheet', *India
    Today*, 3 March 2019, indiatoday.in/india/story/bulandshahr-
    violence-five-charged-with-murder-of-inspector-subodh-kumar-
    singh-1469354-2019-03-03.

15. Web Bureau, '7 Accused In Bulandshahr Cop Lynching Case
    Get Bail, Welcomed With Garlands', *Outlook*, 26 August 2019,
    outlookindia.com/website/story/india-news-out-on-bail-7-
    accused-in-lynching-policeman-in-bulandshahr-welcomed-with-
    garlands/337140.

16.　Anuj Kumar, 'Bulandshahr killing was planned lynching of an officer on duty', *The Hindu*, 3 December 2019, thehindu.com/news/national/bulandshahr-killing-was-planned-lynching-of-an-officer-on-duty/article30143392.ece.

17.　Ibid.

18.　FP Staff, 'Who was Subodh Kumar Singh?'.

19.　Human Rights Watch, 'Violent Cow Protection in India'.

20.　Paula Giddings, *Ida: A sword among Lions* (Amistad, New York: 2008), p. 2.

21.　Ibid., p. 153.

22.　Ralph Ginzburg, *100 Years of Lynchings* (Black Classic Press, Baltimore: 1988), p. 253.

23.　Paula Giddings, *Ida*, p. 431.

24.　Ibid., p. 409.

25.　Ibid., p. 387.

26.　Ibid., p. 413.

27.　Ibid., p. 655.

28.　Emmet Till Antilynching Act, 2020, congress.gov/bill/116th-congress/house-bill/35/text.

29.　The Rajasthan Protection from Lynching Bill, 2019, prsindia.org/files/bills_acts/bills_states/rajasthan/2019/Bill%2022%20of%202019%20RJ.pdf.

30.　The West Bengal (Prevention of Lynching) Bill, 2019, prsindia.org/files/bills_acts/bills_states/west-bengal/2019/Bill%2021%20of%202019%20WB.pdf.

31.　Emmet Till Antilynching Act, 2020.

32.　Harsh Mander, 'Harsh Mander: When our caravan of love defied threats of violence to pay tribute to Pehlu Khan', *Scroll*, 16 September 2017, scroll.in/article/850860/harsh-mander-when-our-caravan-of-love-defied-threats-of-violence-to-pay-tribute-to-pehlu-khan.

33.　Paula Giddings, *Ida*, p. 226.

34.　Philip Dray, *At the Hands of Persons Unknown: The Lynching of Black America* (Modern Library: 2002), p. 72.

35. Hannah Arendt, *The Origins of Totalitarianism* (Harcourt, Brace, Jovanovich, Orlando: 1973), p. 112.

36. Kumar, *The Free Voice* (Speaking Tiger, New Delhi: 2018), p. 60.

37. Ibid., p. 87.

38. Arendt, *The Origins of Totalitarianism*, p. 107.

39. A. Rosenberg, 'Fascism as a mass movement', cf. Jairus Banaji (ed.), *Fascism: Essays on Europe and India* (Three Essays Collective, New Delhi: 2016), p. 39.

40. 'Communal Policing in Dakshina Kannada: Vigilante Attacks on Women and Minorities 2008–2009' (A report by PUCL, Karnataka: March 2009), sacw.net/DC/CommunalismCollection/ArticlesArchive/CulturalPolicing-Karnataka.pdf.

41. Arendt, *The Origins of Totalitarianism*, p. 323.

42. Ibid., p. 356.

43. Jyotirmaya Sharma, *Hindutva* (Penguin, New Delhi: 2003), p. 156. (Republished as *Hindutva: Exploring the Idea of Hindu Nationalism* (Context/Westland, New Delhi: 2019).)

44. Christophe Jaffrelot, (ed.), *Hindu Nationalism: A Reader* (Penguin, New Delhi: 2007), p. 96.

45. Jyotirmaya Sharma, *Terrifying Vision: M.S. Golwakar, the RSS and India* (Penguin Viking, New Delhi: 2007), pp. 4–5. (Republished as *M.S. Golwakar, the RSS and India* (Context/Westland, New Delhi: 2019).)

46. Bhikhu Parekh, *Hannah Arendt and the Search for a New Political Philosophy* (Macmillan Press, London: 1981), p. 115.

47. Ibid., p. xi.

48. Christophe Jaffrelot, (ed.), *Hindu Nationalism*, pp.116–117.

49. Aakar Patel, *Our Hindu Rashtra* (Westland, New Delhi: 2020), pp. 101–102.

50. Bhanwar Meghwanshi, *I Could Not Be Hindu: The Story of a Dalit in the RSS* (Navayana, New Delhi: 2019), p. 119.

51. Ibid., p. 191.

52. M.S. Golwalkar, *Bunch of Thoughts* (Sahitya Sindhu Prakashana, Bangalore: 1980), pp.177–204.

53. M.S. Golwalkar, *We, or Our Nationhood Defined* (ed. Shamshul Islam) (Pharos: 2017), p. 171.

54. Ashish Khetan, *Undercover* (Context/Westland, New Delhi: 2021), p. 90.

55. Walter Andersen and Shridhar D. Damle, *Messengers of Hindu Nationalism* (C. Hurst and Co., London: 2019), pp. 258–59.

56. Padmaja Nair, 'Religious Political Parties and Their Welfare Work: Relations Between the RSS, the Bharatiya Janata Party and the Vidya Bharati Schools in India', University of Birmingham (working paper, 2009), epapers.bham.ac.uk/1570/.

57. Bhanwar Meghwanshi, *I Could Not Be Hindu*, p. 48.

58. Padmaja Nair, 'Religious Political Parties and Their Welfare Work'.

59. Bhanwar Meghwanshi, *I Could Not Be Hindu*, p. 48.

60. Ibid., p. 49.

61. Ibid., p. 185.

62. Ibid., p. 181.

63. Smitha Nair & Sruthisagar Yamunan, 'Special Report: How NIA went soft on Pragya Thakur – and is now delaying the Malegaon trial', *Scroll*, 12 July 2019, scroll.in/article/930093/special-report-how-nia-went-soft-on-pragya-thakur-and-is-now-delaying-the-malegaon-trial.

64. Christophe Jaffrelot, 'Abhinav Bharat, the Malegoan Blast and Hindu Nationalism: Resisting and Emulating Islamist Nationalism', *Economic and Political Weekly*, Vol. 45, No. 36 (4 September 2010), pp. 51–58.

65. 'Report of the Liberhan Commission of Inquiry' (November 2009), para 160.10, https://www.mha.gov.in/sites/default/files/LAC-Chap-XIV-B.pdf.

66. Jairus Banaji (ed.), *Fascism*, p. 7.

67. Klaus Mann, Tagebucher, cf. Volker Ullrich, *Hitler: Vol I. Ascent* (Vintage, London: 2016), p. 496.

68. Ibid., p. 499.

69. Jairus Banaji, (ed.), *Fascism*, p. 70.

70. Daniel Goldhagen, *Hitler's Willing Executioners* (Alfred Knopf, New York: 1997), p. 82.

71. Ibid., p. 92.
72. Ibid., p. 96.
73. Shiv Sunder, Presentation at a meeting of civil society groups (25 May 2019, on file with the author).
74. Sumit Sarkar, 'The fascism of the Sangh Parivar', Jairus Banaji (ed.), *Fascism*, p. 139.
75. 'The Wages of Hate: Journalism in Dark Times' (a report by Campaign Against Hate Speech: 2020), hatespeechbeda.wordpress.com/2020/09/08/report-wages-of-hate-journalism-in-dark-times/.
76. Ibid.
77. Hannah Arendt, *The Origins of Totalitarianism*, p. 336.
78. Martha Nussbaum, *The Clash Within: Democracy, Religious Violence and India's Future* (Permanent Black, New Delhi: 2007), p. 333.
79. Ashish Khetan, *Undercover*, pp. 97–98.
80. Hannah Arendt, *The Origins of Totalitarianism*, p. 113.
81. James Q. Whitman, *Hitler's American Model: The United States and the Making of Nazi Race Law* (Princeton University Press, Princeton: 2017), p. 82.
82. Ibid., p. 83.
83. Krishnadas Rajagopal, '140 pleas against Citizenship Amendment Act hang fire in Supreme Court', *The Hindu*, 6 December 2020, thehindu.com/news/national/concern-over-delay-in-hearing-pleas-against-caa-in-sc/article33264290.ece.
84. Rohan Venkataramakrishnan, 'Who is linking Citizenship Act to NRC? Here are five times Amit Shah did so', *Scroll*, 20 December 2019, scroll.in/article/947436/who-is-linking-citizenship-act-to-nrc-here-are-five-times-amit-shah-did-so.
85. See Citizenship (Registration of Citizens and Issue of National Identity Cards), 2003, under which the NPR is authorised.
86. ICF Team, 'How NPR Is Different from the Census', 2 March 2020, newsclick.in/how-npr-different-census.
87. Under Section 4(3) of the Citizenship Rules.
88. Under Section 4(6)(a) of the Citizenship Rules.

89. Utpal Parashar, 'Those excluded from Assam NRC can vote if their names are on electoral rolls: EC', *Hindustan Times*, 21 January 2021, hindustantimes.com/india-news/those-excluded-from-assam-nrc-can-vote-if-their-names-are-on-electoral-rolls-ec-101611144425805.html.

90. Web Desk, 'Assam final NRC list released: 19,06,657 people excluded, 3.11 crore make it to citizenship list', *India Today*, 21 August 2019, https://www.indiatoday.in/india/story/assam-final-nrc-list-out-over-19-lakh-people-excluded-1593769-2019-08-31.

91. Angana Chatterji, 'Breaking worlds', Center for Race and Gender, University of California, 2021, p.7, https://www.crg.berkeley.edu/wp-content/uploads/2021/08/9-12-21_Update_BREAKING-WORLDS_Monograph_Chatterji-et-al.pdf.

92. Rohini Mohan, 'Worse than a death sentence', *Type Investigations*, 29 July 2019, typeinvestigations.org/investigation/2019/07/29/national-register-citizens-india-assam-bangladesh/.

93. Angana Chatterji, 'Breaking worlds', p. 8.

94. Ibid., p. 10.

95. Kamaljit Kaur Sandhu, 'No detention centres under CAA, NRC, MHA informs Rajya Sabha', *India Today*, 17 March 2021, indiatoday.in/india/story/no-detention-centres-caa-nrc-mha-rajya-sabha-1780324-2021-03-17.

96. Arshdeep, 'CAA — NRC — Detention Centres and its impact on India', *Medium*, 26 December 2019, medium.com/@arshdeep773/caa-nrc-detention-centres-and-its-impact-on-india-e846a87191a3.

97. *The Gambia v Myanmar* (January 2020), https://www.icj-cij.org/public/files/case-related/178/178-20200123-ORD-01-00-EN.pdf.

98. B.E. stands for Burmese Era, which is the Burmese Calendar.

99. Burma Citizenship Law, refworld.org/docid/3ae6b4f71b.html.

100. *The Gambia v Myanmar.*

101. Ibid.

102. James Whitman, *Hitler's American Model*, p. 30.

103. Hannah Arendt, *The Origins of Totalitarianism*, p. 296.

104. Ibid., p. 297.

105. *Shafin Jahan v K.M. Asokan* (March 2018), indiankanoon.org/doc/18303067/.

106. Web Desk, 'Mohabbat Zindabad! It was love, no Jihad, says NIA in Hadiya Case', *National Herald*, 18 October 2018, nationalheraldindia.com/india/mohabbat-zindabad-it-was-love-no-jihad-says-nia-in-hadiya-case.

107. Dionne Bunsha, 'I don't believe in love marriages', *New Internationalist*, 1 May 2007, newint.org/columns/currents/2007/05/01/fundamentalism.

108. The Uttar Pradesh Prohibition of Unlawful Conversion of Religion Ordinance, prsindia.org/files/bills_acts/bills_states/uttar-pradesh/2020/UP%20Prohibition%20of%20Unlawful%20Conversion%20of%20Religion%20Ordinance,%202020%20.pdf.

109. *Rev. Stainislaus v State of Madhya Pradesh and Ors* (January 1977), indiankanoon.org/doc/1308071/.

110. *K.S. Puttaswamy v Union of India* (August 2017), indiankanoon.org/doc/91938676/.

111. See Section 12 of the Uttar Pradesh Prohibition of Unlawful Conversion of Religion Ordinance, 2020.

112. Amita Baviskar, 'Adivasi Encounters with Hindu Nationalism in Madhya Pradesh', *Economic and Political Weekly*, Vol. 40, No. 48 (26 November 2005), p. 5107.

113. Sanya Talwar, 'PIL In Supreme Court Challenges Laws On Religious Conversions "In The Name of Love Jihad" Passed By UP and Uttarakhand', *LiveLaw*, 3 December 2020, livelaw.in/top-stories/up-ordinance-uttarakhand-law-on-religious-conversions-love-jihad-supreme-court-166757.

114. James Whitman, *Hitler's American Model*, p. 31.

115. K.N. Panikkar, 'From Revolt to Agitation: Beginning of the National Movement', *Social Scientist*, Vol. 25, No. 9/10 (September–October: 1997), pp. 28–42 at p. 40.

116. Rohit De, *A People's Constitution: The Everyday Life of Law in the Indian Republic* (Princeton University Press, Princeton: 2018), p. 127.

117. Constituent Assembly Debates, Book no. 7 (24 November 1948), pp. 568–580.

118. Ibid., pp. 568–580.

119. Collated by Human Rights Watch in January 2018, hrw.org/sites/default/files/report_pdf/india0219_appendix_1.pdf.

120. *M.H. Qureshi v State of Bihar* (April 1958), indiankanoon.org/doc/93885/.

121. Rohit De, *A People's Constitution*, p.148.

122. Ibid, p. 163.

123. *State of Gujarat v Mirzapur Moti Kureshi Kassab Jamat and Others,* 2005 8 SCC 534.

124. Article 51A(g) of the Constitution reads:
It shall be the duty of every citizen of India
(g) to protect and improve the natural environment including forests, lakes, rivers and wild life, and to have compassion for living creatures.

125. See Section 5 of the Maharashtra Animal Preservation (Amendment) Act (MAPAA), 2015.

126. Ibid., Section 5A.

127. Ibid., Section 5B.

128. Ibid., Section 5C.

129. Ibid., Section 5D.

130. Ibid., Section 9B.

131. *Shaikh Zahid Mukthar v State of Maharasthra*, indiankanoon.org/doc/153513175/.

132. See Section 2(2) of Karnataka Prevention of Slaughter and Preservation of Cattle Act (KPSPCA), 2020.

133. 'Communal Policing by Hindutva Outfits' (A report by PUCL, Karnataka and Forum Against Atrocities on Women, Mangalore: September 2012), puclkarnataka.org/wp-content/uploads/2012/11/Mangalore-Report.pdf.

134. See Section 8(7) of KPSPCA.

135. Ibid., Section 8.

136. *Jamiat Ulama-E-Hind Gujarat v State of Gujarat* (August 2021),

livelaw.in/pdf_upload/gujarat-inter-faith-marriage-conversion-law-order-aug-19-399000.pdf.

137. Naomi Klein, *The Shock Doctrine: The Rise of Disaster Capitalism* (Metropolitan Books, New York: 2007).

138. Saubhadra Chatterji, 'Parliament panel meetings stalled amid Covid-19 spike', *Hindustan Times*, 2 May 2021, hindustantimes.com/india-news/2nd-wave-of-covid-holds-up-parliamentary-panel-meets-101619895534077.html.

139. Special Correspondent, 'Venkaiah Naidu, Om Birla take the initiative on panels' "virtual" meetings', *The Hindu*, 7 May 2020, thehindu.com/news/national/parliament-officials-to-explore-if-committee-meetings-can-be-held-via-video-conference/article31526490.ece.

140. News Desk, 'COVID: Jairam Ramesh urges parliamentary standing committees be allowed to meet virtually', *India TV*, 27 April 2021, indiatvnews.com/news/india/covid19-jairam-ramesh-urges-parliamentary-standing-committees-allowed-meeting-virtually-coronavirus-pandemic-700936.

141. Maansi Verma, 'Parliaments in the Time of the Pandemic', *Economic and Political Weekly*, Vol. 55, No. 24 (13 June 2020).

142. 'In times like these, transparency matters more than ever', Transparency International, 19 March 2020, transparency.org/en/news/in-times-like-these-transparency-matters-more-than-ever.

143. See the draft notification here: environmentclearance.nic.in/writereaddata/Draft_EIA_2020.pdf.

144. See the letter here: cprindia.org/sites/default/files/Letter%20EIA%202020%20deferment%2C%20covid%2C%2024.3.2020.pdf.

145. Meenakshi Kapoor and Krithika A. Dinesh, 'Throughout the Pandemic, Environmental Clearance Law Has Been Under the Chopping Block', *The Wire*, 23 May 2021, thewire.in/environment/throughout-the-pandemic-environmental-clearance-law-has-been-under-the-chopping-block.

146. Ibid.

147. 'How The Government Diluted Forest Rights Of Adivasis During

Lockdown', *Behan Box*, behanbox.com/how-the-government-of-india-used-the-lockdown-to-dilute-the-forest-rights-of-communities-voices-of-the-people-affected-by-coal-mining-projects/.

148. Arvind Narrain, Maitreyi Krishnan and Clifton D. Rozario, 'COVID-19 Lockdown: Uttar Pradesh and Madhya Pradesh watering down labour laws is a body blow to the working class', *FirstPost*, 11 May 2020, firstpost.com/india/covid-19-lockdown-uttar-pradesh-and-madhya-pradesh-watering-down-labour-laws-is-a-body-blow-to-the-working-class-8355791.html.

149. Anya Bharat Ram, 'Relaxation of labour law across states', PRS Legislative Research, 12 May 2020, prsindia.org/theprsblog/relaxation-of-labour-laws-across-states.

150. These changes are based on recommendations made by the Ministry of Labour and Employment and 'prior instruction' was issued by the president of India through a letter by the Ministry of Home. deccanherald.com/state/karnataka-districts/karnataka-government-tweaks-three-laws-approves-labour-ordinance-864859.html.

151. Arvind Narrain, Maitreyi Krishnan and Clifton D. Rozario, 'COVID-19 Lockdown'.

152. Kavya Bharadkar and Babu Mathew, 'The Journey of Labour Regulation', *Seminar*, No. 758 (February 2021).

153. See Sections 62 and 63 of the Industrial Relations Code, 2020; cpimlnd.org/the-new-labour-codes-depriving-workers-of-rights/.

154. Sudha Narayanan, 'The Three Farm Bills', *The India Forum*, 27 November 2020, theindiaforum.in/article/three-farm-bills.

155. Anumeha Yadav, 'Why landless and marginal farmers are the backbone of farmer protests', *Newslaundry*, 4 December 2020, newslaundry.com/2020/12/04/why-landless-and-marginal-farmers-are-the-backbone-of-farmer-protests.

156. 'P Sainath | All About The New Farm laws & Farmers Protest | On IndiaPodcasts With Anku goyal', youtube.com/watch?v=16Dmm34vK5g (video).

157. Amandeep Sandhu, 'Mahapanchayat; a signal to the regime', *Maktoob*, 6 September 2021, https://maktoobmedia.com/2021/09/07/mahapanchayat-a-signal-to-the-regime/.

158. Arthur Rosenberg, 'Fascism as a Mass Movement', *Fascism*, p. 61.

159. Vijayta Lalwani, '"I kept feeling it was a nightmare": Safoora Zargar on surviving 38 days in solitary confinement', *Scroll*, 8 March 2021, scroll.in/article/988844/i-kept-feeling-it-was-a-nightmare-safoora-zargar-on-surviving-38-days-in-solitary-confinement.

160. Vijayta Lalwani, 'In Delhi violence investigation, a disturbing pattern: Victims end up being prosecuted by police', *Scroll*, 23 May 2020, scroll.in/article/962526/in-delhi-violence-investigation-a-disturbing-pattern-victims-end-up-being-arrested-by-police.

161. The Nazis used the assassination of the German diplomat Ernst vom Rath on 7 November 1938 in *Paris by a* seventeen-year-old Jew, Herschel Grynzslpan, as a pretext to launch Kristallnacht. Volker Ullrich, *Hitler*, p. 668.

162. Volker Ullrich, *Hitler*, p. 678.

163. See the judges' and lawyers' representation at disbandthecommittee.in/assets/documents/statements/3.pdf.

164. 'Representation to the Committee for Reform in Criminal Law', 9 July 2020 (civil society submissions by Ramachandra Guha and others on file with the author).

165. See the judges' and lawyers' representation at disbandthecommittee.in/assets/documents/statements/3.pdf.

5. What Is to Be Done?

1. Varavara Rao, *Captive Imagination* (Penguin Viking, New Delhi: 2010), p. 79.

2. Ernst Fraenkel, *The Dual State: A Contribution to the Theory of Dictatorship* (Oxford University Press, Oxford: 2017), p. lxxii.

3. Jens Meierhenrich, *The Remnants of the Rechtsstaat* (Oxford University Press, Oxford: 2018), p. 36.

4. Mihir Desai, 'COVID-19 and the Indian Supreme Court', sabrangindia.in/article/covid-19-and-indian-supreme-court.

Also see the *Hindu* editorial: 'Belated, but welcome: On Supreme Court move on migrant workers', *The Hindu*, 30 May 2020, https://www.thehindu.com/opinion/editorial/the-hindu-editorial-on-the-supreme-courts-belated-but-welcome-move-on-migrant-workers/article31705341.ece. It notes: 'With a kind of self-effacement and self-abnegation not in keeping with its institutional history, the Court had then accepted the government's sweeping claim that there were no migrants on the roads any more, and that the initial exodus of workers from cities to their home States had been set off by "fake news" to the effect that the lockdown would last for months.'

5. *Mohammed Arif Jameel v Union of India* (March 2020), https://www.legitquest.com/case/mohammed-arif-jameel-v-union-of-india/1c2857. Also see Mohammed Afeef and Basawa Kunale Prasad, 'Justice A.S. Oka: The judge known for taking suffering seriously', *The Leaflet*, 3 September 2021, https://www.theleaflet.in/justice-a-s-oka-the-judge-known-for-taking-suffering-seriously/.

6. Jens Meierhenrich, *The Legacies of Law: Long-run Consequences of Legal Development in South Africa* (Cambridge University Press, Cambridge: 2008), p. 130. Meierhenrich documents how legal victories, though few and far in between, kept alive the spirit of the normative State.

7. Avigdor Feldman, 'Which side are you on, Grandpa Weinstien?', cf. Michael Sfard, *The Wall and the Gate* (Metropolitan Books, New York: 2018), p. 188.

8. Public talk given by Michael Sfard on 'Human rights litigation in Israel and Palestine in the context of the occupation', in an online meeting organised by the All India Lawyers Association for Justice (AILAJ) on 8 August 2021, https://www.facebook.com/AILAJHQ/videos/4288140417932852.

9. Michael Sfard, *The Wall and the Gate*, p. 454.

10. Ibid., p. 455.

11. Jules Lobel, *Success Without Victory* (New York University Press, New York: 2003), p. 7.

12. Pratiksha Baxi, 'Understanding Rape Law Reform', *YOJANA*, Vol. 58 (June 2014), pp. 38–42.

13. 'Justice for Jayaraj and Bennix Means Ending a Culture of Impunity', *The Wire*, 2 July 2020, thewire.in/rights/jayaraj-bennix-custodial-deaths-impunity.

14. Hugo Gorringe and Karthikeyan Damodaran, 'Bound by Brotherhood: India's Failure to End Killings in Police Custody', Human Rights Watch, 19 December 2016, https://www.hrw.org/report/2016/12/19/bound-brotherhood/indias-failure-end-killings-police-custody.

15. Hannah Arendt, *The Origins of Totalitarianism* (Harcourt, Brace, Jovanovich, New York: 1979), p. 434.

16. Gautam Bhatia, 'A Constitutionalism Without the Court', *Indian Constitutional Law and Philosophy*, 1 August 2020, indconlawphil.wordpress.com/2020/08/01/iclp-turns-7-a-constitutionalism-without-the-court/.

17. M.K. Gandhi, *The Law and the Lawyers* (S.B. Kher, ed.) (Navjivan Trust, Ahmedabad: 2001), p. 119.

18. Ravish Kumar, *The Free Voice* (Speaking Tiger, New Delhi: 2018), p. 30.

19. B.R. Ambedkar, *Ranade, Gandhi and Jinnah* (Thacker and Co, Bombay: 1943), columbia.edu/itc/mealac/pritchett/00ambedkar/txt_ambedkar_ranade.html#01.

20. B.R. Ambedkar, *What Congress and Gandhi Have Done to the Untouchables* (Kalpaz, New Delhi: 2017), p. 244.

21. Akash Singh Rathore, *Ambedkar's Preamble: A Secret History of the Constitution of India* (Penguin, New Delhi: 2020), p. 137.

22. Ibid.

23. *Navtej Singh Johar v Union of India*, September 2018, indiankanoon.org/doc/168671544/.

24. Constitutional Assembly Debates, Book no. 2 (4 November 1948), p. 38.

25. Ravish Kumar, *The Free Voice*, p. 143.

26. Ibid., p. 156.

27. Constitutional Assembly Debates, Book no. 7 (4 November 1948), p. 38.

28. 'Jean Dreze speaks at PUCL press conference against arrests in the Bhima Koregaon case', youtube.com/watch?v=Hsp1kbLr6qo (video).

29. Ramachandra Guha, 'The Rise and Fall of the Bilingual Intellectual', *Economic and Political Weekly*, Vol. 44, No. 33 (15 August 2009), pp. 36–42 at p. 38.

30. Ibid., p. 39.

31. Ramachandra Guha, 'The Loss and Recovery of Intellectual Bilingualism', *Economic and Political Weekly*, Vol. xlv, No. 4 (23 January 2010), pp. 70–71 at p. 70.

32. B.R. Ambedkar, *Dr Babasaheb Ambedkar: Writings and Speeches*, Vol. 11 (Department of Education, Government of Maharashtra, Bombay: 2014), p. 14.

33. Romila Thapar, *Voices of Dissent* (Seagull, New Delhi: 2020), p. 41.

34. B.R. Ambedkar, 'My philosophy of life', All India Radio Broadcast Speech, 3 October 1954, cf. Aishwary Kumar, *Radical Equality* (Navayana, New Delhi: 2019), p. 138.

35. Romila Thapar, *Voices of Dissent*, p. 41.

36. Ibid., p. 73.

37. Mukunda Rao, *Sky-clad: The Extraordinary Life and Times of Akka Mahadevi* (Westland, New Delhi: 2018), p. 37.

38. Ibid., p. xii.

39. Girish Karnad, *Collected Plays*, Vol. 2 (Oxford University Press, New Delhi: 2005), p. 45.

40. Omar Rashid, 'Ram temple bhoomi pujan: Symbol of modern Indian culture, says Narendra Modi', *The Hindu*, 5 August 2020, thehindu.com/news/national/ram-temple-bhoomi-pujan-a-golden-chapter-for-country-says-narendra-modi/article32275140.ece.

41. A.K. Ramanujan, *Speaking of Siva* (Penguin, London: 1973), p. 19.

42. Mukunda Rao, *Sky-clad*, p. 37.

43. A.K. Ramanujan, *Speaking of Siva*, p. 19.

44. Ibid., p. 21.

45. Munawar Faruqui, instagram.com/p/CAciDOHFh8F/ (Instagram post).

46. 'Meet Munawar Faruqui, The Man Behind The Comic', youtube. com/watch?v=P4AFnyIGfiw (video).

47. 'Munawar Faruqui: Prison, Comedy & Self-Censorship: Barkha Dutt', youtube.com/watch?v=k7FqswitVrM (video).

48. PUCL statement on Martyrs' Day (on file with the author).

49. The operation of some of the rules have been partially stayed by the Bombay High Court and the Madras High Court. See: internetfreedom.in/intermediaries-rules-2021/; https:// indianexpress.com/article/india/information-technology-rules-madras-high-court-stays-key-clause-may-rob-media-of-its-independence-7513901//; and https://www.thehindu.com/ news/national/bombay-high-court-stays-provisions-of-new-it-rules/article35917008.ece.

50. Shiv Visvanathan, 'The wages of dissent', *Seminar*, https://www. india-seminar.com/2007/569/569_shiv_visvanathan.htm.

51. Ibid.

52. Gaurav Vivek Bhatnagar, 'The Controversial Record of a Modi Aide Who May Head the Enforcement Directorate', *The Wire*, 10 October 2015, https://thewire.in/government/ the-controversial-record-of-a-modi-aide-who-may-head-the-enforcement-directorate.

53. Ibid.

54. Satish Jha, 'Relief for ex-IPS officer Rahul Sharma as CAT allows his plea', *The Indian Express*, 25 December 2018, https://indianexpress. com/article/india/relief-for-ex-ips-officer-rahul-sharma-as-cat-allows-his-plea-5508385/.

55. Satish Jha, 'CAT stays investigation against whistleblower Gujarat IPS officer Rajnish Rai', *The Indian Express*, 18 October 2017, https://indianexpress.com/article/india/cat-stays-investigation-against-whistleblower-ex-gujarat-ips-officer-rajnish-rai-4895855/.

56. Web Desk, 'Jailed IPS officer Sanjiv Bhatt begins to pen prison diary, first entry on CAA protests', *The Week*, 2 January 2020, https://

www.theweek.in/news/india/2020/01/02/jailed-ips-officer-sanjiv-bhatt-begins-to-pen-prison-diary-first-entry-on-caa-protests.html.

57. Ashish Khetan, *Undercover: My Journey into the Darkness of Hindutva* (Context/Westland Books, New Delhi: 2021), p.195.

58. Facebook post, https://www.facebook.com/hashtag/justicefors anjivbhatt?fref=mentions.

59. Arvind Narrain, 'Sexual Violence and the Death Penalty: A Tale of Two Judgements', *Economic and Political Weekly*, Vol. 49, No. 3 (1 January 2014), pp. 34–42.

60. Ashish Khetan, *Undercover*, p. 266.

61. Ibid., p. 266.

62. 'Sessions judge recuses himself from a bail hearing; alleges J&K HC judge tried to influence him', *The Leaflet*, 11 December 2020, https://www.theleaflet.in/sessions-judge-recuses-himself-from-a-bail-hearing-alleges-jk-hc-judge-tried-to-influence-him/#.

63. Gaurav Vivek Bhatnagar, 'Legal Experts Slam Alleged Attempt by HC Judge To Influence Srinagar Sessions Judge', *The Wire*, 11 December 2020, https://thewire.in/law/legal-experts-influence-srinagar-session-judge-directive-high-court-judge-javid-iqbal-wani.

64. Ibid.

65. Hannah Arendt, *The Origins of Totalitarianism*, p. 109.

66. Hannah Arendt, *Eichmann in Jerusalem* (Viking Press, New York: 1963), p.

67. Martha Nussbaum, *Political Emotions: Why Love Matters for Justice* (Belknap Press, Cambridge: 2013), p. 3.

68. Correspondent, 'The forgotten stanzas of Jana, Gana, Mana', NDTV, 16 August 2011, ndtv.com/india-news/the-forgotten-stanzas-of-jana-gana-mana-464590.

69. Ibid.

70. Anikendra Sen et. al., (eds), *Patriots, Poets and Prisoners: Selections from Ramananda Chatterjee's The Modern Review* (HarperCollins, Noida: 2016), p. 72.

71. Rabindranath Tagore, *Nationalism* (Fingerprint Classics, New Delhi: 2019), p. 82.

72. Rabindranath Tagore, *Nationalism*, p. 28.

73. Ashis Nandy, *Illegitimacy of Nationalism: Rabindranath Tagore and the Politics of Self* (Oxford University Press, New Delhi: 1994), p. 81.

74. Ibid., p. 87.

75. Thomas Piketty, *Capital and Ideology* (Belknap Press, London: 2020), p. 139.

76. Ibid., p. 976.

77. Ibid., pp. 20–21.

78. 'Report of the Special Rapporteur on extreme poverty and human rights, Philip Alston', UN Human Rights Council, https://undocs.org/A/HRC/29/31.

79. Ibid., p. 972.

80. Ibid.

81. Ibid., pp. 966–1034.

82. Ibid., p. 1041.

83. Congress Manifesto, Nyay, https://manifesto.inc.in/en/nyay.html.

84. Jean Dreze and Amartya Sen, *An Uncertain Glory* (Penguin, New Delhi: 2013), pp. 213–242.

85. Thomas Piketty, *Capital and Ideology*, p. 971.

86. Hannah Arendt, *The Origins of Totalitarianism*, p. 474.

87. Ibid.

88. Meeting to address the imprisonment of Binayak Sen organized by PUCL-K and PDF, addressed by K. Balagopal in 2007.

89. Deepa Dhanraj's film, *The Advocate*, https://www.youtube.com/watch?v=haGd9ICmD8w.

90. Hannah Arendt, *The Origins of Totalitarianism*, p. 451.

91. Ibid., p. 475.

92. Ibid., p. 451.

93. 'Charter of Principles', World Social Forum of Transformative Economies, https://transformadora.org/en/about/principles.

94. Hannah Arendt, *The Origins of Totalitarianism*, p. 323.

95. W.B. Yeats, 'The Second Coming', https://poets.org/poem/second-coming.

96. Martha Nussbaum, *Political Emotion,* p. 97.

97. Martha Nussbaum, *The Clash Within* (Permanent Black, New Delhi: 2007), p. 121.

98. K. Balagopal, 'Democracy and the Fight Against Communalism', *Economic and Political Weekly* (7 January 1995).

99. Martha Nussbaum, *The Clash Within*, p. 79.

100. Lars T. Lih, *Lenin Rediscovered* (Aakar, New Delhi: 2017). Lih argues that 'What is to be done?' has been misinterpreted as a text which is contemptuous of workers' agency and provides the intellectual arguments on which Stalinism based itself. Instead, Lih argues that the text, by setting out opposition to Tsarist autocracy as the starting point, is a fertile and generative text for a struggle against autocracy. The citations which follow are from Lih's translation of 'What is to be done'.

101. Lars T. Lih, *Lenin Rediscovered*, p. 727.

102. Ibid., p. 739.

103. Ibid., p. 821.

104. Ibid., p. 744.

105. Volker Ullrich, *Hitler* (Vintage, London: 2016), p. 412.

106. Ibid., p. 430.

107. Ibid., p. 416.

108. William L. Shirer, *The Rise and Fall of the Third Reich* (Fawcett Crest, New York: 1992), p. 271.

109. Ibid., p. 423.

110. Ibid., p. 424.

111. William L. Shirer, *The Rise and Fall of the Third Reich,* p. 273.

112. 'Otto Wells', *Holocaust Encyclopaedia*, https://encyclopedia.ushmm.org/content/en/article/otto-wels.

113. 'Otto Wells', The German Resistance Memorial Center, https://www.gdw-berlin.de/en/recess/biographies/index_of_persons/biographie/view-bio/otto-wels/?no_cache=1.

114. William L. Shirer, *The Rise and Fall of the Third Reich,* pp. 280–81.

115. Volker Ullrich, *Hitler*, p. 427.

116. M.S. Golwalkar, *Bunch of Thoughts* (Vikrama Prakashan, Bangalore: 1968), pp. 166–196.

117. Neeraj Chauhan, 'Law giving more power to Delhi L-G now in force', *Hindustan Times*, 29 April 2021, https://www.hindustantimes.com/cities/delhi-news/law-giving-more-power-to-delhi-l-g-now-in-force-101619653101867.html.

118. B.R. Ambedkar, *Babasaheb Ambedkar: Writings and Speeches*, Vol. 8, p. 358.

119. Wire Staff, 'COVID-19 Sharpened Inequalities in India, Billionaires' Wealth Increased by 35%: Report', *The Wire*, 25 January 2021, https://thewire.in/rights/covid-19-sharpened-inequalities-in-india-billionaires-wealth-increased-by-35-report.

120. 'We Must Hang Together or We Will Hang Separately', *History Central*, https://www.historycentral.com/Revolt/stories/Hang.html.

121. United States Holocaust Memorial Museum, 'Martin Niemöller', https://encyclopedia.ushmm.org/content/en/article/martin-niemoeller-first-they-came-for-the-socialists.

Acknowledgements

This book began when I was asked by P.R.S. Mani to speak on the 'undeclared emergency', at a meeting organised by the All India People's Forum, Karnataka, to mark the forty-fifth anniversary of the Emergency on 25 June 2020. My background reading got me interested in the idea of an 'undeclared emergency'. The presentation itself went well and those I shared the write-up with expressed interest in my presentation of the same.

Asmita Basu was intrigued by the initial essay and insisted that I should publish it not as an essay but as a book. She asked me to get in touch with Ajitha G.S. from Westland. When I shared that initial long essay with Ajitha, the theme sparked her curiosity, and she made many useful suggestions on how the essay could become a book.

The journey from presentation to book was helped by other innumerable such conversations and suggestions, all of which added significant sections to the evolving manuscript. I owe a lot to Clifton D'Rozario who, over innumerable small cups of tea, discussed many of the ideas in this book. In particular, I owe the discovery of Michael Sfard's remarkable book on human rights lawyering in Israel / Palestine to him.

Lawrence Liang has been the source of many precious insights in conversations over the years and has generously shared material from his incredible archive, including such gems as A.K. Gopalan's autobiography.

Many ideas have evolved in conversation with Sudhir Krishnaswamy over the years. I particularly remember that it was he who brought to my attention to the fact that fraternity is the ignored stepsister in the trinity of liberty, equality and fraternity, and that it was Ambedkar who insisted that fraternity was the key to unlocking the promise of liberty and equality.

Asmita Basu and Shraddha Chigateri were among the first and most enthusiastic readers of the initial draft and provided many important correctives to the argument.

Madhu Bhushan is someone who has passionately argued the limitations of human rights and the importance of engaging with culture over the years. I hope that important dimension finds its space in the book.

For providing useful and encouraging feedback on drafts of the book, I must thank Babu Matthew, Kunal Ambasta, Aiman Khan, Sharib Ali, Mohammed Afeef, Maitreyi Krishnan, T. Jayashree, Alok Hisarwala and Swathi Seshadri. For conversations on thematics in the book, which were generative of many an idea, I owe a lot to Mayur Suresh, Jawahar Raja, Matthew John, Anuj Bhuwania, Anshuman Singh, Jayna Kothari, Miriam Chinnappa, Neeraj Grover, Siddharth Narrain, Ashish Rajyadhaksha, Rohit De, Subasree Krishnan, Sanjay Bavikatte, Narayana A. and Sarah Khan.

I have to thank Alok Hisarwala for his friendship and suggestions on the manuscript and for pushing me to expand my human rights imagination to be a little less anthropocentric and make space for animal rights!

The space in which the writing was done was that of the Alternative Law Forum, and the ALF is the space where an intense engagement with all the issues I write about in this book is kept alive. For maintaining the ALF as a creative and passionate space where the ideas of justice and freedom matter, I must thank Vinay Sreenivasa in particular. He and his colleagues in the ALF, Lekha Adavi, Basawa Prasad, Mohammed Afeef, Manavi Atri, Poorna Ravishankar, Narasimhappa T.V., Swathi Shivanand, Sivamani, Aishwarya Ravikumar, Saba Syeda and Usha, form a collective whose work speaks to many of the concerns in this book.

When speaking of the ALF, one cannot but speak of Manthan Law, again manned by a remarkably committed bunch of comrades, including Clifton D'Rozario, Maitreyi Krishnan, Shilpa Prasad, Avani Chokshi and Raghupathy, whose 24/7 work as lawyers, activists and organisers in combatting the 'undeclared emergency' is inspirational.

Working with the People's Union for Civil Liberties, which is fronted by the dynamic energy of Kavita Srivastava and the insightful legal acumen of V. Suresh and Mihir Desai, has been deeply enriching. The dogged passion of Y.J. Rajendra, who heads the PUCL-Karnataka, unit, as well the enthusiasm of PUCL members Robin Christopher, Lara Jesani, Apoorvanand, Shujayathulla and so many others has been infectious.

For being an unfailing source of intellectual inspiration, I must thank Kishor Govinda and Ramdas Rao, who have been heading a remarkable reading group on Marx's writings for over three years.

I must also thank the public policy students at the National Law School who opted for the National Security and human rights cluster (which I had jointly taught) in the Public Policy Dialectics course in 2021 for their enthusiasm and comments.

Arun Thiruvengadam's friendship and long conversations on many of the ideas in the book provided the necessary impetus when energy was flagging. It was Arun who gently suggested that the draft would benefit from the pushback and feedback I would get if I were to present it at the faculty seminar at the School of Policy and Governance, Azim Premji University. Thanks to Vishnupad for inviting me to me present at the faculty seminar and for the many thought-provoking questions and insightful comments, and to friends and colleagues at the APU, including Sitharamam Kakarala, Abhayraj Naik, Kanika Gauba, Shrimoyee Ghosh, Vishnupad, Paaritosh Nath, Siddharth Swaminathan, Sunayana Ganguly and Arun Thiruvengadam.

My thanks also to Ram Guha for his comments right through the development of the draft as well as for his warm endorsement of this book. Kavita Krishnan, Mihir Desai and V. Suresh have very kindly taken time out of their many pressing engagements and provided a generous endorsement of the book as well.

I thank Usha Ramanathan for reading the manuscript and pointing out the many ways it could be improved. I was not able to implement many of her suggestions, but the ideas she communicated will structure my thinking in the time to come.

I am also deeply grateful for the outstanding editorial work by Janani Ganesan, whose thoughtful comments made me rework substantial sections of the book, making it a vastly improved text. If the book has the form it has today, it owes a lot to the suggestions of both Janani and Ajitha. Thanks to Dipanjali Chadha for her final, thorough look at the manuscript.

I should also thank Anita Abraham for many insightful conversations over cups of tea and for bringing her magical touch of lightness to everyday life.

Finally, I have to thank my family for their unquestioning support for all my endeavours. My sister Aparna A.S. has insisted that we have fun by persuading me to watch many entertaining films. My mother, A.S. Vijayalakshmi, has provided companionable times around delicious home-cooked meals and tea. My father, A.K. Sathyanarrain, has embodied Hemingway's dictum that courage is 'grace under pressure' by the way he has coped with a series of illnesses that would have broken a lesser person.

Index